First Days/First Nights:
The Beginnings of an NFD Career

First Days/First Nights
The Beginnings of an NFD Career

An Oral History of the Newark Fire Department
1940 - 2016

Neal Stoffers

Springfield and Hunterdon Publishing
Copyright 2022
www.newarkfireoralhistory.com

First Printing: 2022

ISBN: 978-1-970034-31-8
Springfield and Hunterdon Publishing

East Brunswick, NJ 08816-5852

Dedicated to past, present, and future generations of Newark firefighters, and especially to the 67 firefighters who made the ultimate sacrifice upholding their oath to protect the lives and property of Newark's citizens.

Contents

Acknowledgements

First, I must again acknowledge my long-suffering wife Miaoli who has put up with my obsession to preserve the history of the Newark Fire Department for thirty years. I anticipate another four books will come from the interviews I have already conducted, so her sacrifice has not yet ended. My sister Dorothy took the time to read through the manuscript and point out all the typos, omissions, and repetitions I had inserted while transcribing. And finally, my brother Mark made the cover possible. Of course, in the end I am responsible for the final product.

The credit for much of this book goes to the members of the Newark Fire Department who gave so generously of their time to take part in my oral history project. The hours of recorded conversations they contributed will help preserve the history of Newark's fire department and of Newark itself. A list of those interviewed appears at the end of the book. This is their story. I am honored to tell it.

Foreword

First Days/First Nights is one more book that grew out of an idea for a chapter in *The Best Job in the World: Learning the Job.* Like *Remembrances of Newark,* the stories were too long and rich to limit to a single chapter. The title refers to expressions commonly used by Newark firefighters when they worked a "tens and fourteens" schedule, two ten-hour days and two fourteen-hour nights every eight days. The first of the two days or two nights was called first day or first night. It also refers to the probationary period after firefighters are appointed to the job. Many of the stories are about their very first "first day" or "first night." The expressions are a throwback to another time before the present twenty-four-hour shift.

All of the interviews I have conducted over the past thirty years are included. I did not ask a specific question about first days in my early interviews. It was the answers I received to other questions that gave birth to questions focused on career beginnings. This "backing" into the topic, meant that very few of the early interview responses were included in previous books since the topic simply wasn't covered before. Of the 175 interviews included, only fifteen have parts reprinted here.

I have broken the stories into decades, beginning with the 1940s and moving through to the 2010s. This is a convenient way to organize the book, but life is never that precise. The titles of the chapters provide an approximation of the "theme" of each decade. Giving a context for the stories recounted. As is true of firefighting stories in general, sometimes the stories are comical, sometimes they are tragic.

I owe an explanation for the chapter titles. (Keep in mind, these stories are told from the point of view of newly appointed firefighters.) The first chapter, *1940s: Foundations*, refers to what I have found in interviewing men appointed in the 1940s. The extraordinary advances in the fire service over the past eighty years had their beginnings in that decade.

The second chapter, *1950s: Innovation and Expansion* refers to the innovations in firefighting equipment and tactics that permeated the decade, as well as, the growth in manpower. The third tour was appointed in December of 1949 and a fourth was added in March and April of 1959.

I called chapter three *1960s: Social Explosions* for the obvious reason that the 1967 and 1968 civil disturbances have come to define the firefighting experience of the decade.

Next is *1970s: The War Years and Contraction*. This is a reference to the extraordinary fire rate that existed from the 1970s into the 1980s. Accompanying this growth in fires was a fiscal crisis that forced the layoffs and manpower reductions of the 70s and 80s.

1980s: The Height and Then Easing comes from the fact that the number of fires topped out in 1980 and the number of responses peaked in 1981. The rest of the decade saw a gradual "easing" of fires and responses.

1990s: Passing the Torch refers to the generational shift of the decade. Most of the men appointed in the 1940s and 1950s had retired by or would retire in this decade. The core of the fire department now shifted to those appointed in the 60s to 80s.

2000s: A New Millennium, a New Department tells the story of firefighters appointed after the turn of the century. The rapid changes of the 20th Century's second half culminated in a different fire department than had previously existed.

2010s: The Modern Fire Department includes stories from young firefighters on the job today (2022). The department they talk about would be a wonder to the men appointed in the 1940s. But the mission would remain the same. Protecting the lives and property of Newark's citizens and guests.

1940s: Foundations

Conville: Back in 1940 Nine Engine was a very nice neighborhood. It was in the Forest Hill section, predominantly all white, nice houses. In fact, it was called the silk spot in the battalion. The only company up there that was older was at the end of Summer Avenue which was Thirteen Engine. I was told that's the last company that had horses. In Nine Engine, we had a battalion chief that rode out of our building and we had an engine and a wagon. It was kind of hard coming in new. You were called a snot and the men didn't like you because you were young and they were like veterans from the First World War. We had experience with the captains that you just minded your name.

Your house watch was very important. Cleanliness of the house was important. I'll give you an example. When you have those high radiators? They would put a cigarette butte in and then when you didn't clean good, you had to do the cleaning all over again. And then in Nine Engine, the heating room was in the cellar and you had to be detailed to whitewash the wall because the coal came in there and it got dusty. So, every once in a while, you were sent down there with a whitewash brush to make it presentable. And if you were last man on the company, you were assigned as that person to keep the cellar clean.

So, I was detailed to wash all the walls down, paint them down, take care of the coal because it was dusty down there. I said, "Ah, what the hell." So, I couldn't get it clean. But outside the window was a hydrant on Taylor Street. So, I got the small inch and a half hose. I hooked it up to the hydrant. I brought it downstairs. I started washing down all the walls, washing the floor. I opened up the sewer plates. All the water's going down. I look at the coal bin, the coal's dirty so I wash all the coal. You couldn't even get messy if you slept on the coal. Man, that place was spotless. I know they'll give me the Congressional Medal of Honor for this here.

So, the battalion chief went out about 9:30 in the morning to make the rounds. He comes back around 12 o'clock and he's yelling that Nine Engine didn't respond on a couple of fires. The bell never hit. We don't have radios, only the bell. The bell didn't hit. Now it's the battalion chief and the captain. They're at each other's throats. So, they called downtown. Send out a test signal. No God damned test signal comes over. I washed out the bell. Now, the chief lives on the second floor. The phone rings, but it doesn't ring upstairs, doesn't ring downstairs. So, I got assigned to go next door to Ventola's where they got a public phone. I got to put a sign on the thing, Do Not Enter. I had to sit in the telephone booth and then when downtown called, I had to get the chief, but the chief lived up on the second floor. Now he's got to walk all the way down. I think two weeks later I was detailed to Three Truck. And that's how I got to Three Truck. I got thrown the hell out of the place.

I was assigned to the wagon and Thirteen Engine had a fire on Broadway. I was new. I was told to park the engine over there by the hydrant. And I could hook up to the hydrant and then the hose would go across the street if Thirteen Engine needed any more water. So, I'm in the wagon and I'm sitting there and they're fighting a small cellar fire. I see the line go dead. I jumped really quickly and I pulled my booster line all the way across the street. I went down and put the fire out. I went home. I told my wife what a hero I am. The captain did say it was good, so I was very proud of myself. Then we went out on McCarter Highway where there was a diner over on this side. I was told to park over here with the wagon. While I'm looking, Thirteen Engine's not getting any water. So, now I grab the pipe with the two-and-a-half-inch line. I dragged it all the way across the highway where there were no cars. I got in and I knocked the fire down. Now I'm a hero, right? When I got back to quarters, Captain Higgins brings me upstairs and he details me, he says, "Don't you ever take a hose off an engine unless I tell you to."

Fredette: The oldest guy when I came in was Johnny Komstack. He came in I guess around 1914. He was up at Nine Engine. I started at Nine Engine. I worked there maybe a year and a half, then I went to Six. Komstack was about the oldest man I can ever recall, when I came in. I guess he worked with the horses. 1914, Thirteen Engine had them up until 1923. 1923, Thirteen Engine had the last horses on the job. So, he had to do it. He had to shovel manure and take the horses out for a walk at night for exercise.

And then I went to Six. Now generally, the number one driver would work with the captain. They stuck together. They always worked together. In those days it was "Don't touch the apparatus. I'm the driver. Keep your hands off it." Six Engine, we had a guy, he idolized that engine. The way he kept that polished.

We had an old captain, Captain Herman Sherah, he broke a leg, he came in around 1914. He used to hobble at the fires. As soon as the apparatus pulled in front of Six, you would have all your hose piled up on top of the truck, empty booster tank, he would send in the return call. He would say "We don't want to miss any fires." Then he would hobble in. We could not get a cup of coffee. "Get that loaded up, we have to get ready for the next fire."

I think the first year was around 837 runs. In around that period of time, but my last year at Nine Engine was 273 times a year. I got detailed to Six Truck on Christmas Eve and I said "Well, this is living." I want to get transferred to Six Truck. Because we were having a good time New Year's Eve. You did not go out on any fires or anything. Then the next morning I sobered up and looked at the books. They did not even go out 100 times for the whole year. I said "Oh, Jesus. No, I can't."

My wife was the one who got me out of Nine Engine because she knew Bobby Brown very well. They played together on Lily Street. Brown was King's nephew. So, she said "Oh, Bobby, Reggie didn't mean Six Truck, he meant Six Engine." So, I did not know what the hell I was doing. Even though my wife's uncle was the Captain, Sholey was the captain at Six Truck, and I got on his shift, but I was asking to go from 273 to less than 100. I think it was around ninety times a year. Twenty-eight Engine went about seventy times a year.

There was the urn explosion over in Kearny around the end of 1942, beginning of 1943. We went over to Kearny on that. They had a lot of companies from Newark. It was a big four-story brick building. They were making some kind of powder or substance for camouflage nets and it exploded. It took this four-story building right down in a heap. I was in Nine Engine. The explosion occurred just at the change of shifts. We were up from Standard Oil down along the Passaic River and thought it was Standard Oil. We went right down there. Then we looked over across the river and saw it was over in Kearny, so we went back to quarters. The operator picked up and said respond to this explosion. We went there.

The two fireboats had come up originally on the explosion thinking it was Standard Oil. It was a good thing they did because that was really the only way of getting water. There were six outlets on each boat. That meant we could get twelve lines off. These two fire boats were the only ones who had the water. Down there along the Passaic River, all those hydrants were dead. One by one they kept bringing more companies from Newark. They brought in Ten Engine's hose wagon. They brought in Four Engine and Thirteen Engine. They must have stripped the city of thirty percent or thirty-five percent of all the companies. We stayed there a couple of days.

Vetrini: My first assignment was Engine Sixteen. As a temporary I was put to Engine Sixteen. They more or less tried to keep us in our own neighborhood at the time because everybody lived in the city. But at that time, you could be detailed anywhere in the city. Especially the temporaries. We were all over the city. I was not permanent at Sixteen Engine. Then when I went on as a regular, I imagine the officers there wanted me to come back, so that is how I got to Sixteen Engine.

When I first went on, we had a fire in Reilly Tar. It was a three bagger. We were first due down there. The fellow who was the first driver was Art Fagan. I stayed with him. He was a big help to me. They were stretching in at that fire and I guess I was going a little wacky trying to do three things to what I should only be doing one. He grabbed me. He stopped me. He said, "What did you do?" I said, "What?" He said, "Did you start this fire?" I said, "No." He said, "What the hell you running around like crazy, like you started it? Take it easy." So, he taught me a lesson. Be calm. You didn't start it. I felt that was a good lesson.

Redden: Two Engine was my first assignment. On assignments, fellows who knew somebody got better assignments. Two Engine was down at the bottom as far as assignments were concerned. Up on the hill, up in Six, Twelve, Seven, and the trucks, Five Truck. If you knew somebody you got into them. Well, I didn't know anybody, so I got what was left. But they did me a big favor. I had a lot of time to study.

When I came on the job, of course, Two Engine is a three-story building, bunkroom on the second floor. And the third floor the Police and Fire band used to practice upstairs. They had a combination Police and Fire Department band and they would practice on the third floor. Then I think later on they put a boxing ring up there.

Two Engine was not busy at all. It is right on Center Street and McCarter Highway. McCarter goes north and south. There was no response to the east because the river is on the east and we covered the downtown area. You had very few fires in the downtown area. So, we used to go to seconds in the First Battalion, the Third Battalion, and the upper part of the Fifth Battalion. We didn't have too many of them. We had one bad job up on James Street, which is in the First Battalion. But it was a very slow company. That's why nobody wanted to go there.

Kinnear: My father was a battalion chief. He never brought the job home with him. He was a widower. My mother died. The five children were very young, so he never really brought the fire department home with him. In fact, I was kind of dumb when I went on the job. I should have known a lot more. I went to Six Engine and I worked 24 hours the first day. Going to bed that night, I didn't know whether to wear socks in bed or not to wear socks. I never thought to ask my father, so I wore socks the first couple of nights. Then after that, I learned that you didn't really have to wear socks, especially in the summer time.

As I recall, Six was the busiest. Well, Twelve beat them out sometimes or Twenty beat them out sometimes. But as I recall, I would say around 800 runs a year. Somewhere in that vicinity. But that didn't include what we called still runs. Still runs would be what we call a Signal Five today. They didn't total that in. So that was actual bell alarms. Probably with still alarms it was 900 maybe. It was in that area.

When I first went there, there was an old grey-haired man sitting up at the window on the Hunterdon Street side of the building. I figured, well this guy's got to be a hanger on. A civilian who just hung around. I found out he was the first driver. Most of the guys were old. I was the only guy, the only new person assigned to Six Engine. The other guys were what I thought was old. They were probably in their fifties and forties and maybe a few in their thirties.

It was a little hard breaking in because there was a young fellow who had been a temporary, who they wanted to get the job. But because he was under-weight, he couldn't pass the physical test. They knocked him down on weight which they wouldn't do today. They were of course disappointed that he didn't get the job. But as I worked my way in, they kind of accepted me.

I don't believe it was easier for me because I was Chief Kinnear's son. I really don't think so. My father was a well-liked man. He never did anything to make it easier for me. In fact, I could have probably, being his son, have gone to a much slower company if I wanted. He wanted me to go to the busiest companies in the city. Originally, I was supposed to go to Twenty Engine, but when it came out that this fellow hadn't passed the test because of his weight there was an opening in Six. So, I think he did help me get to Six Engine. I just worked my way in with the guys. He wasn't working the same shift as me, so there was no direct contact. I don't think that applies at all really.

I remember the first time we got a new apparatus; we got an American LaFrance. Bert Knight, Gerry Knight's father, he was the driver. Of course, this was a little wider than the apparatus we had in the beginning when I first came on the job. He took the door out his first run out. But I remember that one because we did have a three-alarm fire then. Basically, I remember being on the end of a two-and-a-half-inch line and drowning the thing. You couldn't really do a close approach like you do today. There were masks on the engines, but they weren't used at all. You stayed back. With a two-and-a-half-inch line you could stay back because you had a lot of reach with it. Basically, you drowned them. If it was a one room job, you'd do it the same as you do today, but it would take you a little longer to work your way into the room naturally. But you did it. Of course, you had more men too. So, the guy on the tip, he'd go as far as he could and then there would be another fresh man to relieve him. You'd just work your way into it. It worked. You took a lot of smoke, but nobody knew any different. You took it and that was it. It was part of the job.

Masters: I was first assigned to Ninth Street and Central Avenue, Engine Eleven. I walked into the firehouse with my rubber goods. Signed in, I met the captain and he took me around, told me what was expected of me. You come dressed in your uniform. You do your job, obey orders.

We were doing 500, 600 runs a year. I stayed there ten years. I drove the engine for ten years, the old Ahrens-Fox, then they came with the new apparatus. I was on the engine when we had the Warren Petroleum. I thought I was back in Europe with the devastation that those tanks flying created. I really mean it. I'm not kidding. Let me see. Those tanks were five feet in diameter. They were fifty feet long and half inch steel. I'll tell you; they were flying off like the rockets in Carnival. One of them took off and landed right on a gas station. Demolished the gas station. Another one took off, one in a million shot, came down on the ground, busted a water main. So, we had to relay water from Newark Bay. I was at the dock with the Ahrens-Fox pumping water, relaying. We stayed there for three days. I was up in Irvington shopping with the wife when the alarm came in. We were on our way home. I said, "Oh, my God look at that. It must be in New York." I got to my house, then we get a phone call. I had to report back to duty. I went right down, I lived on Farley Avenue then. They told me where to go and I went right there with my car. That's where I stayed. Then I had my brother-in-law come down and pick my car up.

When I got on the scene, I went with the engine, Eleven Engine. I stayed there with the operator, helping him out. Three days, that Ahrens-Fox shook so much, it went right down in the mud to the hub caps. That's where it stayed. The only time it stopped was to check oil and gas, then started up again. We had to pull it out of the mud. Those old apparatus were all chain driven. It was quite an experience.

F. Grehl: We were the young kids. We were all out of the service. A little bit wild. Being confined to strict discipline for all those times, now you get on the job, but we found out it was still a little strict discipline. The old timers didn't like us too much because we had an attitude. We kids had an attitude. The world owed us a living. We saved the world for you old guys and you wouldn't have this day without us. Those were the arguments going back and forth. Most of them good natured. You wouldn't have this job. The Japanese would be here sitting in your seat if we hadn't won. That's what would go back and forth. Not a lot of them, but many of them used to just hate the guts of these young kids who thought the world owed them a living for fighting the war. There were a lot of old timers out there who loved the young kids coming in there because the old timers liked to see the youth there.

I was assigned to Twenty-nine Engine. Captain Schaeffer was my captain. Very well learned man, a good fireman. The captain in the truck was my father.

When he drilled the truck, Captain Schaffer made sure all the engine men went over and vise-versa. So, I had learned to raise an aerial even though I was never in a truck company.

That worked out because later on I spent quite a few months down in Five Truck as a temp in there. When the underwriters came to town, there I am in Five Truck. They come there and I'm sitting there with a Twenty-nine Engine front piece on. They asked, "What are you doing here?" I said, "I'm detailed here for the day." They said, "Okay, Cap. Take the apparatus out." We took the apparatus out. They said, "Okay, we're going to raise the aerial, but you raise the aerial." They pointed to me. So, the captain said, "He's not in the truck company. He's only detailed." "If he's detailed here today, he's supposed to do all the jobs of a truck man in this thing." Well, having been trained in everything, it was very simple. The aerial went up, beautiful. No problem at all. Of course, the captain was as happy as a lark.

Twenty-nine Engine didn't do very much at the time. First year I was there, I think they had 250 runs total for the year. Because you're in a slow company, as time goes on you realize if you had the extra man you could say to the captain, "Can I go to the store?" He'd say, "Yes, but make sure you make the rig." Make sure you get back on the rig. You run down that street and get back on the rig. So, if you went to the store, you had one ear on the bell and everything and run back and get on the rig and go. We were one and seven in a slow company. The slower companies always got the detail. I guess rightfully so, too. Put the men where you need them and where you're going to get the work out of them.

But I had the opportunity to go to Five Truck and Six Engine because I was in the Fourth Battalion. I enjoyed more work and it was shortly after I went to Five Truck and somebody was out on a long-term injury or sick leave, so they left me there for about four or five months. I enjoyed it. One of the fellows I worked with, Jimmy Nolen, was a fireman there at the time. We had a great time. So, I put in for a transfer to Five Truck. I didn't get it because somebody else had it. I went back to Twenty-nine Engine. The first Captain's list was made and that's when I decided to go to Six Engine. There was a vacancy there and I went to Six Engine as a fireman. There was about a year and a half I was in Twenty-nine Engine. Then I transferred to Six Engine which I was at almost the whole rest of my life. In one position or another, I stayed there.

The early years at Twenty-nine Engine, I had maybe one, two good fires. One multiple that I know of, but most of them in the Jewish neighborhood, the people had nice homes. We didn't have fires over there. It took quite a big fire for us to move from Twenty-nine Engine into the Central Ward. Because there were so many other companies around that went before us in that running schedule. So, I didn't have many until I went to Five Truck. That's when I started hitting constantly, hitting fires.

It's funny when you talk about attitudes. I had worked for really three, four chiefs. Chief Gabrielle was a quiet, stern man. He put me on charges. I was only on the job about three months and I was detailed to Eighteen Engine. The new kid got all the details, so I was the new kid. I was up in Eighteen Engine and the Yankee game was on television.

I played a little ball in my time. We were talking about it and Gabrielle said something about it. He was a real Yankee fan. And I said something else. We got into a heated argument about baseball. The next thing you know I'm on charges. "You don't talk to a Deputy Chief like that. Don't you know a Deputy Chief is God?" So, I'm on charges. The captain of Eighteen Engine got them ripped up before we went home that night and straightened everything out, but I mean he was stern. He was a stern. You couldn't even come up to him without permission no less arguing with him.

I wasn't on the Fire Department that long before I went to Six Engine in which things are changing. Chief Donlon is starting to change things. We had our own masks. We had Teddy Smith, never wore a mask in his life. "I won't put on a gook-gook." He used to call them gook-gooks. "I don't put no gook-gook on." Teddy was right there. I don't care how thick the smoke was, he stood right with you. One time I had a nozzle and we were working our way down a hallway. We get into a room and the thing was hot. It started coming back. I'd say to Teddy, "Teddy come on, we have to back out into the hallway. It's too damn hot in here." "I'm all right kid. I'm all right kid. I stay with you. Don't worry. I won't leave you." I said, "Teddy back up. We're going back to the hallway." "I'm all right kid." Well, then I have to push him. And in pushing him we end up rolling out in the hall. Just about that time the fire comes out over our heads out into the hall. I'm lying on the floor with the hose line trying to push it back in. The captain comes up and says, "What the hell are you two guys doing?" I said, "We're all right, Cap." But Teddy said, "I stay with you kid, I stay with you." He did.

Conover: Being in Twelve Engine, I'll never forget it. The first day at work, was a Friday. Friday was the day the day crew had to clean the windows. I'm out on the roof doing the outside of the window on the second floor when all of the sudden the bells starting to hit. Johnny March was working with me and he was hollering, "Bill, come on in we're going." Away we went and I'll be darned if we didn't have a two-alarm fire. I'll tell you the truth; I was so green I didn't even know which end of the hose water came out. But there I was, I'll never forgot it. I think I was on the job something like maybe an hour and a half. It was in the middle of the morning, somewhere between Tenth and Eleventh. Yeah, those days were something.

Vesey: My first assignment was Nine Truck. Stayed there a couple of years. Had to get away. Then I went to Three Truck. From Three Truck I went to Five Truck. We had a deputy out of Nine Truck, Davy Kinnear's father. Eli Sorita was the captain there. He drove me out. I had to get the hell out of there. I think I was there even less. If I was there a year and a half, I was there a long time. He drove me out of that joint. That was too slow anyway. Eighteen Engine and a deputy, the

First Deputy. I had to leave. No social life. The First Battalion was out of Market Street, but that wasn't bad. He didn't bother us, Chief Cullen, Charlie Cullen.

There weren't that many transfers. In fact, I was told there were no openings. Then one day I got the phone call home. He says, "Your transfer came through." I said, "Yeah, what's that?" He said, "You're going to Three Truck." I said, "I don't give a shit, take me. Get me out of here." That was a good bunch of guys over there. Tommy Rush, Hemmy Gam, Conahan, then you had Bob Melloyd the Captain.

Seven Engine was different. For a double house, it was pretty good. We got along pretty good. We had our own thing. Larry Hagis and Bob Melloyd were the captains. We had a good, pretty square. We had the dungeon. That was the only thing wrong, had to go to the cellar, like Six Engine, the stairs. Bang your head around.

The night my daughter was born, we had a three alarmer on Springfield Avenue and Tenth Street. Yes, she was born that day. That was a goodie. The building like the one in New York, the flat iron building. There was a name in concrete on the side of the building, the Okin Building. They burnt that one out. The old elevator server, dumb waiter shaft. It was a good fire. I came in. I was celebrating all day.

J. Ryan: I started out at Five Engine. I stayed at Five Engine for about a year, year and a half. I went into Four Truck. They were both on Congress Street then. First day in the firehouse at eight o'clock in the morning, you got your first cup of coffee. After you were introduced to everybody, met the officers, then they showed you what had to be done, the house work. Well, they showed you the apparatus, what it was, where the hose was, what the hose tower was. What I had to do was handle the hose, follow one of the senior men. Do what he said and make sure your boots went on the right way. Some fellows had a tendency to mix your boots up, so that you put them on backwards. So, you check your boots. Of course, one fellow I remember, he was in Seventeen Engine, he wrote a left and a right on his boots on the back.

The Fifth Battalion was also in Five Engine on Congress Street, the chief and his driver. They had an acting captain in Five Engine, Tommy O'Boyle, who later became a deputy chief. He was the acting captain in Five Engine. Later on in 1949, they made captains to fill out the third tour for officers, somewhere around the first of the year. Tommy O'Boyle of course made captain and he went down to Eight Truck. I got Patty O'Beirne as a captain; who later became Chief of Department. And then Jim Barry came from Eight Truck. He came into Four Truck. He was the captain there. They had an acting captain in Four Truck when I went there on the tour. So, they had two officers who were made later on.

McCormack: My first assignment was Fifteen Engine. The third tour just came in when I got appointed. I think it was the second tour I was on. I think that my living in the North Ward had something to do with my assignment there. The city tried to assign you to a place near your home. Although I never knew that for a fact or asked for it, but I think that was kind of one of the basis of assignment in those days.

We were told when I first came on the job, in the early days that some of the deadliest places in the building were the clothes closets. The woolens when they burned gave off toxic gases and a closet full of woolen winter clothes was extremely hazardous to your health. We didn't have any plastics. Nobody mentioned plastics at the time. We didn't have foam rubber. The mattresses were stuffed with cotton material and they were always deadly from the standpoint of smoke and burning and everything. That's another factor too, which I hadn't thought of, but I suspect strongly, and I just thought of it this minute, but I suspect that with the advent of the anti-smoking campaign going all around, we've cut down tremendously on mattress fires. Because mattress fires almost invariably in those days were due to some guy smoking in bed. I think you still have mattress fires, but I don't think you have anywhere near the amount you used to have because people don't smoke as much as they used to. That's just a thought. I just thought of that now. But we were always getting mattress fires and invariably it was a guy smoking in bed. He fell asleep in an overstuffed chair or a couch or on a mattress or something with a cigarette and boom you have a fire. But were they worse or better? I don't know. Fires are fires. It's hard to say. It's a tradeoff.

Masterson: Ten Engine was my first assignment. I didn't know much about the fire department. I didn't know what to expect. I hope I don't just stand there sucking my thumb when things start to happen. They were good, Brenner and those guys were good. The guys who were there were new too. Well, Pete Dobak was one guy. He had a couple of years on the job, so he was helpful. Paul Delvere, he came from Thirty-five Engine. He was down there about a year when he was on the job. I came walking into Ten Engine, we were practically a new crew. Those guys had a year or so on before me. But they had no fire duty except for Pete. Out of 500 runs a year, how much do you get? But we learned fast. That's how you learn. You go out and you just work. You make mistakes. You don't do it the next time.

Ten Engine was doing about 500, 600 runs a year. They were getting close to a thousand when I left. But that was the '50s in Ten Engine.

I only remember big fires at Ten Engine. You didn't do anything really. The propane tanks and a big school on Washington Street, they're big fires. They're all deck pipe jobs and you really don't get inside on those big jobs. A couple of more, the platinum houses on High Street, especially on the hill. In those days they had stables with horses when I first came on, up on Prince Street and Charlton Street. We were pulling the horses out, whacking them on the ass and chasing them down Charlton Street. Smacking them and chasing them. They were really getting excited in there. The smoke was getting to them. It wasn't that much, so they were all right. I was at Ten until 1959. Then I went to Five Truck.

J. Doherty: I took the fire department in December of '49 which was the institution of the fifty-six-hour week. Started in Twenty-three Engine, but I did take a job when I was in the fire department about six months. Essex County jail guard came up. And Emmet Mathews was the secretary of the fire department. He was a very, very, very distant relation. So, I went down to see if I could get a leave of absence. I got a three month leave of absence. And I didn't even take the whole three months. No, no jail guard. I wasn't suited for that. I think it was six or eight weeks and I came back into the fire department. And I don't know, within a month the FMBA came around, tells me I owe three months dues. I said, "What are you talking about?" "Well, you didn't take out a slip or a withdrawal." So, naturally, I was just married and money was tight. And I said, "To hell with it. I'm not paying it." I just quit the FMBA.

So, then I was transferred to Thirty-two Engine. That was a punishment house. And I mean they had some real characters down there. You couldn't believe it. I was there for about six months, but I had been qualified as an Ahrens-Fox driver of apparatus. That was the supposed reason I went down there, to drive. They left me there for about six months. And from there I was transferred to Five Engine. And I stayed in Five Engine about two years.

1950s: Expansion and Innovation

Gibson: First day in the firehouse was Thirty-two Engine. It was like a one-story building, brick and a garage at the other end of the house. And that's where they fire engine was. That building is still there. It's at Port and Airport Street. It was an old fashion Ahrens-Fox with the ball on the front. I stayed there about sixteen months. Harold Titcomb, he told me, "Kid, don't stay here. Get in the busiest company in the city." So, I kept asking for transfers out. I got transferred to Two Engine. They did maybe 100 runs a year. I developed a program up there with a guy, Chief Crowley, Fred Crowley. Well, he and I became friends, true friends. He was a mask man, an old Rescue Squad guy. So, listening to him and Jimmy McAlinden, I started taking the masks out of the box. They made me the driver in Two Engine and I thought that was a great thing. Then I realized they put the guy there that could do nothing.

So, I took the mask and I hung it on the searchlight in the back. When we'd go to a fire, I'd go inside with the mask and it killed me because I couldn't breathe with it on. But I'm glad I did because it turned out to be a great thing for the whole fire department. Then I went from there to Eleven. I didn't like that. That was a house of partying. I called Frank McCarthy up and I says, "Frank, you got to get me out of here. I'm gonna knock someone on his ass around here. The way they act." "This is a rule and that's a rule." Buy ten cents worth of butter and two slices of bread for lunch. Well, then they put me in Twenty Engine and they made it a one and eight company. We responded to fires in half of the city, from High Street up. They had another one in One Engine which responded to the other half of the city from High Street down. I liked it, but then Caufield came in and he did away with that. McAlinden dubbed them the flying squad, cause New York had flying squads. He had somebody make a thing with wings. He mounted it on the hood of the apparatus.

G. Alfano: I went to Washington Street across from Bamberger's and I stayed there until it closed. It was a nice house and I really enjoyed it. And of course, all the pretty girls used to come out of the Prudential and we used to sit out and watch them when we could. I was fortunate that I knew a couple of the guys before I went on and they were there. They were supposed to be bad boys and that's why they were there, but they weren't bad boys, they were terrific guys. We had a great company. They were all good firemen. A good fireman's a guy that works. That's the way I figure a good fireman and they worked. Like I said, I knew most of them before I went on. That helped because I think if I didn't know anybody, I might have been kind of shy. I didn't have to be because when I walked in it's like having a friend there. If you're not a fireman, I don't think you know what to except. I didn't. That's for sure. They said, "Don't worry about a thing. Just stay with me. You'll pick up by yourself." And I did.

It was a little different than going to an engine company or a truck company because it was a different kind of work. We ran on everything. We went into the fourth battalion. If we threw a few covers, the chief would get us to do anything. We may take a line, pull ceilings, anything. Sometimes I think us being there and the Squad, I think he didn't have to send the second. So, I really feel that we did a nice job. And I did love it, so that's the big thing.

We put the net out one time. We caught this guy from the third floor and he had a cast on his leg. I'll never forget it. And when he came down, he hit the second-floor window sill and did a somersault and landed perfect right in the net. I was in Salvage at the time. We had a terrible net. It wasn't like the kind on a truck. It was canvas and it had rope all around it. It was nowhere near the truck nets, but that's what we used. We caught him and the next week we caught another guy. The flames must have been licking them, so they jumped. The one guy was only on the second floor, so that wasn't too bad. The other guy was the third floor So Bobby Howard said, "You guys are going to need catcher's mitts."

Deutch: I was assigned to the foam truck, Thirty-five Engine at Newark Airport, the traffic circle for eighteen months, When I was down there, Chief Shanahan said, being I'm a young fireman, I shouldn't be stuck down here with the old timers. I worked with two old time men down there in the foam truck. It was such a quiet house. He said, "I'm going to put you on detail." He detailed me to all the houses in the Fifth Battalion. So, I spent like three months at Eight Truck, time on Congress Street and Fourteen Engine for my eighteen months.

I saw a few fires with Eight Truck where we did work. My Captain was Chief O'Boyle, Captain O'Boyle then. And he later was my chief when I went up to Five Truck. He followed me up. He became Chief. In fact, I'll never forget Eight Truck, my first week there they had a four-alarm fire. We could see the smoke, but we never moved. It was like another Twelve Truck, Saint Bridget's, four-alarm fire. We never moved.

I transferred up onto the hill at Five Truck which was really hard to do in those days, to get a spot. You really had to know somebody. I knew Hop Fagan; John Fagan's father had a lot of power down City Hall. Just a fireman, he was just a fireman, but he knew everybody. The man was so popular that in 1938 he won a car from the Down Neck association. A 1938 Dodge he won for being the most popular fireman in Newark. He got me into Five Truck and he had to know somebody because Chief Schaeffer couldn't get his own son in. Georgie Schaeffer always said to me, "Chuck, who did you know?" Because he had in for Five Truck before me and I got the spot.

There were a lot of old timers up in the Burg and also in North Newark, but there were a few older Captains around in the busy companies yet, who were hanging on. We had a couple of them used to visit us at Five Truck. I know Cap Reiss used to walk down and the man was almost in his nineties. He used to come down to visit the firemen. And talk about the old days with the horses.

R. Griffith: When I first came up to dispatch, it was a lot different than now. First of all, it was almost like there was a vast separation between operators and firemen, with very little or no friendship. It was always the good guys and the bad guys. It just seemed there wasn't a blending of people or personalities. They just didn't seem to get along. Why? I don't know. When I got here, I knew a lot of firemen and I was always kind of discouraged from being with them socially or talking with them and things like that. I don't know why, but they wanted this job isolated from the actual field units. It did break down, but it took quite a while before it did. That's the way it was then. Now, it's a lot different. I think that the people up here are a lot closer as a unit to the people in the field than they were then, by far.

When I first got here, the personnel were all fire alarm operators. They all took a test for fire alarm operator and were assigned here. There were four men on each individual trick. There were five particular tricks. As opposed to four tours in the firehouse and I'd say maybe eighteen or nineteen years ago, we started losing operators and they weren't replacing them. At that time, they started to detail firemen who were on light duty here. At the very beginning, it didn't work out to well because first of all they were bringing people up here, firemen up here, who really didn't want to be here. I don't know what they thought it was here, but they cared little or nothing about it. Really, they were of no help. The only help they were was it gave some of the guys a chance to get a summer vacation. But as time went on the firemen who came here and are here now really, they're top-grade operators, top grade dispatchers right now

The type of equipment used was like night and day. You know the one thing I hate to say. This place was better then. It was. When I came here, this was a class act. All the equipment we had was old, but first class. It was something that people used to come from all around just to see. It never failed. It never failed. Which is the big thing in fire alarms. But it was a thing of beauty from the checking of each individual circuit. They had things here where you could almost tell how many box doors would be open on a circuit. The alarms coming in, even the bells that they had here were all brass. The sound, the look, the cleanliness.

Of course, the telephone switch board was an old type of PBX switch board, before they had the Centrex here where they could dial from firehouse to firehouse. In those days every phone call whether it be firehouse to firehouse, firehouse to here to Eighteenth Avenue, to any of the offices, everything had to go through here. You had to be connected by the operator. There was no such thing as you calling Twenty Engine or Nine Engine or Six and Twelve. It had to come through here. That was a big thing for us because you can imagine in the course of a day the amount of phone calls that went through here. Now of course, we don't have anything like that. But the equipment itself, the receiving and the transmitting, things of that nature. By far was superior then than now. I know that sounds silly, but I think if you look around now this place was immaculate. The floors were swept clean, waxed. The equipment was always clean.

As far as work, I'd go back to a New Year's Eve. It's quite a while back. I'm just sorry I can't give you the date or the time, but I got in here about eleven o'clock because we wanted to give the off going people a chance to get to where they were going. I brought in a nice spread. The others fellows did. We put it out on a little table right in the middle here. We were all set to have a little party and watch Guy Lombardo at midnight and it started just about maybe a quarter of twelve. As I said after a while you can get a feel here and you can feel it building to the climax. Well, the way we left everything out was the way it was at eight o'clock when we left here.

It was the first time that anyone ever heard of Newark not having any engines left. Was something really memorable. At that time, it was a first. It was a first. In fact, they started to release companies as quickly as possible. Something they never did before. They never had where they ran out of them. I'm sure it was two three-alarm fires and one or two two-alarm fires. Absolutely stripped the city. We had nothing left. And to me, I was a new fellow here. I wasn't here all that long. I forget how many years, but years. That to me was the most memorable night

Wall: From the Academy I went to Ten Truck, Lehigh and Bergen. That was considered Hollywood and Vine. The young guys didn't want to stay there because at that time Ten Truck wasn't a busy truck. I was initially assigned to Nine Truck which I wanted. But Nick DiDaminico was president of the F.M.B.A. at the time. I was assigned to Nine Truck and then they said, "Oh, Nick is still on the rolls here." At that time, they detailed the president of the FMBA out, but they carried them on the rooster. So, they transferred me over to Ten Truck which didn't make me too happy.

Bergen and Lehigh was in the Jewish section. The truck didn't know how to turn left. Whenever you went out on a run you went right. Very rarely did you ever go over towards Lyons Avenue. Chancellor Avenue, you didn't know what that looked like except for in service inspection. That was a beautiful area, large one family houses. And the only action you got is when you caught fires over on Hawthorne Avenue in that area. We used to respond like second due truck down to Frelinghuysen Avenue, so you would get some action down there in the industrial section. But Ten Truck at the time was a relatively slow truck.

On some companies there was a permanent first driver who was next to God. There was the captain and then there was the first driver. In Ten Truck I eventually became the first tiller man. And the first driver we had, whose name will remain nameless, thought that his responsibility ended at the fifth wheel and that the tiller man took care of the tools and everything else back to the tiller wheel. So that was the first driver. If you had a rigid captain, that's the way it was. Where you had more liberal Captains, they rotated the driving as is common today.

Freeman: I went to Twelve Engine. We got sworn in February 14, 1956. Probably because I knew everybody on Belmont Avenue, I got along pretty good with the guys. There were a few incidents, but I never let that bother me. Was it a subdued bigotry? I would say in a way yes. I'm a little different than maybe some of the guys. I guess everybody's different. You're an individual. Now there were two of us there. I didn't know what was happening with the other guys, like Willie Thomas and Shelly Harris. They were down in Salvage across from Bamberger's on Washington Street.

When we came on the job, I knew all the guys there. When I was an auxiliary, I got along pretty good with some of the guys. They used to get telephone calls sometimes. "Oh, I see you're carrying the only smoke around." When I used to ride in Five Truck. That was one of the phone calls that day. It kind of made me feel kind of rough, kind of bad, but I just kind of shook it off. I just kept going and the guys who were there at Five Truck were really good to me.

I had some good guys I worked with. Sherman Dubois, he passed away now. Caufield, Andrew Caufield. He quit the job. We had Jan Taucsh, Chief Jan Taucsh was our Captain. I didn't have any problems like the other black guy in the house. I never argued with anybody. If certain guys wouldn't talk to me, so what. Hey, I would say hello to you. If you didn't want to speak to me, you don't speak. But I'm not going to say, "Hey, how come you don't speak to me?" Then you cause a whole lot of problems. I think that's what happened with this other guy. Certain things went down and he was verbal about it and he ran into a lot of problems.

A lot of guys would say I always wanted to be around white guys, rather than around black guys. I didn't do what a lot of the black guys did. I was more or less doing my own thing. I didn't hang around black guys that often not because I didn't want to, but just because my life style was totally different from theirs. All these guys drank. A lot of them were married and so they had families. I didn't have a family. I liked scuba diving, flying, and all that stuff. They didn't do things like that. I invited them. I just kind of kept to myself. I had certain activities that I did, my athletics, my lifting. All the other stuff I just couldn't get involved in it. I heard about a lot of stuff. Some guys would come to me and ask, "Hey, Rich. What would you do in a case like this?" Sometimes they wouldn't go by what I said. But then sometimes you couldn't. You had to say something.

I remember my first death, up around Fourteenth Avenue, maybe Hunterdon Street. We went into the back. I don't think there was that much fire, but I remember we went in and I thought this was a little doll on the bed, but it was a dead baby. I just couldn't get that in my mind. It was charred.

I saw a guy sitting at a table once dead. He had been drinking and he was just sitting there just like you're sitting. I guess he was asphyxiated, but he had been drinking. It's just part of the job. Sometimes you can get in. Sometimes it's too late.

I had a captain and he didn't like me for beans. I came in late one day about a minute and I had maybe come in late maybe one or two other times, a minute late. That just kind of ticked him off and that particular last time he said he didn't want me in his company anymore. He called the chief down, said, "I don't want him anymore. I don't care where he goes." I didn't know where to go. I was appalled. I couldn't understand what was wrong with this guy. I never did a bad job with this guy. Maybe he didn't think I was a good firefighter. I don't know, but he always gave me a hard time. In fact, nobody really liked him. He's the only captain I ever had a problem with. Well, I had to go to Ten Truck. In fact, Chief Finucan's father was in Ten Truck then on that tour. That's where I went for a short period of time. Then I had to go in the hospital to have a back operation. When I came back, I came back to Twelve Engine. I guess it was a temporary thing to get away from him. And Finucan's father took me in. It wasn't even a temporary transfer. I was detailed there.

Ch. Griggs: There were thirty of us appointed the same day; they split us up. The first fifteen guys they sent up to Eighteen Avenue for two weeks. The second group which I was in, they assigned us companies. I went to Eighteen Engine on the third tour, with Chief Donlon and my captain was young Jimmy Caufield. So,

I was assigned to Eighteen Engine and I would occasionally get detailed to Nine Truck while I was assigned there. After two weeks, we went up to the Training Academy and then right after that we got our assignments. And I went to Fourteen Engine on the third tour with Black Jack Brady.

What happened was Chief Donlon put a plug in for me to stay up in Eighteen Engine, but I got cut out of the picture. Somebody that lived in the neighborhood that had a little better influence than I did. Maybe somebody that had family on the department got a hold of that spot. I was asked to go there by the captain and I said I would be interested, but it didn't work out.

I had never spent any time in the firehouse. I walked into the Eighteen Engine and young Captain Caufield had me walking around the apparatus, opening up the compartments. And he says, "John if I send you out for a tool, I want you to know where to go and get it. And you stick with me, thick and thin, if we get something. You stay right by my side." And that's what I did.

I had to sit with the book guy, whoever had the book during the day and lean over his shoulder. That was my assignment up there. They didn't put me on the watch, but I was with the man on the watch during the day. I knew they were going to send us to school. I knew it wasn't a permanent assignment, but it was just the meeting of the personnel. How you're going to be accepted. But it was a nice reception except for the Deputy Chief. He caught me with the wrong shoes on one day. I didn't have a locker and I came out of Down Neck. I had a pair of shoes on. I had my regular uniform on, but I forgot the work shoes. So, the captain pulls me aside. He says, "John, those are your dress shoes. Where are your working shoes?" I said, "Cap, I accidentally left them at home. It's only a short ride. I'm Down Neck. I'll go right out and get them if you want." He said, "No, the Deputy spotted you. He said he'd like you in uniform." And I said, "I'd like to be in uniform, but I forgot."

They called him the cobra. He'd snap. Isolated individual. He'd come in. You'd stay clear of him. That was like the old days. He was like the walking god of the firehouse. He had his own TV. Naturally, his own room and he didn't exactly sit and have coffee with us. He kept himself apart, but he didn't miss a trick.

As far as having turnout gear, here's what happened there. Prior to going to the firehouses, while we were getting appointed, we were asked if we were members of the credit union. And some fellows knew about the credit union. And I didn't and I said, I'm not a member. "Well, we would like you to sign up because you'll be charging everything out of Cairn's. You'll have to pick up boots, the helmet, the front piece, the coat and gloves and that's it."

When I got to Fourteen Engine, we had an American LaFrance there. They didn't have the wagon. It was a nice location, quiet, industrial area. John McVey and I, we reported at the same time, the same day, and we were shown around. We were explained the house duties, the watch duties, and that we would alternate the two days. The two veterans that were there, John Scalia and Sammy DeMitio, would take the night watch and then the next tour we would take days again and then we would fall right into the night watches.

We had a fire on Raymond Boulevard. A waitress had come home, early morning hours. Went up to her room in a tax building, very heavy-duty smoker. Fell asleep and she lost her life. And now we had a couple building going by the time we got here. That was right near the pool, Hayes Pool. And that was a big one. I mean we had two-and-a-half inside the building. That's how much fire was going on. I was on the line with Captain Lopez that night. I drove Chief Kelly there. I got him all set up, second alarm. It went to a second. In fact, it went to a third. Then I checked with him where I could be used. I wasn't a chief hanger. I did not hold the chief's hand. Whatever he needed done was done immediately.

C. Stoffers: I went to Ten Truck when I first came out of the academy and I was there for two nights. Then I came in and the captain was on vacation. The captain in the engine company got a phone call from the chief. So, I went up to

Nine Engine and I stayed up in Nine Engine until about ten months, until October. Then I transferred to Five Truck.

When I transferred to Five Truck, they were making them one and five. They had been one and four. So, that's how the openings came in.

We filled up spots that were already vacant. The forty-two hours didn't go in until March of '59. Which was a couple of years later. Over the course of the next couple of years they hired more and more. The busier companies got one and six.

McGee: There were quite a few elderly guys in this job. And places like Special Service literally had thirty-five guys assigned to them. As opposed to what they have now. There was a theater bureau which was strictly a good little spot. The guy actually went to different theaters. I'm sure he went to the burlesque show more than any of the other theaters and that was his job. There was a hospital detail. But there were more service-connected jobs than there are with strictly fire department. I think it had to do with the extra personnel. As salaries went up and everything else went up after that, they had to cut these different pancake jobs out basically. They were jobs given supposedly to firemen who had been injured in the line of duty or had been ill. So, nobody complained they didn't get it. They were happy to see somebody get the job who had been injured or something.

We would do this with new firemen. The first night we worked after a new fireman was assigned to us, Pete Sheridan would have a meal welcoming the guy into the company. What a great feeling that is for some guy who's just coming. We don't know the guy. Whatever you did, we forgive you and he would have this great meal. It was a very good public relations gimmick. I've had guys comment later and say, "That was such a great night." There were a lot of great things that went on.

Very early in the job, I was in Eleven Truck. We had a fire on Seventh Street. The normal procedure was to bring a twenty-four-foot ladder in with you into the alleyway. It was a very heavy smoke condition. In that area alleyways were literally arms' length from the next building. We raised this ladder because there was a fellow sitting in the third-floor window and he was on his way out. That's how much heavy smoke was coming out of the windows. The ladder was short. We didn't have time to go back and get another ladder. Chief Schaeffer said, "Put that ladder on your shoulders." Two big firemen from Eleven Truck put the ladder on their shoulders. I climbed up the ladder because I was the smallest, skinniest guy.

We brought the man down the ladder. That man definitely would have died. That was very impressive to me because it was one of the earliest fires that I went to. What I'm saying is impressive is not so much for my part because it's probably the easiest part. The two guys backed themselves up against the other building, which was close enough to hold them, and raised the ladder. I climbed up, literally climbed up one of the guys, climbed up the ladder, and brought the man down. What impressed me the most was the Chief had the presence of mind to realize that we didn't have time to back out and get another ladder. Had we raised that ladder it would have been maybe eight or ten feet lower than where the man was. He would have never gone on that ladder and we might have even been hurt.

McGrory: When I first came on the job it was a little different. I think there were quite a few of the old timers. This is my idea. You have a group of people who came on after the Second World War II who were very energetic. They were educated in the services. They knew a lot about what was going on. They were taught to do what you had to do. I think that differentiated the fire department from before 1940 or so. I think it was a whole different department. The department really came into its own after the Second World War because you got an influx of those veterans and they were people who really wanted to do the job. The city was changing too. So as the time went on, you got into the '50s and '60s when the fire problems changed. The root cause of fires started to change. They started to burn down whole areas of the city. Which wasn't like the accidental fire in the cannery or things like that.

My first assignment was Twelve Engine on the third tour and I thought I was going there. Deputy Chief Gabriel came in one day. He says, "Who is McGrory?" I said, "I am, I am." He said, "Okay. We'll take care of you when we get you to Twelve Engine." And he walked out. Anyway, the fellow I was supposed to replace had asked for a transfer out of Twelve to Seventeen, didn't want it at the time. So, I ended up in Seventeen on the first tour working with Captain Eddy Brock. Eddy Brock, Bill Quirk, Johnny Cosman, Joe Mariano, and myself. We had a one-piece engine company which was fine. I lived on Wainwright Street so I wasn't far from Seventeen Engine. I could walk there. I did in some of the storms. I was working there. I liked it. It wasn't too busy. It was 600 or 700 runs a year where maybe the busy companies might have been doing a thousand or somewhere around there. I stayed there.

My first good job, we had a three-story frame on West Runyon down near Bergen Street. A lot of us had rubber turn out coats, rubber boots, and the leather helmets. I'm riding on the back with Willie Quirk and we had our coats draped over the back handrail. It's blowing out the third-floor windows of a three-story frame. It's a hot summer day, during the day. I did everything Willie did. He jumped off, threw his coat on the ground. I threw my coat on the ground. He grabbed a two and a half. I grabbed a two and a half. We start pulling the two and a half off.

Now we're going to go upstairs. Captain Brock is yelling. We don't stand on the outside. We take this two and a half to the third floor without masks. I think I got my coat on. We have to wait for water. We're in the staircase and the whole cockloft's going. The third floor is going. It's a six-family duplex, three-story frame. We got on the left side. We're going up, can't get up to the third-floor landing. We have to wait. We have fire all over. We hit it and it just banks down on us. He yells for me, "Go get a mask!" I run all the way down to the corner. Grab two masks. Run all the way back. Give him a mask.

By that time Danny McCoy is on a two-and-a-half-inch line. Willie yells to me, "Put your mask on kid!" I'm panting, but I put my mask on. I get up and Danny McCoy and I go in with that. They're lightening up. Danny yells to me, "Tell them to lighten up!" The truck men are coming up the stairs. "Lighten up!" "Get the hell out of here." So, we go in. The truck gets the roof, but I'm telling you it's hot. My eyes are crossing. I'm bow legged. I'm exhausted because of the excitement, running, and heat.

We get in. We work our way into the front room. By that time somebody else comes up behind us and they go into the rear. Danny McCoy gets it pretty well knocked down then he gives the line to me. "Hey, kid. Hold this line up in the air." He walks over to wave out the front window. Now he doesn't know that I can't control it too well. I almost knocked him out the front window. By that time, I'm just staggering around.

The Deputy asked, "What's the matter with you, kid?" Then he told me, "Go sit over there." I go into another apartment and sit in a big, overstuffed chair. I'm sitting there. My tongue is hanging out. I'm finished. I can't move. Now, they all have to come up, "What's the matter with you." I can't even talk. I'm saying to myself, "What the hell did I take this job for? This is crazy."

I was told very early on, "Don't let anyone take your line. Don't let anyone take your line." So, we're in a place and I have the inch and a half. It's pretty well knocked down, but it was in a factory building. So, Duke Zeller from Eighteen Engine was coming and trying to get the line off me. They had told me that they're going to come back in. "Kid, I'll take that and move that." "No! No, you won't." I wouldn't give it to him. I got a detail over there one day a couple of weeks later. Over to Eighteen Engine and Duke grabbed me, "Hey, listen kid, I didn't try to grabbed that line off of you." He was explaining himself.

Duerr: I was first assigned to Nine Truck. Captain Thaddeus Haraza was my first captain. He was a great, great fireman. One of the finest firemen Newark ever had, like a bull at a fire, really. He had a problem, a speech impediment and when he got excited you couldn't understand him. I remember our first job. I came to work at night and I was up. I was nervous, so I stayed up. I didn't bother going to sleep. We got a small fire on Rose Terrace which was about four and a half, five blocks from the firehouse and the captain was a little excited to a point where you couldn't understand him. So, he would direct his order by pointing to either the ladder or what he wanted you to do. I had to get used to that.

Of course, he didn't like to leave either. Chief Donlon used to order us up and Captain Haraza would be in the fire building pulling, knocking out a window, or taking a channel out or something. The Chief would say, "Didn't I order you up?" You know he'd come to one of the firemen and say, "Didn't I order you up?" "Yeah, we told Captain Haraza but he's still inside." "Go inside and tell him that it's time to leave."

One of my first deaths was a tragic comedy. There was a job on Fifteenth Avenue. I wasn't on the job that long, maybe six, seven months. On Fifteenth Avenue down by Bruce, I think it was. And there was a tavern on the first floor. There were two residential apartments upstairs. When we responded it was going pretty good. I went up and did a search pattern with Bobby Silk and Kenny Patune. We found this guy in bed and he was dead. So, Captain Haraza asked one of the guys to go down and get the body bag. Well, at that time the body bag was canvas and it had leather straps. So, this guy had an erection, that's why it's a comedy. He had a big erection, let me tell you. Anyway, we put him in the body bag and we can't get it closed because you know. So, I had an axe. I said if I knock it with just the side of the axe the blood may flow out. When I take the axe, Haraza thinks I'm going to chop it off or something. He says, "Wh —wh-what are you going to d-d-do?" So, I just touched it and it went down. Then we tied up the body bag and brought it down. It was a tragic comedy there.

Schoemer: In Three Truck we had a bunch of World War II veterans, which were pretty decent. It seems like veterans are much nicer, more disciplined. The guys I worked with were Tommy Rush, Emmet Gamms, Leo Fay, Bill Dorney, and Milt Januse. Milt came on with me the first day. So, on the truck you had, Bob Malloy was the Captain, Tommy Rush the driver, Emmet the tiller man, and Milt Januse and myself on the side. The Engine crew was Buddy Pulogic, who was driving, Leo Fay, Bill Dorney, and then there was an Italian fellow who got scared. He was blown off a ladder. He had a ladder up to the second floor. I think I was probably in the building, but he went out and I think it had a flashover and it scared him. He fell off the ladder and quit the job. I can't think of his name. But anyway, he quit the job.

Chief George Schaefer, he was a good German guy. A real smart man, I loved working with him. I even got trapped in a fire with him and he said to me, "Rich, let's get out of here." We were on the third floor of a six family. I worked that line and we got on the back porch and I threw the line down and the guys hit it with a two and a half. We got down to the first floor and the whole back porch fell out, just fell off the building.

In the early days you learned to smell the smoke. As you were riding up, you'd say, "Another wet mattress." or "Hey, it's meat on the stove." that kind of stuff. You'd get to know. Then little by little the furniture started changing, become vinyl and then you didn't go in without a muzzle anymore. That stuff just stuck in your throat and you couldn't get it out. That was terrible stuff.

But we had a number of fires. We had that big one up by Eleven Engine on Central Avenue. Of course, the apparatus is on an angle and we had this one wall of this great big building. I put the aerial out. I think somebody from Twenty Engine went up the aerial and the aerial bent. I couldn't get it to lock, so I just pulled it in and it tore the rung out with lock, the ladder lock. When I put it down, it's stronger. No. no, no. This guy's scared saying I'm gonna catch his arms or legs. And I'm yelling, "Just keep your fingers clear." I bring it back down.

A. Prachar The best thing that ever happened to me was going right to the firehouse and not going to the Academy. Because if you went to the Academy and you did the job the way they taught you it, it's no good. According to the book, you do everything you're supposed to do, but there's nothing like practical experience. Learning the job on the street. Learning the job from guys that did the job. Guys that would protect you, but at the same time would be behind you and push you so that you would do the job. Not to the point where you got hurt. Make sure you got low when you had to get low and make sure you did what you were supposed to. It was the best thing going to the firehouse for that time and then going to the Academy and saying, "What are you talking about? That's not the way you do it in the firehouse." Start you off that way. It was an experience.

We had a two-piece company. We rode a captain and five men. I can remember being on the job a week and having four six-family homes on Ridgewood Avenue. That was my first multiple alarm. It was in March. It was cold. It was my first experience with the water running in the eyelids and the eyelids closing. Oh my God. And I'm saying to myself, "Am I crazy?" I can remember my first body was on Sherman and Wright in a three-story wood frame. There was woman screaming about her baby being trapped on the third floor and the captain took me up there. We searched the third floor. We couldn't find a baby. I remember crawling through what I thought was talcum powder or something like that. It turned out later on to be part of a body. And the baby we were looking for was over six-foot tall. Those are the things that you learn. That was my first experience with a body, that part of it was so crisply burnt. Like I said, it was like talcum powder. We worked in a team of two. I was with the captain. And he said, "You found the body." I had no idea what he was talking about. But he had thirty years of experience, so he certainly knew what he was talking about.

Bitter: When I went into the firehouse, my brother-in-law Chris Larson was already working there. He worked days. I says, "Oh, they got a hook and ladder here too." He said, "Shut up you dummy. That's your company." I didn't know a truck from an engine.

Nine Truck, everything was happy. I spent six years there. I remember my wife saying to me, you know, about making captain. And I says, "Captain? Do realize what a captain is?" This is like way up there, next to God. Chief, don't even look in his directions at the time.

At the time I was a worker. I would work until I dropped. I used to be like Mister Nine Truck. I remember Chief McCormack searching me out at a fire, "Rich, I need those windows opened." They had confidence in me. I wasn't going to let anybody down. I remember going up and crawling on my belly to get these windows opened. Angelo Ricca was the captain at Five Truck and he wanted me down there because of my work. So, eventually we did a swap. I swapped with a guy named Harry Digger and he went to Nine Truck.

I went to Five Truck and my work ability was almost like in competition with Captain Ricca. It was me, the captain was Angelo Ricca, Eddy Chrystal, who had just come there, Boisy Cosby, and Elton Fisher, Fishcakes. Fishcakes became my partner. I used to go places and do things and he used to curse me out. "You bastard, you're going to get us killed." Doing what we were doing.

Charpentier: My first assignment on the fire department was Engine Six. Right on the second tour with Chief Rushek. I was an auxiliary before I was on the job. I would have liked to have gone to Twenty Engine. I was a little disappointed when I went to Six, but after I got there, I was glad. At that time, when you went in, both tours stood roll call at eight in the morning and six at night and then you left. That only lasted maybe a year, if it was a year when I first came on. Then later on as your relief came in you went. Whether it was four o'clock in the afternoon, five o'clock. As long as it was before six.

Having a first driver was up to the discretion of the captain. Some captains wanted to rotate. Others just wanted the one driver, then designate a backup driver.

When I first went on, we had Reggie Fredette who was a real old timer and Jimmy Cavanaugh, an old timer. Henny Richter and myself both came on together. So, Reggie didn't want to drive and Jimmy was stuck. He didn't care that much about driving, so they broke me in and Henny. But Henny didn't go for driving. He wanted to go in and I got stuck most of the time. But Henny or Jimmy were there for back up. I worked under captains who just wanted one driver, so I got stuck being the first driver for quite a few years.

Cardillo: When I went to Seventeen, they were running about 300 times a year. Because I lived in that area, I knew every street. So, Captain Whittick said, "Listen Phil, you be the driver." We were two-piece and McGrory drove the second piece. I drove the first piece. I would go to the fire and I would go in front of the fire. I would take the nozzle and go in. McGrory was the pumper at the fire hydrant. He would take a hose from me to his rig. And that's how we worked it. It was super. Because I knew where the locations were. McGrory was there before me, but he didn't know the locations. He didn't know the streets.

Well, the minute I walked in, the bell hit and I don't know who the hell was there, but I didn't even have boots or anything. A guy says "Here use these, use my helmet and he put me on the back step and that was it. We went to this fire on Johnson Avenue and Clinton Avenue. That was the first. And Whittick says, "Come with me." I don't know why the hell he said come with me, but we didn't do much there. I think Twelve Engine took care of it. That was the first job I went to.

Denvir: My first assignment was Truck Twelve. I was there for about seven months. That year they had about 150 runs. But then I went down to Three Truck on the third tour. I was supposed to go to Five Truck, but there were a few transfers that were in the works, so I wound up in Three Truck and I just stayed there.

George Quackenbush was the captain. Then there was John Kelly, then Jankowski, Stanley Kossup.

When I walked into the firehouse, I had my old boots from Public Service. They weren't good, but they were a pair of boots. I didn't have to lay out the money for them then. Everybody wore what they wanted. There was no uniform coat that everybody had. Some had turnout coats, cotton duck turnout coats. Some guys had rubber. Whatever they wanted, back in those days.

I was told to follow the big guy. Follow Eddie Jankowski. He was a hell of a fireman, Eddie. The first rescue, I don't recall where the fire was, but there was a child trapped in the building. The fire was on the first floor. They didn't know where the kid was. So, we came in. Went around the back. I think Eddie went in the second floor. I think Dick Kelly and I went to the third floor looking. The door closed behind me. I heard a *thunk*. I went around the room and I was having a hard time finding the door. We had the canister mask on, but the breathing wasn't too bad. It was a little warm and I was starting to panic. Am I going to find my way out of this room? I find the door. Then I said, "Now where's the door to get out of the building?" I did one room. I heard the door. I said, "Who's that?" He says, "It's Jankowski." I grabbed hold of him. I said, "Boy am I glad to see you." He said, "They found the kid downstairs." Skippy Linhoff had grabbed the kid in one of the bedrooms on the first floor. Pulled him out. He said, "They got the kid." So, I followed him down the stairs. That I've never forgotten. That was something.

Another memorable one was when Kossup and I rescued the five kids. Five Truck had broken down and we got the extra call. So, we went all the way over there. They said there were five kids in the building. So, we went up. They had knocked the fire down. There was still a lot of smoke. We went up on the fire escape. Bill Olvaney, Captain Maron from Twenty, and Rocco Piegaro were on the fire escape. So, I went in the window and Stanley came in behind me. I says, "You go to the right. I'll go to the left." We found out later, it was a small room. He went to the right and I went to the left. I found a doorway. I went into the room and I felt a leg. I says, "Stan, I've got one. I've got a kid here." So, I passed it to him and he handed him out the window. I went back and I found another one and handed it to him. Found another one and handed it to him. Now they're going out the window. When I found the little baby, I handed it to him. There was nobody else there so, he went out the fire escape and passed it down. I went and found the other one. They were twins. I passed them out and that's where that picture came from. He went out on the fire escape and gave it mouth to mouth and brought it around. I went looking to see if there were any more kids. But that was it. That was a night that you never forget. We were only on the job about a year when that happened. That's a good memory.

Freda: When I came on the job, I was assigned to an engine company, Engine Company Fifteen on Park Avenue. I was there for approximately four or five years. I happened to be assigned to a captain who became a captain later on in life. In fact, he was made a captain when he was in his fifties and took the job very seriously. He was still into some of the old school thinking of cleaning the apparatus after each run, especially if you went out in the rain. You'd have to come back and wipe all the rain off the apparatus. The house was always kept spotless. If the schedule called for brass to be cleaned on Wednesday, you would clean the brass on Wednesday. If Friday was window day, you would clean windows. And you would drill every day. He was more or less a man who ran things by the book. And he didn't deviate too much from the book.

In those days there were steady pump operators too. That was another change. A steady pump driver and a truck driver on the truck who was steady. They guarded their positions. If you would ask the pump driver whose name was Jimmy Page and I loved the man. He was in that firehouse while the horse and wagon were in there. He was just at the end of his career when I came. If I had asked Jimmy what the relief valve was about, he wouldn't tell me. He didn't want me to know anything about that rig because that was his job. I wasn't taking it off him. He wasn't hanging on the back step. If I asked him, how did he know how much pressure to pump, he'd say things like, "Well you put your foot on the hose and you press down. If it gives a little bit, that's enough. Too solid, back down a hundred." I asked him about the pressure. "How do you know how much pressure to put in an inch and a half?" He said, "When they holler out the window 'Give us more.' or 'Cut the pressure down' you'll know." He was very vague. He wouldn't tell me.

The captain would take us out on drills because every fire we went to, me and the other new fireman would drive back. It got to be a pain in the neck because you had to keep switching. We would go on occasional drills. Until the time that Jimmy Page went on vacation, then you'd be called on to drive. And I loved it because I couldn't wait to drive this big red fire engine around. This was fun. Until I found a spare in the house that had a magneto on it.

The fire department had a spare. This thing was an antique. A magneto has two levers that sit underneath the steering wheel that you had to set by sliding them back and forth. It set the spark. That was the ignition. The siren was a chain coming into the cab on the captain's side that was hooked up to the fly wheel and you pulled on it. The siren went up. It hit the fly wheel and spun. That's what made the siren noise. But the motor was so loud that you couldn't hear the siren because they did not have mufflers on the rigs then. So, they could hear it coming without the siren. You could hear this thing coming a block or two away. When I saw that, I didn't even know how to start the engine. I had no idea how to start it. But it was interesting how guarded the position was. How the driver or the pump operator really had to learn on their own because the first driver was not going to tell you anything. The symbol of their authority was they always had rags hanging out of their back pocket.

I was trying to impress my captain at one of the first fires I ever had. Show how brave I was. It was a job on Bloomfield Avenue in an interior decorator place. I was there no more than two minutes. I ran in the front door. A beam came down, hit me on the head, and knocked me the hell out. I'd say five minutes after the fire started, I was outside, knocked out. Doctor Ciccone, who was the fire surgeon then, examined me and said, "You have a little concussion, go home." And I remember within an hour of me dropping my wife off at her mother's house, I was back at her mother's house telling this harrowing story of how I was almost killed at this fire. I remember Doctor Ciccone telling me, "If you get nauseous call me up because it could mean something else." I threw up all night and I never told him. I said to hell with it because I wanted to go to work the next night.

The tradition was, if the chief ever came in, always look busy. Never be sitting around doing nothing. Traditionally the chief would hit the bell. You knew when he was coming. You got up and did something. Jimmy Page would take the rag, I don't care what time day or night it was, he would take the rag out and would be wiping the chrome on the apparatus. The chief walked in; the rag was always there.

Smith: My first assignment was Engine Twenty-one. I was there about two weeks, then they had some injuries and vacations down in Engine Seven. I was sent there. Then I think it was in July, I was sent to Ten Engine on the third tour. That's where I was until I got hurt.

There was a first driver. One man drove the engine, but on the wagon, they used to switch. What happened one night was they needed a driver so they got a guy from another company. I had to go down to fill in for the man who came up. Don't know how it came about, but the captain said, "This is ridiculous." So, everybody started driving either piece. I mean not as the first driver, but just so that you wouldn't have to do that.

You knew the captain was the boss. You didn't argue with him. You went into the firehouse in the morning. We knew just what had to be done. You did it. You didn't have to be told to do it. You simply did it. Then after everything was done. The captain was off the hook. Now if you had wanted to fix your car or read, you could do it. But you never hung the captain up. In other words, you went to a fire. He didn't stand there and tell you what to do. You did your job. You did it well. The Chief would say, "Nice job Cap." His job was made easier, ergo, your job was made easier. That was the philosophy. I know in Ten Engine and I assume it was all over.

One time I was up on Prince Street before they had knocked all the houses down right across from the firehouse. They had a three-alarm fire up there. I pulled up on the corner. There's a tavern on the corner. There's a hydrant there and a guy in front of the hydrant. He wouldn't move. The Chief was down there going, "Water, water, water." The wagon goes down. They stretch a line off. So, I said, "Okay." I got in back of the guy's car. I put it in low, low and I drove him right up on the sidewalk. We had the rear hook up. I pulled out, hooked up. This guy called for the Police. The Police come down. He says, "What's the trouble?" I says, "This bum wouldn't move. Look at what's going on up there." People were killed there. "Oh." So, he gave him a ticket. I said, "What are you getting him for?" He said something about, "Failure to comply with the motor vehicle statue of the State of New Jersey." So, I asked a friend who was a deputy chief on the Newark Police. And he says, "Oh, he got him. That's an automatic five hundred dollar fine."

J. Miller: First assignment was Six Truck. That was on Broadway, right across the street from Rutgers, the old chemistry college. My first captain was Captain Drew Hagel. I worked with Frank Graff. He was an old timer. At the time he was in his sixties. He was getting ready to retire. Eugene O'Hara. Both of them are dead. Captain Hagel is dead. Dominic LaTorre who was killed in 1972 at that fire on Pennington and Orchard Streets and that was it. I made us one and four. I was the fourth person at that time. And when Honsey Graff retired, we got Jerry Lifliss who came on about a year later. And that was the tour.

My first assignment the first night was to get the old pickle jar out. It was a glass jar and go across the street on Broadway to the tavern and bring back a pitcher of beer. Fill it up. I made, I think the first night I worked, three trips. As a greenhorn, you were at the bottom of the totem pole. It wasn't like today where everybody's equal. The old timers sort of had an edge on you. You had to do whatever they told you and the captain would back them. You were their lackey. They told you to go to the store. You did it. They told you to do this or that. You couldn't answer them back or say, "No I won't." Because right away you'd be in big trouble with the captain.

Dominic LaTorre was a hardworking guy. He drove a cab at the time part time for himself. And he just had bought a house up on Belair Place. He had a couple of young kids and his wife. Eugene O'Hara did painting on the side and Honsey Graff did some landscaping. I know he was still fretting over the fact that his son had died in the war right before that, the Korean War. He had a young son who was killed and he refused to cash the $10,000 life insurance policy that the government had award him. Because he figured that it was the duty of the family. They didn't want that money.

Captain Hagel got to be a nice guy. As far as teaching me anything, I didn't learn too much from him in that respect because there weren't that many fires. Their experience was limited also. They didn't have the teaching academy to know the basics of how to stay alive. I never really learned how to stay alive. The first fire I had, I ran into the building without a mask and almost got trapped. He didn't tell me to stay with my captain. So that you stay with the guy who knows the most so you can stay alive. That's the main thing you should learn when you come on this job. Take care of yourself and stay alive so you can help other people.

I was kind of embarrassed because I would get detailed out of the battalion, to Twenty-eight Engine, Thirteen Engine and I would go to the Captain and I would say, "Cap, what do you want me to do?" "Just hang on the back step." That was it. Nothing specific, take me over and show me. "Well, you grabbed this line, wrap it around a hydrant, wait there when we tell you to give us water. Give us water. Alright you follow me with the inch and a half. We're going to go in." None of that at all. Forget about that. Just jump the back step. They could care less because they figure they weren't going to get any fire anyway. And ninety percent of the time you didn't get any fires. And of all the details I had to engine companies, believe this, I never got a fire. I never caught a fire where I had to go in with that inch and a half line for some reason in all those years. And the details were infrequent because the manpower was much more.

At Truck Six I think we had 300 runs a year. That was a lot and in my first year I went to several fires. The biggest one I can remember was a school fire up on Mount Prospect Avenue where we spent the whole night. We had to raise a forty-five-foot extension ladder that night up to the roof. The roof had collapsed and we could basically help the engine companies with their big lines, their deluge sets, and two and a half inch lines on the building all night long. A few structural fires, not many. We had the old Pittsburgh Plate Glass which was a pretty big fire down by the river side there, Riverside Drive. Really, nothing to talk about as far as firefighting in Six Truck at all. Even in the years I was there. I didn't go to any major fires.

Dunn: My first assignment was to Engine Company Eight, on the third tour. The crew was made up of one, what I'd call a senior fireman, a guy named Walter Speck, a three-year fireman, Billy Walsh, and two new guys, Richie Hettinger and myself. A new captain, who came from Engine Sixteen which was a very slow company like Engine Eight.

I was assigned to Eight Engine because the Vice-President of the FMBA at that time, Lester Price, used to hang in Joyce's Tavern. My father was in Joyce's Tavern and he says, "Where do you want your son to go?" So, my father, knowing nothing about the city of Newark, he says "What's open Down Neck? How about Sixteen Engine." He says "Well, that's full, but there's an opening in Eight Engine." That's how I wound up in Eight Engine. That has nothing to do with the city placing you close to where you lived. It's the same political system that's in place today. People are coming out of the Academy tomorrow; being assigned to companies.

Phone calls are made. And if it can be entertained it was. I had no idea where I was going. I thought at that time that I was going to where ever the fire department needed me. But I didn't know you can arrange this over two beers in a tavern.

I spent eight months there and in eight months I never went to a fire. The reason I left the company was as a youth growing up down there and knowing the firehouse, you think it's busy. But when you're maturing; you're in your twenties; you get a job and you sit somewhere for seven or eight months and you don't get a fire, you say "Well, wait a minute, something's wrong here." I misconstrued what was going on or my conception was misguided. I had an uncle I wasn't close to who at that time was in the salvage corps. I went to see him to say "This is fun being a fireman, but I don't go to any fires, how do I get out of there?" Based on his phone call, I went down to Six Engine and I met with Deputy Chief Crowley. At that time, I told him where I was and what my problem was; I wanted to go to a busy company. He says "Come with me." We had three runs there while I was talking to the man. I think I went to a working fire with them and that was more fire than I'd seen in my eight months. I said, "Yes, Chief, this is what I want." He said, "Well, I have some openings coming up in Twenty Engine in the next couple of weeks. If you want that, tell me tomorrow. Give me a call and I'll make sure you get one of the spots."

I went down to Twenty Engine after that and met the captain down there. He was James McAlinden. There were several people, one guy was quitting the job to become a truck driver and another fireman was quitting also at that time. They were both leaving the job. About a month or two later I was assigned to Engine Twenty on Prince Street.

That was a fairly young crew. They filled up the house at that time. We had, George Fredette was the senior fireman there; Stevie Bobcheck was a fireman there; Ray Fredette was a fireman there; and myself. That was the crew. As time moved on Chief Crowley was transferred to a different tour and we were assigned Chief Rusheck. At that time Jimmy McAlinden, who was an excellent fire captain, was having trouble with the new chief. He eventually transferred through political means or something to Three Truck. He was replaced by Captain Singer. He took over the company about two weeks later. That became another exciting span of life because at that time George Feely was also assigned to Twenty Engine to make us a one and five company. Both Fredette and Feely worked in Eighteen Engine with Captain Singer. They had a very strong dislike for Captain Singer.

I didn't think that was working out after the almost two years in the company. Even though I liked the company and I had a very interesting and nice Battalion Chief, Jimmy Nolan. He came down one day and I told him my problem. He says, "Well I have a vacancy coming up in Six Engine. Why don't you come up to Six Engine for a while?" Because I enjoyed the work, it was the house problem I was having trouble with. That was my next transfer. I went from Twenty Engine after two years to Six Engine.

Belzger: I went into Eighteen Engine and we were doing 350 runs a year. That was in '59. Well, I guess it must have been two or three years later, we broke into the thousands. When I went over to Seventeen Engine, sometimes we'd average two, three, even up to five workers a night. We always had the idea that it was competition when we fought fires. We tried to beat Eighteen Engine in and we tried to beat Six Engine in and we tried to beat Twelve Engine in. And Twenty-nine was always easy. They were slow. It was that way with the job. As quick as we could get on. We used to pride ourselves in getting out of the firehouse before two minutes elapsed. When a box came in, the guy on the book would yell and you'd put your night rig on and we'd be down the pole and we'd ride off the back end. We were supposed to be one and five with two pieces, but most of the time we were one and four and then towards the end it was one and three all the time.

Davey Kinnear was a great captain too. Probably my first worker with him that was in a cockloft. We had the Burrell masks in those days and we took a beating. He kept me back, patting me on the back for doing a good job. I stayed with him. I didn't do very much. I coughed and choked my head off.

There was another guy, Chief O'Boyle, who I worked with. What a bull that guy was. He was a tough firefighter. We had a job off Avon Avenue and it was a mattress in a basement and I couldn't take it. I had the mask, a filter mask. They don't work and I couldn't catch my breath. I was only a rookie at the time, so I kind of backed off from it a little bit, try to get some air, then I went back in. After they got all the wood pulled off all the windows, because it was air tight, then the job went pretty easy. But this guy was right in there, never bothered him a bit. Maybe that's why he's not here anymore.

1960s: Social Explosions

Carragher: My first assignment was Nine Engine. That first year on the job, 1960 in December we had two major snowstorms. Both were around twenty or twenty-two inches of snow. I worked two hundred hours on recall in December of that first year on the job. We had two hundred hours of recall. No pay, nothing, they just told you to stay. We had the four shifts on duty at one time in the firehouse. Being that Nine Engine was a two-piece company, we could man two apparatus and could go out. Some of the guys went out and shoveled snow and the two apparatus could ride as two different companies. The first piece would go out to this fire and the second piece would pull up and be in service as Nine Engine. So, Nine wouldn't go out of service. It would be there. And that's how they worked it then.

The captain was Herbie Plank and he came on the job in '42 or '41. Then I had Ray Shea who probably at the time had thirteen years on the job, Johnny Heinze who probably had about eleven or twelve on the job and Chris Healy who had just come in '59. So, when I came in, they were very accepting. I had a good crew there.

I lived in a house with Battalion Chief Donohue, Andy Donohue was our Battalion Chief. And Ben Martorano was the Chief's Aide. Benny came on right after the war. We had a good rapport. There was no problem either way. I could accept them. They accepted me. Of course, I was twenty-eight when I came on the job. I wasn't like a real young person.

I stayed in Nine Engine I think probably about eight or nine months. I was guided very wisely by Benny Martorano, Chief Donohue's driver. Chief Donohue and Benny came from the Rescue Squad. When Donohue was promoted, he came to the Third Battalion as a Battalion Chief and Benny came with him as his aide. Sitting talking to Benny every day, I'll tell you one thing that I did realize doesn't happen today. When I worked with these fellows, particularly Ray Shea and

Benny. They always talked about working at fires, what to do at a fire, what not to do at a fire. It seems to me it's lost today because we don't have enough older people around anymore to tell the younger guys what's going on or what to do. It's gotten to be a young job. But I used to talk to Benny and Ray Shea all the time about this. I said to Benny, "I can't last in this house. It's too slow for me, Nine Engine." At the time we used to separate the Signal Fives from the box alarms. I think Nine Engine was the busiest in the Third Battalion. We had 575 runs for alarms of boxes. And maybe 150 Signal Fives for car fires or something like that. That was our total. Less than 700 or a little over 700 for the year. They were the busiest in the Third Battalion.

Benny mentioned to me one day. He said, "You know there's a guy on the Rescue Squad on the First Tour who wants out of there." I says, "Oh?" He says, "Yes. I know the captain. A lot of people have a problem with the captain, but he's a good captain. Maybe you'd like to try it." I says, "Okay." A month prior to this I was talking to Benny and he mentioned to the chief that I wanted some action, a little bit more action. So, the chief said to me, "All right. We'll move you around a little bit." From there, between him and Deputy O'Boyle, who was my first Deputy Chief, they said that I could move around in the division. So, I moved from Nine Engine. I went to One Truck for a while, One Engine. Then I went to Fourteen Engine and I came down to Congress Street here to Salvage One, rode with Salvage One for a while. Now I'm getting the feel of the city and liking it.

When Benny told me about the Rescue Squad, I decided I'm going to put in for the transfer. Benny made a call and I went to the Rescue Squad within a couple of weeks. When I went to Rescue, I liked it right away. I worked over there. I had another nice, good crew there. Frank Combel was my Captain. I worked with Barney Fabo and Johnny Coxton and Artie Knispel on the first tour. Captain Combel was deep into training. Every day we had to train. And every day a different compartment on the apparatus had to be emptied out and if it looked a little marred or scratched, we painted the compartment, took care of the tools, and put them back in the compartment. Every day that we worked, we did a different compartment and worked around the rig. Then the fires started picking up like in the early '60s. With the Rescue Squad I went to New and Colden. That's where we were stationed, New and Colden Streets. They were going to start tearing down that area from Central Avenue to West Market Street and from Halsey Street up to Lock Street. They were tearing down for the colleges, for NJIT and Rutgers. It wasn't Rutgers there at the time, NJIT mostly. And our firehouse was slated to be torn down. In that period of time I was there, we had a lot of fires in that area. I saw quite a bit of action there. Plus, also in the Rescue Squad, you know it's city wide. You go all over the city, so anything happening in the city, you saw it. It was interesting, really nice.

Harris: We were assigned to firehouses when we came on. I stayed in the firehouse that whole winter. It was something like around the end of May, the first of June before we went to the Fire Academy which was on Eighteenth Avenue at the time. Joe Dinardo and I were both assigned to Engine Company Twelve at the time. It was interesting because when we went there, they said, "Okay, go up there. The tour you're going to be working on, they're working right now. So, go introduce yourself." So, that's what we did.

We walked in and they were eating and I remember they had a big pot of hot dogs and beans. Everybody is sitting around eating. When I walked in, I knew one guy, Kenny Gibson and only because Kenny lived a block away from me in North Newark at the time. We weren't friends, but I knew Kenny Gibson and his brother Hooter. We went in. They offered us something to eat. Then what they did was the captain, who was going to be in Engine Company Twelve, he took Joe and said, "Come on, you don't have the gear, but I'm going to give you some gear. Try this on." Do this and everything. My captain never said a word. We worked the second tour's first night. Reggie Evelyn had old stuff and he said, "Come here kid. You use this." My captain offered me nothing, showed me nothing.

Then the next interesting part was when we went upstairs, Joe's captain took him upstairs and said, "Pick out any bed you want." My captain took me upstairs and said, "If nobody is sleeping in those beds when we work, you guys have those three beds." I said, "What do you mean those three beds?" Those were the only three beds blacks would sleep in. Whites had eight bunks on that side. They can pick and choose and there were two in the middle that they can choose to sleep in. We had three bunks in the corner and that was it.

But we had a good house. The guys in the house themselves changed the bed situation. One day Charlie Chapman got tired of sleeping in that corner. He was on the third tour; Captain Ryan was his captain. Charlie decides one night, "I'm not sleeping in that hot corner anymore. I'm moving out of that corner." Because right next door was a house and it butted right up against the building. So, you had no air or anything coming in there. Charlie went out and made his rack up right in the middle because we had one, two beds right in the middle, then all the other beds against the side. Ryan told him, "You move that out of there or you're on charges." Charlie said, "Well, put me on charges, I'm not sleeping in that corner anymore. This is where I'm going to sleep and that is that." He called in the Deputy. He came in. They discussed all this. They decided, leave it alone. In the summertime you died in that corner. In the winter time you froze. After Charlie did that, we had no more troubles in the firehouse where the guys could sleep.

The only time I ran into a problem, Joe DiNardo and I we had a problem in the city. We were detailed. The chief came and picked us up, took us to Six Truck. At that time Six Truck sat on Broadway right across from the Esso gas station. We went in there. Then it dawned on the captain. These guys got to stay here all night. So, he says, "Wait a minute. Don't make-up your racks yet." He goes and gets on the phone. He's talking to the chief. Next thing about ten minutes later here comes the chief back. "Come on Midge, you go back with us." "What's the problem?" "You can't sleep here. The captain doesn't want you to sleep here." So, they took me back and let the company ride short because the captain didn't want me to sleep in the firehouse.

The first big fire I ever had was right across the street from Twenty Engine. We had a four-alarm fire. There was like a factory right next door to a church, right directly across. And Captain Schoemer and myself and somebody else, we took a line to the top of the church roof. It's a gable roof. We hadn't even been to the Academy. Thick ice on the roof and every time I take a step, I'm sliding back at the same time Schoemer's reaching out. "Come on kid, you can make it. You're going to have to do this the rest of your career." And he's hollering.

What is wrong with this man? We better get the hell off of here. So, we get up there and we like get to the chimney and we kind of brace ourselves, locking our arms around the chimney. Trying to control this line and everything and shoot it into the top of the building next door. Then finally somebody said, "Off the roof." This is my first big job. I've had about six, seven, maybe ten jobs. This is my first good fire. We get to the edge of the roof. Somebody took our ladder. We don't have a ladder. Schoemer starts calling. I don't know who it was. Somebody brought our ladder back over and put it back. But we had no ladder to get down. Not long after we had gotten down, part of the church on that side, the roof and the roof of that building went. The church roof went only because this building collapsed on to it. Then as they were giving us a break, we went across the street to Twenty Engine, freezing. I mean you couldn't even take your coat off. It was frozen solid. I said to myself then, "This ain't no God damn job for me. I'm quitting. That's it. I'm not going to do this."

They put us in as an engine company fighting the fire at first. Now once the fire got knocked down, we had to go into the church and start covering the pews and the altar and stuff like that. That's where we had to go. When we got back to the firehouse, I'm sitting down. We're drinking the coffee and I'm saying to myself, "I quit. I quit. I'm not doing this." I didn't know you had to be up two stories on a roof. You're going to slide back down. This doesn't make any damn sense to me. But that is exactly what happened to us. I just wanted to get back to that. That was my first big job.

Haran: Well, there were two salvage corps at that particular time. There was Salvage One and Salvage Two. Salvage Two was stationed with Twelve Engine and Five Truck on Belmont Avenue. Salvage One was in the quarters of Engine Five, which was on Congress Street just off of Ferry Street. That's the one that I was assigned to, Salvage One. Salvage Corps responded to every fire in the city. Salvage Two responded to everything from High Street from the Elizabeth line all the way over to Belleville. So, they responded to everything west of High Street. Salvage One responded to everything east of High Street from the Belleville line to the Elizabeth line. If Salvage Two was out, Salvage One took the next alarm in and vise-versa. If Salvage One was out then Salvage Two took the next alarm in. We also filled in as Rescue Squad. We had one Rescue Squad in the city and when they were out on whatever it may be, a heart attack, a shooting, a knifing, or a building collapse. Whatever it may be, there was always a Rescue Squad or a Salvage Corps responding to that alarm. So, we filled in as secondary Rescue Squad. We had the old E&J resuscitators on the apparatus. We were all trained in CPR and the use of these E&J resuscitators and so forth. We all filled in as a secondary Rescue Unit, aside from going to all the fires and there were a lot of fires back then. We went to a lot of fires. We responded to every full assignment. Things were different back then. It was full assignments. Today they have reduced alarms. Back then mostly they were full assignments, so there was always a Salvage Corps going on the alarm. Maybe there were 13,000 alarms back then. So, it was nothing to do 6,000 or 7,000 runs a year back then in Salvage Corps. There were a lot of fires.

To me, I enjoyed it. It was new to me. I didn't know any different. I didn't realize there were slow companies doing 250 runs a year up in the Burg or Twenty-seven Engine or Four Truck, Thirty-two Engine down the Port doing maybe 100 runs a year. But I'm a new guy. This is how I'm broken in doing 6,000, 7,000 runs a year. Going to a lot of fires. I enjoyed it. I liked it. The only thing was I also wanted to do engine duty. I wanted to do engine or truck duty too. So, I worked with a lot of good guys. A lot of guys went on to become captains and chiefs there because a lot of guys who were there were there because they wanted to be there. They volunteered to be there. They knew it was busy. They knew they were going to get fires. So, they wanted to be there. You had guys who were interested in the job. Although I was interested in it and enjoyed it, I also wanted to do engine work and truck work. I put in a transfer for Twenty Engine and Six Engine, but of course those companies were in big demand back then. There was a waiting list to get there. At that time, you had to go through the union. The union used to control all the transfers. There was a waiting list to get into those companies. I figured I wanted to get out of the Ironbound section, get up town. Maybe I thought it would be easier to get there from some other place, so I went to Fifteen Engine. I stayed in Salvage about two and a half years and I transferred up to Fifteen Engine.

When I came on in Salvage, we rode one and five. Which is unheard of today. As a result of being one and five, we used to get details a lot and we always got detailed to trucks or engines. Details back then weren't for a day or two days. You used to take the whole trick. You'd take two days, two nights, two days or two nights. It was for a whole vacation pick. You caught fires in there, so you got used to stretching the hose or if you were in a truck, you got used to pulling the ceilings or doing the truck work. I caught a lot of details while I was in there. Me personally, after I put two and a half years in Salvage, I wanted to also do engine work. I wanted to go up to Six Engine, Twenty Engine. It was Six, Twenty, and Twelve and Nine and Five Truck at that time, they were the busier companies. But there were other companies that rolled in with them on the second alarms, Three Truck, Two Truck, Eleven Truck, Eleven Engine and all those companies came in. They caught a lot of work, too, those companies. But by far Six, Twenty, Twelve and maybe Ten Engine. They by far caught most of the work at that particular time.

But then over the years, those particular areas became blighted, especially after the riots. There was nothing left in there. Then the busy companies started to become Seven, Eleven, Eighteen and moving down.

One of my first fires within my first couple of weeks on the job was probably one of my worst fires ever. It was on Broad and Camp Streets, down by Pennington there just on the other side of 1060 Broad Street which was the old draft board. I'll never forget. We used to pull out of Salvage. We'd come up Lafayette Street and make our left onto Broad Street. Ten Engine, One Engine, and One Truck were the first two engines and truck on it. We turned the corner and the sky was lit up. We pulled in. I saw one of the best rescues I've ever seen on the Newark Fire Department that never got mentioned.

I worked with a fellow by the name of John Miele. His name was Luciano Miele. He was an older fellow, good shape. I tell this story quite often when guys start talking about rescues because I've seen one of the greatest rescues on the Newark Fire Department and the guy never even got a mention.

What had happened was we pulled around coming off of Lafayette Street onto Broad Street. The sky was lit up. We could see it down on our lefthand side. So, we pulled down there and sure enough there was this three-story duplex, three-story six family house that they were using for senior citizen housing. There were people in there with wheel chairs, sickly, elderly. There was a fellow in One Truck at the time by the name of Artie Farrow. He went to go into the front door. Somebody jumped off the third floor. As he got to the top of the stairs, they landed on top of him and broke both his legs. That was just one of the things that developed down at this fire. That same fire, we're on Salvage Corps, so we had two ladders. We had a sixteen-foot roof ladder and a twenty-four-foot two-piece extension ladder. We didn't take them off. The building was a three story, six family home with a one -story garage right next door to it.

John Miele went over to one of the trucks there, pulled a sixteen-foot roof ladder off the truck. Threw it up to the one-story garage, went up, pulled the ladder up onto the one-story garage because there was a guy hanging out the third-floor window against the side of the building who wasn't going to be hanging there in another minute. He pulled the ladder up behind him and he pinned the guy to the building and he held him there until the truck could come in with other ladders and take the guy off the side of the building. He pinned him there between the two rails of the ladder. To me that was one of the best rescues I ever saw. Quick thinking, to pull a ladder off a truck, up to the garage, pull the ladder up on top of the garage, run across the garage roof, and pin the guy against the building until they were able to take him down and never get an honorable mention.

Probably my first big fire on the Newark Fire Department. There were six deaths in that building. It's very vivid to me. Monsignor McCabe was the chaplain of the Newark Fire Department at the time and Captain Guiliano was the captain in Rescue Squad. That was the fourth tour. I was on the fourth tour at that time when I came on. We're looking all through the building and I'll never forget. We found an old man in bed. These were all very elderly people, sick, sickly people, wheel chairs, bedridden. We stick him onto the floor and he was pretty burnt, too. We started to give him CPR and I can remember the guy's hand went right down into his chest. Then we started walking around the building looking for other victims. This building was burnt out. They were jumping out of the building. We already removed six people out to the parking lot next door. They were all lined up in the parking lot and Monsignor McCabe was giving them the last rites.

We're looking through the building. We open the closet door in the hallway and there was a woman, an elderly woman sitting in there in a wheel chair still alive. That was my first big fire and all that ensued at that particular fire. A guy coming out the window and landing on Artie Farrow, breaking both his legs. John Miele doing that rescue, six deaths, the woman in the closet, the CPR. It was a memorable fire.

Elward: When you got out of the Academy, you didn't get a company. You got a battalion. And I think most of us ended up in the Fourth. So, my first day was Six Engine. And you'd go from Six Engine to Five Truck. All busy companies and then things are popping. That was the era of the enclosed back porches.

My first day at Six Engine. They were super greeting me. Chief Donlon, Sammy Lomax, Captain Greeley. Tommy D'Anglese, Pete Delone, Willie Olvaney, and Richie Barrett. I'm the fifth guy. Terrific, and Donlon emphasized that, maybe it wouldn't be a bad idea, when we're working days, to take me out. We had the John Bean with the high-pressure gun. Six Engine had it first. The guys would stand back. And everything was a house divided, but some of the chiefs like it.

I had a lot of small stuff, bedroom stuff. They made damn sure there was always somebody with me. I was gung-ho, but every move I made was practically wrong. There was nothing like learning on the job. First big fire was on one of the numbered streets. It was funny. We never really had anything bad at Six Engine at night. The bad stuff was daytime. It might be a Monday, Tuesday, or Wednesday. Weekends weren't bad. I just lucked out. Other tours like Johnny Hoffman's tour, they were brutal.

Then I went to Eleven Truck. That was almost like a semi country club. But in about a month's time, then the back porches, the enclosed things, it was like an epidemic. Like they talk about AIDS. Well for us it was the back porches. At Eleven was my first rescue. It was down on Orange Street and it didn't look bad when we arrived. I nailed the baby and at the time I got the baby she was up against the wall, sitting like that doll. Somebody left her in a room. And there was no getting back. We were ahead of the line. They were only running lines in. And one of them tries to gives us information. They said there's a kid in there. When I got to up there, it wasn't bad. So, it wasn't like nothing like I raced through a wall of flames. I got there and sure enough, there's the kid. Evidently somebody left the kid, figuring that we'd put the fire out and they screwed. They left the kid flopped up against the wall. Freddy and these guys are just running a line up. This is on the third floor and it got hot as a bitch. I could hear the ladder hit the window. As a matter of fact, they cracked it. And it was a good thing. I felt this whole thing coming. It wasn't really a back draft, but I could feel a lot of shit. I took the rest of the window out. And there was one of our guys right there. He took the baby and I came on there. But then it got bad. It did get bad because they didn't charge the line yet. So, after it was all over, said and done, the whole thing took about maybe a minute. It was bang, bang and Davis was happy as a pig in shit.

Coming on like we did, we got a lot of experience. Chief Donlon said, "You're not a truck man. You're not an engine man. You're a fireman." So, I got a lot of experience working and I had it before ever getting to Eleven Truck. So, the eight of us that came on together could really crack it both ways. Participated in a few rescues. Participated in the Orange fire.

It's our last day in. And we were going to play softball that night. We had a game. Guys were throwing the ball. They look up Central Avenue. "Wow, what the hell is that? God, it looks like Morristown or something is burning down." From the vantage point on Central Avenue, you look straight up. Phone rings. Chief Davis, follow me. What are you talking about? Up comes the gig. Seven Engine right behind it. In convoy, up we go. It was Eleven and Seven and off we go. You know, I was tillering. I don't know. So off we go. So, we go up to Lincoln Avenue. An Orange fireman got killed at this. We went to this building. I think it was on Lincoln Avenue. We went one way. A guy says we're trying to get an aerial to the building. So, we took the aerial. We did the best we could. It only went up to the front. We couldn't get to the roof. We put the truck onto the lawn, but our ladder just wouldn't take the roof. No big deal. We extended it to a window. Jumped down, and says "Eh, this is clear as a bell." Damn right. So, we just went all the way up.

The guys were just starting to stretch. The fire was all the way over on the other side. So, you go around. This is a new building being built, an extension of this other building. So, that makes it an "L". They already have an established common cockloft with this new building. Original building is hooked into the extension although the extension is brand new. The Orange fireman got killed in the original building. It was roaring like hell when we got there. Now, when we went up the center staircase, the thinking by that time was other companies are getting called in. And they were stretching in. They bring water in from blocks away. We needed it.

So, we go up and I'm on the top landing. Guys go on the right. Guys go on the left. And Chief Davis says, "I don't like it. I don't like this." Everything as close as hell. Right? If you looked out the window, you could look into the yard and you could see the guys over here at the new building working their chops off. And they're not making a dent on it. And Davis says, "What's down there?" Guy opens the door. "Nothing Chief." "Okay, wye off and let's just leave the line here." And then he says to me, "Did you check down the end of the corridor on the left?" And I went down with Ronnie O'Neill, who was working for Charlie McFadden. We took a light and we were just walking down the hall. Ronnie twists the door to open it. "Ow, God damn it." I had gloves. Whoa. Davis by this time now is about five feet behind me. "What'd you got Jimmy?" I was getting ready to say, "Nothing." Whoa! And I closed the door. "What is it?" "We got everything. It's going this way chief. It's got to be in the cockloft." He says, "I thought so. God damn it, I thought so."

So, we did it one by one. And it was just that way. We went all the way down the floor. We worked the whole time. We went up there a little after lunch time. Got relieved at the fire. We were whipped ass. Nobody could lift their arms up. And Ronnie O'Neill says, "Charlie owes me another day."

But this thing, this was bad news. I'm talking about the consistent working. Newark was doing the whole thing. And one of their guys, from where they're standing in the street and don't forget now, this whole cockloft went and every apartment was on fire. They were telling us to abandon the building. Davis was not going to abandon this building. We're not going to lose it. But then I see maybe we are going to lose it. We had everything wyed. We had two-and-a-half and we had it wyed down to inch-and-a-half. We must have had at least ten inch-and-a-half lines.

Dalton: My first assignment was Seven Truck. Walking in I'm a little not sure. I'm not coming in like, "Hey, I'm here." They made me welcome, they made me welcome. Puffy Freda was a fireman there and he more or less took me under his wings and he made life very easy from the very beginning of the fire department. In fact, we got so good, me and him had a floor waxing business. That was our part time job. He really took me under his wing. And taught me the little bit I could learn there. My problem was I didn't get many fires to train at. But he would tell me things to be careful of, what you've got to do in case you're in there in this type of predicament. He was a help.

When I walked into the firehouse, some of the older guys were there. They were all at the table drinking coffee. They look you over and everything else. They knew I was a red ass coming in. They looked up and introduced themselves and somebody asked me what high school I went to. I went to St. Benedict's. Sure enough, Red Quinn graduated there. We talked about it and he knew my cousin, Pat Dalton. And they took me under their wings. Got me started.

And then I realized that they weren't very busy at that time. The Third Battalion was very, very nice. There wasn't too much going on and I used to hear the fires, hear the guys screaming. They got to rescue this person up on the third floor. Five Truck get that up and all that. Oh, man, how I'd like to see that. So, I eventually transferred to Ten Engine.

Butler: The first year I came on was 1963. I was in Truck Eleven. The total company runs for the year were 399 and some of the fellows who had been there a while were looking to go to Vailsburg. What they called the old men's home because those guys had around 100 runs a year. As time progressed it got busier. In the early '70s, Eleven Truck was running 2000 runs a year. I enjoyed it. Enjoyed the work. The firehouse was starting to fall apart back then, but it was still home and you looked forward to going to work. I had the good fortune of working with a lot of really good guys, good firemen, good friends, and just good to be with, good comrades both on and off the job. They were a lot of fun. Made a lot of great friendships out of those years on Central Avenue.

My very first fire was in late February and it was about three blocks from my home. It was on Halsted Street in Vailsburg, two-story frame house. It was heavily involved. At that time when an alarm was sent out you always had a full response of four engines and two trucks no matter time of day or conditions or anything. As we were responding a working fire was called in. The only break with that was there were wide lots on each side of the building, so there was no exposure problem. But as instructed the first day I showed up in the firehouse, I went with the captain. Stayed right with him because he was my teacher, mentor, and guardian. Went right into the building with him.

The first-floor fire was under control. Went up to the second floor. Started opening ceilings, pulling walls, and it got hot up there. My captain, Freddy Kormeyer was right alongside of me. Telling me what to do. Telling me how to do it. It's funny. I laugh, but he said open the window, try to get some air in there and I was very naïve. I went over and tried to open the window, which I couldn't find the lock for it. Discovered later that it was nailed shut. But the Captain came, he said, "Here, I'll teach you how to open windows." He grabbed the hook I had in my hand and just smashed through the panes of glass and swept it around the window. We had an upper and lower section of window wide open. He said, "That's the way we open windows." So, then I learn how to open windows in the fire department method, where if there's a lot of damage in the building a couple of pieces of broken glass are not going to make any difference.

Schofield: My first day, okay, well I knew my captain, Cliff Boan. He was buddies with my brother-in-law. I had known him for years. He introduced me to everybody. He had George Werdann. He was a real quiet guy. He's the driver. We used to have a first driver on our tour. Some guys had one guy who would drive for a month then the next guy would take a turn and so forth, but on our tour, George Werdann was the first driver. He'd always drive unless he was on vacation and then somebody else would take a shot at it; Tony DeTroia, he retired as a battalion chief; Peter Vincent McGraph, the jokester; and myself, that comprised the engine. Then you had, Frank Reheis was the battalion chief. Chief Ho-ho we'd call him. He's this real big guy. And Frank Hale, a great cook. And then on the truck, I think at the time I came on it was Bob Schultz, he was the captain. Joe Kelly was the driver. Cliff Fox was the tiller man. And we had Bob Melillo and Dick Watson and Joe Smith. That comprised the truck. But great guys, great guys made the job.

One fire early on was a big apartment house on West Market, just before you got to Bergen Street. We had a big fire there one night. At that time, we had a lot of back porch fires and we had just come back from one on Second Avenue. We just backed into quarters when an alarm came in. We had just come down the street, West Market and here the street was full of smoke. The fire we came back from was multiple alarms. We were there for quite a while before other guys showed up. There were a lot of rescues. And when the commendations came out for the rescues made at that place, Frank Hale made a comment. It looked like the lineup for the NBA. Because it was engine captain so and so and all the firemen and truck captain so and so all the way down the line. Everybody got a commendation that day.

One time we had a fire just around the corner from the firehouse off of Hudson Street. The alarm came in and we responded. A guy came running out. He said there's a kid in there and he didn't hear her screaming anymore. We went in, put the fire out, couldn't find her. Found out it was a girl. Found the girl in a closet. All the clothes had fallen down on top of her. But she had died in the fire.

Cahill: First assignment was Five Engine, Five Engine on the third tour. I was there for about a year and a half then I went over Salvage. We were in quarters with Salvage. I probably spent three or four years with Salvage. John Tartis came down to Five Engine and I was getting kind of tired of Salvage anyway, so I jumped back over to Five Engine.

Work in Salvage depended pretty much on who you worked for. Some chiefs utilized them for salvage, first aid, overhauling, or stretching lines. Some chiefs used it strictly just for salvage, so it really depended on who you worked for. Salvage gave you the opportunity to do a little more freelancing than an engine company did. You could go around and help people. With an engine company you're committed to a line. One room and that's it. With Salvage you could float around.

We worked for a Chief who wanted you to do pretty much everything. We tried to help people out with their property and things like that. Sometimes there was nothing you could do to protect their property. But it gave a tremendous amount of good will for the fire department. People loved us, especially insurance companies. And then the city secured the building for you. Times were a little different then. You didn't have break-ins. We did it with tarpaper. Today that would last about thirteen seconds. But basically, that was it.

On the engine, we had a tool that nobody in the First Division had that was probably unique to the firefighting industry in the country. We had the O'Beirne roller for brush fires. I don't know if you ever heard of this or not. Before the airport was expanded and the Turnpike was expanded there was an awful lot of meadowlands down in Newark along Route One and the Turnpike. Brush fires in the spring were very common. Chief O'Beirne, who has long since retired, designed the O'Beirne roller, which was simply a garden roller. I mean if you put in a new lawn, you would roll it. And his theory was you could roll this thing over the brush and put it out. Its longevity was not very long. That was one of the lighter moments of brush fires.

B. Cosby: I went to Five Truck. When the chief brought me in, he said, "Here's a new man here. He doesn't have turnout gear. We need guys and they don't have a class in the Academy, so we got to put him in the firehouse first. And go to the class whenever they plan." They said, "We don't have anybody here that has extra gear." So, Charlie Chapman was in Salvage. He loaned me his boots and I wore his coat sometimes. But in the summertime, they had a shorter coat. I used that for the time being because I came on in May. It wasn't too bad in the summertime. After that I got my own coat and boots.

But when I first walked in the firehouse, a lot of guys they didn't look too happy. What do you do about it? What do you have here? I knew there was going to be a lot of static, but I just started to talk, told them where I've been. In most places you go, if you are one of the first, it's anywhere. Sometimes it's good if you're Italian or whether you're Polish or whatever you are. It depends on who's there, if they accept you or not. I didn't feel like scared or nervous because I'd been working in a lot of places and got teased. So, it wasn't like I was afraid or anything. I just wasn't accepted at first. But I said that's alright coming in.

At that time, I knew Charlie Chapman, Cliff Evelyn, Curtiss Moore, and Richard Freeman in that firehouse. I knew those guys. And I think it was Coxman, also, he was in Truck Five. Elton Fisher. So, I met them as I came in. And at that time, they assigned me to a bed with Fisher. but we were on the same tour. So, we couldn't share the bed. They had to get another bed. They didn't want to do it because black guys had a bed. They only had one bed for the blacks and beds for the whites.

Now I had a problem. I had to find a bed. They got a bed for me and they put it in a room that had no heat. So, I took my bed and I put it in a room that had heat in it. They didn't want me back there. And we had a squabble back and forth. I'd put it back in there and I 'd come in and they'd take it out. I'm talking about Five Truck. The back room was the weight room. The middle room had the heat. The front room had no heat, the big room didn't have any heat. The tour that I'm on, I was allowed to sleep back there because I was on duty, so they consented. But when I went off, they dragged the bed back to where it started.

That went on back and forth until finally, I guess they accepted me. Chief Donlon came down and he talked to the guys and they were saying "Well, why are you punishing us? Why are you sending us the black guy?" He said, "Well, he's assigned here." They said, "Well, we're doing all right. You're sending us a black guy. Is that punishment or something?" He said, "No, I'm not punishing you." We had a back and forth for about six months. They finally said, "Well, if you do this stuff, you can stay here."

I guess they felt like if I was the type that could do the job as good as they could or better and they'd accept me. They thought they were hot stuff; they were number one. At that time, it was Five Truck and Engine Twelve and Engine Twenty. Engine Six and Engine Ten were the two hottest companies in the Central Ward. They wanted to be all prima donnas, didn't want any blacks. Five Truck and Engine Twelve were the first ones to have the blacks. When I came on, I became one of them so they said if I can do what they can do and do it a lot better, I was good to stay. I made a few rescues and got a few commendations and they finally accepted me. We got along good. They took care of things. We did a lot of things together, went out together

The first night on the job I had five or six deaths and a couple of dogs, cats and we got to handle the bodies. At that time, that was a truck job. That was the first time I ever did it in my life and I was petrified. It's like, "Oh, man." So, I told my wife, I said, "You know, I don't know if I can handle this job. I'm having deaths. Every time I turn around, we're having deaths." And I said, "One fire we went to, after the fire was out. We had to go through the ashes and find the bones."

And the last part I went to I found this bone of a lady. After that they started to turn it over to the Squad. But at first, we did all that. But the first deaths that we had, I would find somebody, touch them and the skin would come off. Even though they're dead, sometimes they're all puffed up and like foam rubber. That was scary. But I needed to get used to it really quick. That first year I saw so much death and destruction, I guess I got kind of hardened to it.

Highsmith: When I first came on the job, it was like a new experience to me being I was just recently, about a year, released from the Army. I met a lot of people. Minatee was the first one I met outside of John Coxton. When I got on the job, first week I spent at the Academy up there on Eighteenth Avenue, December 16, 1963. We stayed in the Academy for one week and then my first assignment was Engine Company Nineteen, Fenwick and Frelinghuysen Avenue.

Christmas day was my first day working in the firehouse. I was the first black there in Nineteen Engine. I was the only black in the Second Battalion. We had five battalions at the time. I was in the Second Battalion. In Engine Nineteen I met nineteen of the nicest guys that I would ever want to meet. They all became my friends. There were no problems with me with race, that never came about. We just did things together. We knew each other's families. We helped each other out when we could. And I had a very enjoyable time down there.

Well, my first memorable fire was my first big fire. I was on the book and somebody started knocking at the door and the bells started hitting at the same time. I lifted up the overhead door and the guy said, "There's a fire down the street." So, I looked down Frelinghuysen Avenue going north and I saw a fire rolling out in the street, actually rolling in big balls out in the street. I hit the bell. Everybody comes downstairs. We jump on the engine and we go down to the fire. The fire is still rolling down the street. We put up a ladder to the roof because it took One Truck a while to get there and Five Truck a while and Ten Truck a while to get over. So, we're going to see what we can do on the roof. Try and ventilate or something, get some water in there. Mistake for me.

I get up on the roof. I lose my partner. I'm surrounded by nothing but smoke, my first big fire. I said, "Lord if I ever get off this roof, I'm quitting this job." So, I thought about what little training I had. I got down on my hands and my knees and I crawled and I groped and I groped until I found the ledge of the roof. Then from the ledge of the roof, I groped all the way around until I found the ladder. I said, "No Lord, you trained me enough to keep me on this job." Then I got down. That was one of the most horrifying events then because I was brand new on the job. Then Freddy grabbed me and he cussed me out for getting lost up on the roof. I'm not supposed to be up there without anybody. Make sure somebody's with me and I started learning.

The only problem the whole company ran into was when we had something like a four-alarm fire in the Dreamland skating rink, right on the border of Elizabeth and Newark. Well, we were first due down there. We got down there. We didn't use our hose wagon because we were so near the fire with our engine. So, we left our hose wagon sitting while we went and fought the fire. We came back out after the fire. Our hose was laid out all over the street. Where other companies had used it and didn't even give us the courtesy of rolling it up and putting it back on or piling it by our wagon, that's the only problem I've ever had, other than that, no problem.

The truck companies had it the easiest. They could come to a fire, get finished at a fire, and go home. But the truck companies in those days, like Ten Truck with Twenty-nine Engine, One Truck with One Engine, they would help. They would stay and help the engine company roll up because they have to live in the same house. They'd come back together and it was no problem. We'd all help each other. Each engine company, if you'd all pick up at the same time and you have hose stretched, you'd help each other. First one finished, we'd help the other guys. We were all part of the same fire department, just different firehouses that's all.

Wargo: Actually, my first assignment when I came on the job was Salvage Two on Congress Street, but when I went in there to see everybody they said "You're going to be permanently detailed to Eight Truck." Because the guy that was supposed to go there, they didn't want there. It turned out later, they didn't want him there because he had some problems. So, being I was detailed there, they asked if I wanted to put in to stay there. I did. That's how I got there. Plus, I lived within like walking distance. I lived on Solomon Street, within walking distance of Eight Truck, so it was convenient for me.

I remember coming out of the Academy and everybody told me, "You go to Eight Truck and you won't see a fire for a year." I walked into the firehouse and the captain said, "You're working here?" I said, "Yes." "Well, put your stuff on the seat." He's talking to me and the bell hits. All of the sudden I see people running around putting their clothing on. He said, "Put your equipment on and sit in this seat. When we get to where we're going, you just hold onto my coat." Well, we got to where we were going. It was a signal eleven in a chemical factory on Avenue P. It was a good smokey working fire. That was my first night on the job, so I thought it was going to be like that forever and ever. I did find out that you went quite a way between fires. When you did get a fire down there, you had a good spectacular fire most of the time because of the chemical plants and things of that nature. There weren't that many dwelling fires. We had a lot of factories. You were there for a while.

Cody: I was assigned to Four Engine. When I walked into the firehouse it was kind of scary. I remember walking in and the captain said, "Find a helmet that fits you." because we didn't have our own stuff. We had our own coats, but we didn't have helmets. We had gotten the coats in the Academy. He said, "Just find a helmet that fits you and ride on the back step." He showed me where to stand. I wasn't in the firehouse twenty minutes. We had a run to the projects, at the Columbus Homes. I remember coming back. When I came back, I found out that I had a captain's helmet on. Not knowing that the white in it was captain, but that's the one that fit me. I wore the captain's helmet just to that fire. The captain pointed it out that it was a captain's helmet. That's was Tommy Boyle. He was the captain at Four Engine.

He was a very good captain, who used to drill us a lot. We learned a lot there, but the people who made up Four Engine, Truck Two seem to have met by appointment because most of them were nuts. We had Lenny Guidera. We had Tommy DeLuca, Jack Hall, and it was mostly laughing. We laughed. There were water fights and things like that. We had that fireplace there. Everything went into the fireplace. It was considered a punishment house. It was the Third Battalion punishment house. No one really wanted to go there, but the guys who were there never wanted to go anywhere else. You just liked it there. It was a good place to be.

Garrity: I went from three days of training to Truck Two on the first Tour. It was one of the funniest places to work in the whole world. It was a riot. We had so much fun in that place. Well, first of all the firehouse had a fireplace in it. How many firehouses have fireplaces in them? We used to keep warm by burning rubber tires and pallets and any other damn thing we could find to keep warm with. It was just one of those places where everybody fit in. I had Tommy Boyle as a captain. He was one of the nicest guys I ever met in my life. Bill Green was a captain. Bill didn't stay there that long. Then we had Dicky O'Donnell for a captain on the truck and then Jack Hall. I had good guys to work for and we just had a lot of fun. We used to do some crazy things. Water fights. Chasing one another around. Chasing the Rescue Squad with water. We would throw water on them. We had a running battle with the Rescue Squad. We used to play softball with them up in Tom's parking lot on the weekends. Chief Magnusson was a deputy over there. After working in a real job and then to go to the fire department, it was like being released from prison. It was just fantastic.

My captain's instructions to me the first night I went to work were, "I want you to grab the back of my mask strap and don't let go until I tell you. And just follow me wherever I take you." Those were his only instructions to me. He showed me where my bed was. He gave me a locker and then I didn't see him the rest of the night. Those were his instructions. I think we had one run to the projects or two runs to the projects and nothing after that. Of course, I couldn't sleep all night; lying in bed waiting for the bells to ring.

My first fire was on my second night, a three-story frame over on New and Arlene which is where they built Rutgers. I remember because after we had the fire knocked down, my captain came over and says, "Come here kid, I want to show you something." So, he brings me over to the corner, it's all dark, and he shines a flashlight on this guy. He was burned in the corner. It's my first job, my very first job I had. It turned out he was murdered and that's what the fire was all about. I guess I was supposed to have some kind of sick reaction. Obviously, he's dead. I worked for a funeral director once in a while, so dead bodies didn't bother me too much.

Knight: I was assigned to Engine Twenty-nine on the third tour. I went over there in July of 1964. That section of town was called little Tel Aviv because it was all Jewish over there; some beautiful one family homes. But in the house that I was in, Twenty-nine Engine and Ten Truck, if there was a multiple that came in, in the Fourth Battalion, a lot of times we wouldn't catch it on the second alarm or the third alarm. The guys in the house always said, "We go after the kitchen sinks." It was something to sit out in the summertime over there; look down Bergen Street; see a two or a three-alarm fire going down Bergen Street; and you're not going to it. Here your house was on Bergen Street.

In January of '65 I went over to Three Truck. I wanted to get out of Twenty-nine Engine because it was a slow house. It was the slowest house in the Fourth Battalion and being a young kid, twenty-three years old, I didn't want to rot over there. So, I wanted some action. I had talked to my Deputy Chief, who at the time was Chief Donlon, and he told me he had an opening in Three Truck on the third tour; to try it out for a while; see if I liked it. If I liked it, he'd make the arrangements for me to stay there permanently. If I didn't like it, then I'd have to come back to Twenty-nine Engine until such time as I can get a transfer someplace else.

My father was always in an engine company and I thought I would like engine work. But I went over to Three Truck and I must have done something right over there because I spent January of '65 to June of 1980 in Three Truck. I loved truck work, to this day I love truck work.

Gaynor: I was assigned, on completion of my training, to Engine Sixteen down on Ferry and Brill. Engine Sixteen was one of ten two-piece engine companies. Out of twenty-five engine companies in the city, ten were two-piece. I knew I wasn't staying down there. I was on the first tour. So, when I reported for work either my first morning or my first night at relief time, I ran into my longtime friend, Robert J. Miller. Who was also there at that company on the third tour. He was, I would say, well prepared for his first captain's exam which is coming about in 1966 or 1967. He befriended me and I knew this is not where a young man ought to be and you would want to go somewhere else.

I stayed there for approximately fourteen months, fifteen months. And I went over to Engine Fourteen, the busy company in the battalion. They were approaching a thousand runs. But at least they went to house fires. Things were looking up.

I didn't have a structural fire at Sixteen. However, when I went to Fourteen that changed. Then we started getting some work. I had a young man, Arthur Linhoff, as my captain. A nice man, Arthur Schmidt was my Battalion Chief. He was a former Engine Fourteen captain. I worked with John Finney, Michael James Whalen, and Mike D'Ambrosio.

John Finney moved to drive Schmidt as the battalion chief when he got promoted. Bob Radecke came over. Who was my friend from the Training Academy and from before we came on the Fire Department. Eventually, Mike Whalen left and Mike Catalon came over, so you had the three of us from the Training Academy within a year, a year and half time we're all in the same fire company on the same tour and aren't we happy. And we got Michael D'Ambrosio to teach us. He is a gentleman and we are not yet. He's a few years older, but not many. But we always took his advice well.

We had the dumps on New Year's Day, 1966. We're laying it must have been eight-inch pipes in the dumps to move the water. The firefighters, they're laying pipes. Right on top of the ground surface, so you could move water into the dump. Barrone's dump had a large, large fire. Deep seated, can't get at it. Right around Christmas is when it started. But it went on for weeks. Two men or four, would carry a ten, twelve-foot length of maybe eight-inch diameter pipe. And you laid the pipe so you could move the water a large distance. You could have put hose, but two-and-a-half-inch hose didn't move that much water. So, they had to end up hooking up pumps and convert back to manifolds so you could hook the hose onto to distribute the water.

We were down there when the Military Park Hotel came in that we would have gone to on the fourth alarm. We didn't because we were sitting in the dumps with two engines. I think that may have been Christmas Eve.

That may have been the highlights of being in Sixteen Engine. You used to go down and sit by yourself as a night watch. One man would get a detail with an old gig. You'd take a thermos of coffee and you'd go down there for four hours until someone would come and relieve you. That's what Down Neck companies did at that time. They all took a shot at the dump. Twenty-seven Engine used to dump a lot of hose down there.

If you had 428 runs and you divide it by four tours, it's 100 runs and change for a whole year. At Fourteen it changed. Now we do get structural fires. Fourteen went up on the twenty-three boxes and the twenty-four boxes. And then you start getting into structural fires and you're starting to get the feel of things, but when you go from Sixteen to Fourteen you really didn't bring any experience with you other than maybe you were a pump operator. You might have had some enthusiasm, but you really didn't have any experience to speak of.

Fourteen we had a wonderful time. Three young men, Michael D'Ambrosio, our captain was a relatively young man too. And it was a good time. I was twenty-three, twenty-four, just before I was twenty-five. And I got married while I was there in '67. But I knew it wasn't busy enough. There I was waiting for Andy Masterson to get promoted. He was a fireman in Five Truck. They were one and five. So, I had my eyes set on that and when he was going to get promoted, I was going to Five Truck. With Eddy Vesey, Jimmy Reeds, Tommy Jones, maybe Hoot Gibson was the other member.

Frank Lieber was the captain. I must have talked to Tommy Jones. Yeah, that was the place to go.

In the meantime, Arthur Schmidt, our Battalion Chief had gotten promoted. When he got promoted, his drive Feeney wanted to go back to Fourteen Engine. To make room for him in Fourteen Engine they called me up. Would you want to go to Twenty Engine? We have an opening there immediately. I said, "Yes I would." I must leave. That happened in a day, two days. I remain on the first tour. I never go to Five Truck. John Feeney goes back to Fourteen in my spot. A man named Russel Schoemer goes to Five Truck.

We had a good time at Fourteen. We started going to some fires. You started to feel like a firefighter. It was a lot of socializing. You're young, full of enthusiasm and the devil. Come to work, not afraid to work. Call up the operator and ask if we could have the move up. Ten Engine was a company nearby. We worked with them pretty often in Fourteen Engine. We also worked with them all the way in Twenty Engine. By remaining on the same tour, you kept a lot of the friends you had cultivated. And made some new ones. But in Twenty Engine we now have action.

Calvetti: My first day on the job, I go to Salvage Two. Back then you came right to the firehouse. It was all on the job training. They told me to come into the firehouse around seven-thirty. So, I got there about seven-thirty, seven-thirty-five. I come in the firehouse and the captain, George Lackey, says, "Who are you?" I tell him my name. He says, "Okay, we don't start housework until eight o'clock. Sit down, watch TV for a while." I says, "Okay." I sat in the chair in front of the TV. I fell asleep. One of the guys wakes me up, says, "Hey, who told you about this job?"

I didn't know what the hell was going on. I walked into the firehouse without turnout gear. The guys took me into the back room at eight o'clock. They find me a helmet that fits fairly decent, a coat, boots, the whole bit. And lucky thing, the guy had gloves in his pockets. So, I had gloves. I can't work without gloves. I don't know how these guys do it. I always had gloves on.

But Salvage had the filtered masks and everybody shared the masks. The first day I came on the job, they started training me in the firehouse and I was quick to learn. They showed me how to do the E and J oxygen.

I was only on the job a week and I had a couple of jobs. Now we get this fire and Eleven Engine or Eleven Truck pulled these two women out. When I got there, they were already in the hallway. So, I ended up working on one with my captain and Rescue worked on the other one. It was sad. They both ended up dying. They were pronounced dead. They died because of a door knob. There was no door knob on the door to the bedroom. If there was a door knob on that door they could have gotten out into the hallway and gotten out. The fire was in the kitchen area. To get from the bedroom to the door to get out to the hall or to the back porch they had to go through the kitchen. Their bedroom door had no door knobs on it. They were forced into the kitchen or go out the window, four stories, no fire escape. It's a shame. They both died. That was my first death on the job and I didn't sleep too good that night.

Lawless: They sent me to the firehouse with nothing. No clothes, no boots, no helmet, no coat, no nothing. What do you do? Start borrowing stuff. I walked into Seventeen Engine, "Hi, I'm the new guy." "What do you have?" "Nothing, what am I supposed to have?" "Well try these boots on." I tried putting the boots on with shoes on. That's how dumb I was. First thing they showed you was how to put the mask on. And if it heats up and everything.

About three hours later I got my first fire. I was dragged into a cellar by my captain saying hold onto my mask. I'm scared shitless, pal. We had to drill in the service with the tear gas canisters, but that don't prepare you for when it's hot and smoky. I just stayed close to him, like we were stuck together. The noise and the shit breaking and the people yelling. Sounds like mass confusion the first time you go through it.

And an interesting experience, the first one. You never forget your first one. It took me a couple of fires to make up my mind to stay. It really did. It really did. My second, third, or fourth fire I said, "This ain't bad." Now I started to like it. This job, you like it or you hate it. There's no in between, no in between. You like it or you hate it. That's it.

Benderoth: I was on tour four, Truck Three on West Market Street. I got sworn in Monday. Tuesday morning, I went to work. The first fire that we had, they try to teach us how to fight fires. There were three new guys at Seven Engine and Three Truck. Well, they try to teach us. Okay, you grab a mask. You put this on. It was fine. Then we had our first fire on Bergen Street, kitchen fire. I'm on the truck company. I go backdoor, the fire rolls out at you. Where the hell's the water? Well, they got tied up with the engine. We didn't get water right away. And I'm inside the back door with only the guys from the truck company. I didn't know what was going on, but I did it. That was about three weeks after we were on the job. That was my first fire.

McGovern: I walked into Twenty-seven Engine my first day in the firehouse and at the time I lived right around the corner on Gotthardt Street. Strange enough, I walked in the first day, they told me you had to be there at eight o'clock and I happen to be late and I only lived like four doors away from the firehouse. That was the last time I was ever late on the job. My captain, he wizened me up to the way of the Lord. "Most guys get in here an hour early." So, that was the last day I was ever late on the job. I walked in five minutes late.

At the time we were having a lot of brush fires, a lot of dump fires and the deal was to conserve your water. Because all you had is what you had in your tank. You get into the middle of the meadows down there you don't just spray all your water on a fire. You do it sparingly, in short bursts. That's one of the main things he impressed on me. "Save your water Tom." We did a lot of broom work. I mentioned that to a few guys when I was in Rescue. "Get a broom." What? McGovern finally lost it. He wants me to get a broom to put a fire out. They had no concept of fighting a fire without water. I spent hours chasing fires with brooms. Well, anyway I was down there for two years and from there I went up to Rescue.

If I was going to be a fireman, I wanted to be a good one. You just couldn't get the experience down there. At the time Twenty-seven was averaging around 800 runs a year and Rescue was doing like 5,000 at the time. I wanted to learn the job. I saw no opportunities to learn it down there, not on garbage fires and brush fires. You very rarely had a structural fire. As it would happen, the day I reported to Rescue we had seven jobs. I said to myself, "What did I get myself into? I could have been sleeping." We had four multiples and three signal elevens that night. We were going from one to the other. Bitter was my Captain at the time. He said, "We do this every night, kid." I said, "Yeah, tear my papers up because I'm leaving."

D. Prachar: My first assignment was Eleven Truck, tour three Captain Melody. My brother had connections. I fit in there for six months. Then I was transferred out.

Then I went Nine Truck where I had Captain Bitter. Worked with another fine crew. I never had a problem back then as far as crew because you lived together. You lived together as a crew. You lived together as a family. You had your little spats here and there, but you didn't have one guy who didn't talk to another guy for two months. Because everybody just got along together and you did your job. Plus, we were busy back in the late '60s, early '70s, so you're always happy. If you wanted to do the job as far as fighting fires, you're always happy. I lasted in Nine Truck about a year and a half, then I went down to Five Truck with Eddie Cassidy as a Captain.

My first job was Fourteenth Avenue and Seventeenth Street, two and a half story frame, second floor fully involved. We pulled up. First due truck, went in, did our ventilation, and that's when I started learning, right then and there. When the fire was knocked down, Captain Melody took me, showed me the proper way of pulling ceilings, opening windows, taking the sills off, demonstrated how you take the pike axe, take the pike, into the sill, and pull. I thought it was fantastic, so he gave me the axe, went to the window next to it. Rotted sill, right through the sill, the pike went right into my foot. Scared to death to tell my Captain I was hurt because I didn't want to be known as a pussy. Got back to the firehouse, took my boot off. My boot was full of blood. Never forget it. He just said, "Did you learn a lesson?" I said, "Yes, don't hit it so hard the first time."

Nine Truck, we had a fire on Tenth Street and Kent, right off of Springfield Avenue. There's a large apartment house there. We came down Tenth Street to Kent, Eighteen Engine, in front of us, took a line right in the building. We put the aerial to the building. The building on fire was the one behind it. We couldn't see that. We thought it was in the back of the apartment building. People yelling kids are in the building. All we could hear from outside was "Daddy, get us out." Well, the three kids ended up dying. Rescue finally got in, got the kids, but they all died within the next week or so. That was my first real taste of kids dying in a fire. Something I'll never forget. Went home, I had two of my own kids. Just hugged them; played with them all day long. Most of my memorable fires are something involving kids.

Weber: First assignment, Engine Company Seventeen on tour four. No Academy, I was thrown right to the dogs. Right into the firehouse. I walked into the firehouse my first day without turnout gear. I looked like a Halloween outfit with a mishmash of all kinds of inadequate equipment from other firefighters. I had very little idea what I was walking into. The reason for that is because life in the firehouse had changed from the time my father was assigned to a company. His last field assignment was Engine Twenty-nine. Then he was detailed to City Hall working with the dispatchers. So, he actually had lost touch with what life was like inside the firehouses. It was totally new to me, totally new experience.

It was intimidating walking in because I was a twenty-one-year-old snot-nosed kid and the next youngest member of that crew was forty-two years old which equates to being twice my age,

The old timers were very concerned with me because of my having a father on the job. And I was immediately taken under their wings. It turned out that I went to high school with Myles and Jimmy McDonald and I worked with their father John. There was a connection there right away. Which was evident as we went on our first few runs for small fires. I was under the protective wing of the father figures. And all I kept hearing was, "Keep an eye on the kid." I knew they were talking about me.

Part of my learning curve when I was still in Seventeen Engine was, I used to volunteer for all details, took all details to truck companies because I wanted to learn my trade. I recall being sent to Truck Five on Belmont Avenue on a detail. And in I walk, maybe a year on the job, maybe less and the captain at the time on that particular day was Andy Masterson. He looked at me and said, "Who the hell are you?" I told him who I was. And he said, "How long you on the job?" I told him whatever it was. Let's say a year. And he said, "Pack your shit and get the hell out of here and go back where you came from." He threw me out of the firehouse because I had no experience. True story. So, I got back in my car, drove back up to Clinton Place. Told my captain what happened. He just laughed. Sent somebody else.

So, subsequently I would go on details to Truck Ten. And the captain on our tour was Al Paine. One of the nicest men you'd even want to meet. He took me under his wing, taught me what he felt as though I needed to know at that stage of my education. Taught me how to tiller, taught me how to drive the truck in the front. And to do the tiller, that was a whole lot of fun. A whole different thought process going to a ladder company. My first fire was small. Location I can't tell you precisely, but I think it was somewhere along Fabian Place near maybe Lyons Avenue. It was in the daytime. It was a vacant house, smoke coming out of a couple of windows in the back of the building on the first floor. And that was when I first heard what I said before. "Keep your eye on the kid." It was a booster job, a bunch of trash in the back room. No masks were involved because of the nature of the fire that didn't require it. I wasn't allowed to do anything, but basically follow in, put my hands on the hose and drag it into the building. Signal three oh eight, one engine, one truck, and a battalion chief, who like in most three oh eights, never showed up. It was a nothing fire, but it was my first snoot full of smoke.

I can remember many times at Seventeen going down West Runyon Street, especially at night because West Runyon Street went downhill from Clinton Place heading toward Bergen Street. So, you had an elevated view of seeing columns of smoke pour out over the rooftop and then turning the corner and seeing the glow. Then heart rates would go up and our eyeballs would start popping out of our heads. But as far as anything spectacular, houses fully involved which I never, ever thought could possibly happen. A lot of excitement in that regard, but probably the biggest thing to me, when you would get to a fire, say on a second alarm assignment and a battalion chief or chief officer would meet you and they would already have determined the building was lost. He'd tell you what he wanted you to do. Which I learned later as a battalion chief myself, strategy. You can't do anything with it as it is, but we're going to do this and that to protect the rest of the block. And pulling up and seeing three or four houses on fire at the same time and ignoring them. As a youngster, that was interesting to me.

I was in Seventeen from my appointment in January of 1969 until I was transferred to Engine Six. I believe that was in 1973. It was a total change in culture. A different type of a neighborhood with all the projects and Engine Six's first due area. You went from a neighborhood of one- and two-family homes where there was more private ownership, to an area where it was all projects.

K. Miller: My first day, I walked into Eighteen Engine on the third tour. My captain was Charlie Plath and the firemen in the company at the time were Eddie McCarthy and Eddie Conklin. We walk in and of course firemen being firemen, I was welcomed with open arms. They commandeered a helmet, turnout coat, and boots for me. The first thing they showed me was how to put on and wear the Burrell mask. Prior to that I never had any experience putting anything over my face and having to breathe out of it. Forty-five minutes later we went to a fire and I put the Burrell on, I thought the way I was told how to do it. I went with my company into the building and I took all kinds of smoke. I come out choking and coughing and thinking, "What am I doing? I don't need this job." Deputy Chief James Donlon, who was the First Deputy and was riding out of Avon Avenue, saw I was having trouble. He came over to me and says, "Alright kid, here put your mask over your face. Pull this strap. Pull that strap. Hold onto my coat. We're going inside." I held onto the Deputy Chief's coat and we walked inside. And that's my first real big introduction to being inside a structure with a fire in it. I think from there, I got back to my company and they actually let me operate the hose line for the wash down. After the fire I went back to the firehouse and seriously thought whether I want to do this. I think the support and the friendship from the guys in the company was so strong that that over weighed any of the negatives that I had encountered.

I remember the first fire where I actually saw like a super man and I don't mean that in the true sense of the word, but a real fireman. Up until that point I had been in an engine company and you went where the line went. We had some fires, but nothing out of the extraordinary. We responded down to Belmont Avenue. And just down the street from the Belmont Avenue firehouse, there was a four-story brick. Going good in the back section, probably one of the lower floors, which was sending the fire up every place it could go. The building was really starting to take off. Frank Calvetti, was a fireman in Five Truck at the time. I saw him climb up the fire escape on the outside of the building and go in. I was in Nine Truck at the time and we had just pulled up.

I was waiting for our aerial to get put to the roof. And I see Frank Calvetti come flying out the window he went into with the fire right on his tail. I mean when he got out, it was like the barrel of a gun. He just jumped out and just stepped away from the window and the fire came blowing out like eight feet out the window, almost like it was shot out of a gun. It wasn't like he had jumped in and jumped out. He was in there for a few minutes. So, I know he was done making his moves in on that floor and all of the sudden he came flying out and the fire chased him out of it. It may have dawned on me that there are risks to be taken, but there are guys who take them on an everyday basis. And to me all through my career those were the heroes of the job. Through the course of my career, I saw many more guys do exactly that same thing.

J. Cosby: My first assignment was Engine Eighteen, Avon Avenue and South Thirteenth Street. I was very excited being assigned to Engine Eighteen because I only lived like two blocks from the firehouse. I could basically walk to work.

I was the first black firefighter assigned to Engine Eighteen. I didn't have that many problems there. Naturally you always hear racial remarks, not only against black guys, but you hear against white guys too. You always hear racial remarks concerning Polish, Italians. I think the only kind of remarks I didn't hear were against Anglo-Saxon Protestants. I guess, nobody had anything to say about them. But basically, it wasn't that bad because I was in the house with Chief Donlon. He was the Deputy Chief at that time assigned to Eighteen's house. He was pretty strict. He wouldn't let them get away with anything in his companies.

I would say I was accepted. I would say blacks were accepted pretty good at that time. Compared to stories I'd heard when the first guys came on. There really weren't that many blacks on the job even when I came on. There was only maybe probably about thirty-five or forty. A lot of times you would have a fear of being isolated because you were more or less the only black in the firehouse. A lot of times you would find yourself in situations where you wouldn't have that much in common with a lot of the fellows, they being from different backgrounds. But I feel like I always had to do a job really, not to basically socialize.

One particular fire stands out in my mind. It was a fire that involved an ambulance and a car. It was at the intersection of Avon and South Tenth Street. The ambulance was going down Avon Avenue and the car was on South Tenth Street, heading south on South Tenth Street. The car came through the intersection and hit the ambulance and hit it right in the center part of the vehicle. It just tipped the whole thing over. The impact was where the gas tank of the ambulance was. It ruptured the gas tank. I guess it was about four blocks from the firehouse. When we got ready to respond from Eighteen Engine our apparatus wouldn't start. So, we grabbed all the fire extinguishers we could off the apparatus and ran down about four blocks. When we got there, the two guys in the ambulance had crawled out, but they were on fire. We managed to extinguish the fire with the fire extinguishers, but I think later on, a couple of days later, I think one of them died. I think one survived. That one particular fire kind of stood out in my mind. It wasn't a real big fire, but it was the circumstances that it occurred under.

Saccone: My first firehouse when I came on the job was Eighteen Engine. I started on the second tour and my first captain was Captain Gower. And he hasn't changed a bit. And if you want to know anything else, my first two weeks on the job, my wife said to me when I went home, "Did you start up the boilers?" Because at that time when I started, we were wearing chambray pants and boiler engineer shirts.

Did I know anyone on the fire department at the time? No. I was scared shit. All I can say is when I walked into that firehouse, Eighteen Engine, I was scared shit. Especially when I looked at big bojo guys, monsters of men. Like the jolly green giant. Some of these guys are not around and they were very good firemen, like Teddy Skinner, God bless him. Fredette, George Fredette. My mentor who recently retired, John Harrobin, he taught me the most. Danny Prachar, he was practically new on the job. And one guy he retired. I didn't really get to know him. He won two hundred thousand dollars and left the job, Charlie Martin. I think he hit the Irish sweepstakes or something. He didn't stay very long.

My first night is the toughest because you don't really know anybody in the firehouse. You have to set yourself in. My biggest experience, and I was a nervous wreck, was being on the house watch and looking at that red phone and wondering when it was going to ring. The captain said, "Don't worry about it, kid. You'll be alright and handed me the first edition of the Oklahoma ventilation book saying, "Look, kid, you got a long time to go. Why don't you read this book? Someday you'll make captain."

We went to a fire one time I'll never forget, especially since it was around the neighborhood of Orchard and Pennington which was notorious for a lot of fires at that time. I remember responding to a fire on Pennsylvania Avenue. We were a two-piece company. There's good points and disadvantages to having a two-piece company. The advantage to having a two-piece is you could lay from a hydrant, piece in, have a long stretch, and you would have water immediately. The bad thing is the guy on the second piece is alone. When we had this working fire, it was night time. And Ten Engine was first due. We responded and the engine was in front of me. I had to stay back three hundred feet. Just like any normal person. So, I would stay in the back, but I wasn't that far. It was like a half a block away. But I kept up. A lot of times people used to see an engine pass by. They didn't think another engine would pass by right away, too. So, you had to keep the siren on. All the sudden the motor just cut out. Everything went dead. They lost an apparatus and they had no way of knowing that I was out of commission because the radio went dead. So, it could have been a battery problem that cut everything out. And I just stood there if it wasn't for Headquarters Fifty-two at that time, the Arson Squad. I don't know if it was Headquarters Fifty-two back then, but if it wasn't for them, I don't know what I would have done. They stood by me and called apparatus repair. But I was there. I think the three guys always rode on the front piece. I think I just drove that. I don't think I drove anybody. But they lost me and they lost a pumper. That was a disadvantage. But that didn't happen too frequently.

1970s: The War Years and Contraction

Daudelin: Well, my first assignment was Salvage One, Belmont Avenue. I tell you. I'd go back to Salvage. It was a good company. Although we had nothing to do with salvage in those days. But when I went, I went on the second tour and my first assignment was Salvage One. It was me; Jimmy Clemens was the new captain there and Mike Cosentino was the crew. One and two, that's all in Salvage at that time.

We had no salvage covers whatsoever. Every once in a while, we had tar paper and we did have some sheeting. If it was like a small fire, they busted out one or two windows, we would tar paper the window up. At times we would use the plastic, but for the most part we were used as manpower. My first Deputy Chief was Chief Grehl. We would just pull right in and then we would take Six Engine's second line or whoever we could pull a line from and we were used more for manpower.

I put in for Five Truck almost right away because I liked the guys and I liked that tillering thing. That to me was sharp. Unfortunately, I was assigned to Five Truck right after the accident when Dominic LaTorre and Russel Schoemer got killed. So, I went over there on an emergency transfer onto the second tour to take Russel Schoemer's place and I wound up staying there. I was working that night. But we didn't catch the fire. Remember, Salvage One and Salvage Two split the city.

I would venture to say, my first year on the fire department, we probably did close to six thousand runs. We had half the city. We had the worst half. All the four boxes, the one boxes, the forty-five boxes and we had the upper half of North Newark. Anything above the park was all Salvage Two. Salvage One was down on Congress Street. So, with the false alarm situation in those days, we would leave on a run and we'd get ten runs while we were out. We used to go on every box alarm. A lot of the captains in Salvage held back for fires, especially the older guys.

But Clemens having two brand new guys, because Mike Costantino only had a couple of months more than me, we would respond all the time. We used to go up and down Belmont Avenue.

I put my transfer in before the accident because it was known that Eddy Vesey was getting out. There were going to be a couple of changes, so Russel Schoemer told me to put in my papers. I put them in right before the accident. And then when it happened, they moved me over there right away. Because after the accident, I actually didn't go back to Salvage, I went right to Five Truck on detail. I was there several weeks and I was then permanently transferred.

Pianka: My first day, I went to Five Truck. I introduced myself to the captain, Danny McCoy. He said, "Okay, kid, don't worry. Do you have any equipment?" I said, "Nah." He said, "Don't worry about it." We went around the firehouse and he rustled a pair of boots, coat, helmet. And all he told me was, "If the bell hits you stick with me. Get on the rig. If we get on, you get on. We go to a fire. You hang on to me. I'll take care of you." Well, I didn't have any fires that first day. Actually, I didn't work with him because he was on the first tour. He was in only for a couple hours with me.

Captain Jorda was my first captain. I did have a fire with him and that's exactly what he did. We had the old Burrells. He showed me how to put the mask on. "If we get a job. You hold onto the back straps. Just follow me." We had a job. He dragged me. I mean literally into it. And that's when I realized, "What the hell did I get myself into? This is ridiculous." But it didn't take long. Because I was with good people and I got into the swing of things. Joe Ricca was one of the fellows in the company. I spent two weeks with the fourth tour and they got me into the swing of things. Then I went to the third tour and again, it was the guys who you are initially with who set the pace. I loved it. I thought I died and went to heaven. Especially when we went to a fire, came back, and the beers were popping. "Here you go kid. You did well."

Perez: I went straight to the firehouse. About nine months later they sent us to the Academy. I walked into Seven Engine. I had no turnout gear. They let me use somebody else's equipment. Then when I went to the Academy, they told me what to get. So, I worked for nine months using other people's equipment. That's the way it was done. The only things I think I had to buy were my boots and the helmet.

I was there about a half hour. The bell goes off. Captain Formisano, told me jump on the rig and listen to Harry Uhde and do anything he does. I'm on the job not even half an hour. We go up to a working fire, I mean a good working fire, on Springfield and Norfolk. It's like three stories, going. A big furniture joint, I mean with houses and all. So, Harry Uhde takes a line. He's gone. I don't know any better. I go right behind him. And we're throwing water and the heat, smoke. And I'm choking. Everything burned for hours. That was my first fire. We lost four buildings at that fire, half a block.

Marcell: I was assigned to Four Engine on tour one. The first day I got to the firehouse, the guys were really friendly. They said, "Oh, the new guy's here. Come and sit down." I reported at a quarter after seven, at a quarter to eight they had a working fire. So, the captain said, "No, let the new guy stay there. I don't want him getting killed on the first day." They were gone for about two hours and I just sat in the firehouse until they came back.

So, when they came back, they broke me in. I saw that Tommy DeLuca was the senior firefighter. So, I tried to make friends with him right away. And we went upstairs and I said, "Where should I go?" And he said, "That bed up there. That's not taken. That's open." It was a bed right outside the captain's room. I said, "What do we do here?" I didn't know how to make beds. I was never in the military or anything like that. So, he showed me what to do. I had a bag of sheets that they had given me. And he showed me how to do it. He said, "You have to get your bed made." and so on and so forth. But we had a lot of fun. There was a lot of ball breaking in that firehouse. If you had one little thing wrong with you, they knew it. They'd find out what it is and they wouldn't let go of that. It was a lot of fun.

I remember the very first fire, maybe about a week on the job. We were first due on Seventh Avenue. It was Lenny Guidera and Jim Cody on the line. Tommy DeLuca was pumping. The captain had off that night. I remember the glass all breaking around us. I was lightening up on the line inside. And I thought to myself, "What am I doing here?" But it all worked out. They broke me slow. First, I was lightening up and then I was right near the captain and then I had the tip. I had mattress fires and garbage fires first, Then I would get a room of fire and then I would get a couple of rooms on the tip and so on and so forth.

Rotunda: My first day I went right to the firehouse, Ten Truck/Twenty-nine Engine on Bergen and Leigh. I think they registered you according to size more or less, if you went on a truck or an engine company. You went into the firehouse and they watched over you and told you what to watch out for more or less. Then you went to the Academy afterwards, but the basics you learned right from the guys in the firehouse. Then there were always fires so you learned fairly fast because it wasn't that you got to sit down too much. We had the jobs coming like crazy at that time. So, you learned on the job.

I mean we were going from one job to another job, to another job. That was the Fourth Battalion. That was the good part, where I went. That was my area when I worked in Coca-Cola, so I knew all the streets. The first fire that I had was a customer, so I knew the lay out of the place. They had the fire in the supermarket and I knew the lay out of the supermarket, so I could lead the guys through almost blindfolded. The other fire we had on Bergen Street, a couple of houses, where a woman and kid died. This is when I first came on the job. They had the picture in the paper of me up on the aerial ladder pointing to the guy. That's when I found out the fascination of a straight tip on a nozzle. It would cut the wall like you were using a laser. Or watching the fire, being a truckman you don't usually have water.

So, you get in before other people, you get into a part where you're watching the fire go around the doorway real nice. Just like doing a dance and you sit there fascinated, watching it. Then all of the sudden you see the whole room just burst into flames. You jump out the door and close the door really quick because you don't have any way of fighting that fire. You don't have the water with you. That was the first big fire I had. An old lady and a granddaughter passed away. She was only on the second floor. She was afraid to drop the kid to a guy who was trying to get her to drop the kid on a car. He was standing on top of a car. She wouldn't let go. She went back into the fire and disappeared. That was it. That was a little tough. Some of them are tough.

McDonnell: I was assigned to One Truck on the first tour. It was a Saturday. My first day and I got up, I thought I was going to be late. I had no car. I took a cab to the firehouse. Carried my rubber coat and my rubber boots and I walked into One Engine. The first person I met was Emil Nardone. I walked in and told him my name. "I'm new, I'm assigned here." He looked, "One Truck, you're next-door kid." So, I went next door and my captain was Leo Chapin. He was the captain on the first tour. The crew was Tommy Farley, Donald McPhee, myself, and another new fireman name Steve Jablonski, a guy who came on the job with me. So, there were two new guys and those two. That was my first day and I remember my first day particularly because I remember going in and I was ready. I was ready for the three bagger because I heard my brother and my brother-in-law talking about the three baggers and the two baggers and this bagger and that, fires everywhere. So, I figure I'm going out all day long. I'll be working eight hours a day fighting fires. I remember we sat in the firehouse all day, had one run. We made it around to Hamilton Street which is a block away and turned around. I was so disappointed. I said "What the hell are they talking about." We had one run all day long. That was my first day in the firehouse. I never forgot that. I was ready for these fires.

One Truck used to do about 1800 runs a year. My two years in '70 and '71 we could have done 1800 to 2000 runs a year. It was a kind of middle of middle. It wasn't a busy company; it wasn't a slow one. It was kind of in the middle. We were in the high value district I think they called it. I think it's because of that, for some reason. I don't think its response area was very big. We didn't go in any direction except south. We went south far. The other directions we really didn't go far at all. I don't know if when they set it up, they wanted to keep the high value district covered. The insurance underwriters were still coming into the city every year. Evaluating the city.

I didn't have a working fire for almost two months. The first fire I had was on Williams and Shipman. I don't know if the street is there anymore. In the back of Saint Benedict's, it was an abandoned building, two and a half story, and I was gung-ho. I'm gonna be a good fireman. I have to prove myself. I remember going in, we had no masks on, the fire climbed up the porch into the second-floor window off the porch roof and I tore that second floor to shreds. I ripped it apart and the fire was on the third floor. I just went into there. I ripped everything, pulling ceilings and walls. The water was coming down. Everybody was walking up the stairway. I had no idea. I was in there tearing the place to Sunder and when the smoke cleared the fire was on the third floor. Good thing it was an abandoned building.

The captain wasn't with me. I think I was with Tommy Farley. "Pull that ceiling." I tore everything apart. Everybody going up and the companies were probably looking, "What the hell's he doing?" I didn't know where they were going. They were all going to the fire upstairs. That was my first fire. At that time, for One Truck, most of the fires were on Orchard Street around South Broad Street. That was a real busy area, Orchard, Pennington, Tichenor in there. We had most of our fires in the summer. They would keep you busy all summer long. I don't know the first time we didn't have a fire there for a couple of months, probably until sometime in August, maybe. That was my first fire on Shipman.

Then the next fire was down at the farmers' market at night, down in there. Then we started getting a lot of fires on Orchard Street for several months. In the winter, both winters in One Truck, I had one fire, each winter. They could have closed the place.

But Orchard Street was bad. There were tons of fire. It was Hispanic and they were into that gang stuff and burning the city down. We would go to fires, put the fire out, and be walking out. They'd be standing there saying, "You'll be back." And an hour later you were back. The place was going again. They burnt every frame building in that neighborhood down. All the brick buildings, we had fires galore in those buildings. I remember going in the building and people walking out, coming out carrying everything. They were experts in bailing out. Come out with their television sets. Then you'd have a report of a kid in there. How the hell could somebody leave their kid and walk out with the television set?

They were pretty wild times. It was all new not only to the city, to the country. I can remember going in thinking one time, probably after the fire, but going in to one of those apartment houses and everybody coming out smoking. Thinking, "Everything in this building is leaving, rats are jumping out windows, roaches, people and we're going in."

When I was in One Truck there was one, it always stuck with me through my whole time on the job. It was probably the biggest fire I ever went to. It was a four-alarm fire where Camden Street School is now. It was that block. It was the biggest single fire that I can remember, thirteen six-family houses. It was the only fire that I can ever remember where it went across the backyards. It was on Bergen Street and Camden. I think the fire started on Camden Street. There were seven six-family houses, three story frames going. Across onto Bergen, they were burning in the back on both sides. We went on the fourth alarm. We weren't supposed to go. Tommy Farley was on the book. Fourth Alarm, "We're next!" No truck goes on the fourth alarm.

He was driving and for some reason went up Avon Avenue. I remember riding up Avon Avenue and looking up at the sky. It looked like orange snow. That far away from the fire. Embers were coming down on Avon. It looked like it was snowing orange. I remember getting to that fire, getting off, and looking down the block. There were buildings burning all the way down the block. I was on the job maybe a year. I think it was 1971 when it happened. That fire, I remembered that my whole time on the job. It was probably, I'd say the single biggest fire. All the time I was on the fire department. All the big fires we had. I never saw fire burn across the backyard. You couldn't go in the backyard. You would have been toasted. You would have been a marshmallow back there. It was burning. It ended up thirteen six-family houses. Some of them were down, gutted, to the ground. The ones at the end, they put it out. We stopped it, a lot stopped it on the one side and a street stopped it on the other. It was really a big, big fire.

I had said I wanted to go to Five Truck. The Chief's driver used to eat lunch in One Truck every day, Dick Stienhien. He was Joe Redden's driver. He was over there in the morning. He used to stay there and then when the Chief would want him, he would call up. He'd go over, drive over and pick him up. He said, "You want to go to Five Truck?" I said "Yes" So he went over to City Hall. Came back at lunch time ad said "You're going to Five Truck." It was that quick. That was like a Friday. Monday I was starting in Five Truck.

So, I went up to Five Truck on the second tour. I was on the first tour at One Truck. I went to Five Truck up there. They were going to eat you alive. Frank Liber was the captain. This was the Hoot Gibson, Hiemy, Eddy Vesey, Andy Masterson tour. They had the accident in May when the guys got killed on Orchard Street. Russell Schoemer was there. When I went there Vesey left after Russell had been killed. George Daudelin took his place and Eddy Vesey left after that. He left, he transferred out. I took Eddy Vesey's spot. So, it was me, George Daudelin which was lucky for me because I knew George since he was a kid, so I had someone there, and Hiemy and Hoot. Richy Schoemer was assigned there too. He was out on injury leave from the fire. He was in the building collapse, too. So, he was out for quite a while, maybe nine months or so before he came back.

I was up on the hill with the big guys now. Things were a lot busier, starting to go, go to a lot more fires. Without anybody really saying it, there's just a whole different attitude about it. I was there now. I was going to fires with these guys before, when I was in One Truck. But I wasn't really aware. I learned in a month more about firefighting actually doing it. And I had great teachers. I mean Hoot Gibson was a tremendous fireman, a really bright guy. He's a rough, gruff kind of guy, but he's a very, very smart guy. That was the thing. They all knew their firefighting. Hiemy, he was another one. That was the thing that over time I came to realize. These guys really knew their business. They talked firefighting. We would come back from a fire at two o'clock in the morning. They'd clean the tools. They always used to say, "When the bell hits the shit stops." They'd be going wild, but when the bell hit you had to do your job. There is no other way. Nothing else is acceptable. You've got to do your job. No one asked you if you liked it or not. There was none of that "Oh, I'm afraid." Who gives a shit? You're afraid? So am I. You got to do the job and they knew the job. They knew different kinds of fires and what to do at this kind of fire. What do you do here? When I was at One Truck, I would get off the rig before it stopped and run to the building, but I had no idea what the hell I was doing. From them I learned the whole idea of firefighting. I got a good understanding of what you're supposed to do.

I started studying when I was up there, but I just learned from them. Like the size up, Captain Liber was great at that. He would stop and go look down the alley ways. Take the time to look and size up what you've got. It was like, "Okay, what have we got? Now what am I supposed to do?" So that when you went in the building, you knew where you were going in there, what you were going to do when you got in there. You didn't just run into the building and then get in there and say "Oh". Because a lot of times you got in the building and there was smoke all over the place and you didn't know where the hell the fire was. That's why he always told us, look around. You'll see smoke pouring out of the third floor. Look down, there's fire coming out the back window in the basement or the first floor or something.

That was the thing that was really good for me. They knew their business. They knew it backwards and forwards. They knew what to do at every kind of fire that you went to. This is what you do. This is how you do it. I think I got a really good idea how to fight a fire with them. That was truck work, even engine work. I mean they talked about fires. It was a different attitude. Guys always talked about fires. You're supposed to have that after fire chat. They didn't do it formally, but they did come back and talk and they always talked firefighting. How to do it. What was the best way? You should do this. You shouldn't do that. That's the asshole way. How's it in the back yard? You got to get in there. Get the lines in. Get up. You know a back porch fire, got to get to the third floor, stop the fire from coming across the cockloft. Everything, they just knew the job. They were interested in it. A whole different attitude. I think I was really lucky to go there.

P. Doherty: The evolutions that we were taught in the Academy were exactly what happened in the field because we had some pretty decent people up there that were teaching us. Not the upper echelon, the people that were actually teaching us to stretch the hose lines. What they would do was they would call up an engine company that had a lot of experience. When we would go down to check lines and everything, we would be with that engine company and truck company. Truck Five was up there teaching us with the saw and all of that. Twelve Engine and Twenty so, they had some quality people teaching you the evolutions when you went to the Academy.

You learned from stretching in the Academy up the stairs. You had to do the whole thing and they monitored you all the way up and around and everything. And basically, that was how it really was done that way. A little minor tweak here and there, but you really didn't have to concern yourself about because you really knew how to do it. That was the way they did it in the field. And with the Burrells and the fog when you were fighting a fire, I didn't have too much time to really worry about what he was teaching me because the first night I was there we were busy as hell. We had a two bagger and I was with Hettinger and Robshaw, backing up Robshaw on the tip and they showed this is how you move it in. This is how you put it on fog to move the heat and the smoke and everything away so you can breathe and move down the hallway into the room, put it out. Put it on fog, blow it out the window, ventilate so you can get overhaul. That was the first fire I went to that night and the second fire I put that into practice myself because I was on the tip.

It was because of Twenty Engine's reputation. They didn't want to waste time with anybody that wasn't going to measure up to their standards. So, if you didn't measure up the first night, they were going to ask you to go. First couple of fires we had, they would tell you and test you. If you passed you stayed. If you didn't, you were out.

Dainty: When we were getting our assignments and if my memory serves me correctly, we got our assignments on a Thursday, Chief Kossup is reading off the assignments. He gets down to my name. He's reading out who's going here, who's going there. Gets to my name, "Dainty, Twelve Engine, tour three. Who'd you piss off." Now I don't know one company from another. I have no clue what this man is talking about. I'm kind of insulted about it because he's the only one to call me out by name and made disparaging remarks.

Alright, maybe I don't know something that I'll find out. Then Ray Fredette was very, very good at giving you real firehouse type information. And what he said was, "Look, you're going to be off for the weekend. Some of you are going to go to work Monday morning, some of you are going to go to work Monday night. Everybody, go to the firehouse you're assigned to; introduce yourself before you go to work. If you're lucky, you'll hit your tour working. If not, you just go in.

You say 'I'm so and so. I'm assigned here. I'll be here on this date and I'm on this tour.' and the guys will usually say, "Okay, see you then." They may, depending on how they are, may talk to you a little bit more. So, John Salvato and I were assigned to Twelve Engine, tour two. We went there, took our gear, and they said, "Yeah, just hang it up there." Our tour wasn't working and that was my introduction to Twelve Engine.

Now I'm assigned to Twelve Engine and I'm in the middle of it. The first night we report to the firehouse, Captain LaTorre is out on injury leave. He had knee surgery, so it was Bobby Wiggins, John Delk, myself, and John Salvato, no captain and two brand new firefighters. So, the chief made his rounds. I think it was Chief Farley back then. He comes in the firehouse. We did the formal lineup back then. We rang the gong; the chief was here. The chief comes in and he says, "I can't have two brand new firemen working without an officer. One of you will go next door to Five Truck and I'll take a man from Five Truck and bring him here and that's how we'll do it for the two nights." We flipped and John went next door with Five Truck and I stayed with the engine.

The captain in the truck sent Hiemy Reed, who is a little Scotsman. Had a pipe about two inches long that he used to constantly smoke. Really super nice guy and he was assigned to Twelve Engine for the two nights. Delky and Wiggins took me around, showed me this and that, what to do, where to go, what they wanted from me. It was basically, push the line, don't go anywhere without anybody, and stay right there. It was good advice. We had an old Mack that had bucket seats behind the cab, but it was out of service. It was being repaired for something, so we had a spare and of course we had the back step. It wasn't bad for me because I was young. I was in good shape, but Hiemy was an older guy, was a little bit short in stature and as the night progressed, he's having a harder time getting onto the back step. I had no idea why. You know your body starts to give out. Your legs are shot and he's got a long coat and that's not helping him.

But we had a couple of runs, a garbage can fire, the projects. The incinerator's blocked which is a common occurrence. It's going through the night. It's busy. Now it's somewhere in the middle of the night. I'm upstairs. We were able to go to bed after ten o'clock. I don't know who had the book. It was either Delk or Wiggins, someone who had a chance to know what was going on, and we had a fire. I can't remember what the street was, but it was right by the firehouse. As soon as the doors went up, you saw the glow. Delk was driving, Wiggins was the acting captain. We go out and it's a typical three-story frame. It's got a front porch on it and the first floor is pretty well involved. Wiggins got the tip; Delk is driving; and we got to the point where we were really good about the engine operator getting water. We got it down to a science. We get there, pull past to leave room for the truck, and Wiggins goes in the front door, starts hitting the fire.

Hiemy is between him and me; he's moving line; and he finds a hole in the porch. So, he falls half way through the hole in the porch and he can't get his leg out. He's hung up with his coat. I don't know how he got on the job because I was five eight and he seemed to be about six inches shorter than I was. So, we had an issue getting him out of there. Now I had to kind of drop the line, get him out of the hole, and then we go in. We knock down the fire. Everybody had quick responses. It was a very well-oiled machine. Things got handled very well and that was that. It was a normal run of the mill fire that I became used to. The irony of it was, after we got back to the firehouse and I was sitting there thinking, "You stupid ass. You went through Vietnam, came out virtually unscathed. You go to your first fire. The very senior firefighter falls through the floor, can't get himself out, stuff is falling on you. What the hell are you doing? Did you really make a stupid mistake or is this an oddity?"

Melodick: The first night in the firehouse on Belmont Avenue, I remember walking in there. Had no idea who was going to be there. I'm looking for this one captain. I guess I got there, it was probably about ten minutes to five, so the shift I was working on wasn't in there yet. I'm meeting other guys. I have no clue who's working with me, who's going home or whatever. So, it was kind of like, who's on first, who's this guy? Is he going to be with me? All I remember telling them is "I'm the new guy." They said, "Your guys will be coming in."

When they came in, they took me upstairs and they showed me around. Gave me an idea of how things are run there and what to expect. All they told me was, "Just stay with us. Just stay with us. No matter where we go, just be with us." I remember one of the first fires we had. It was Belmont Avenue just before Clinton Avenue, like around Madison Avenue. Here's this two-and-a-half story, fire on the top floor, going like anything and they're putting the aerial ladder up, Five Truck. I'm saying, "Oh, my God." All I remember was flames shooting out of the window. I'm totally fascinated. I'm just saying, "Oh my God. Look at this thing. This thing is roaring and they're going up in a window?" I said, "Well, we have to go up in a window."

So, we went up there. We had a line. We went inside. It happened so quickly. I had no idea what I was doing. I was playing follow the leader, but I was there. I don't remember who said it, but they said, "You did a good job." I said to myself, "Did a good job? I didn't know what I was doing." But I was there. And I said, "This isn't bad at all." I had a friend of mine who worked on Avon Avenue, Chief Miller, so I went there because I was on Belmont Avenue for a short time and I wanted to work with Kenny Miller. I went up there and it seemed that that's when it even got better, if that's possible. He's a great guy. I worked for a Captain who was a real die hard from the old school and I mean some situations that came about while I was working on Avon Avenue were unreal. Things that you see inside the firehouse and outside the firehouse. It was a great place to work. We were just like a big family. All the tours, all the guys, diehards, everybody loved it. Didn't want to go home. Wanted to stay there. Didn't want to go home. I couldn't wait to work the weekends, nights. I would always tell the other guys, "I'll work for you." Me and Teddy Holod, we'd always want to work the nights because we felt like we had more fires at night and we probably did.

Kelly: I was first assigned to Twenty-seven Engine on Chestnut and Wheeler Point and it stunk. I'd go to work and it's real slow there. I'd hear the bell ringing off the wall and we'd never go. I'd say, "When are we going to go?" They had a lot of older guys there and they'd say, "Shut up. Don't complain." Sometimes they'd bang in a second, I'd go out into the yard and look at the glow that was in the sky there. I go back and look at the card. When are we due? Are we due on the third or the fourth? We were in the dead wood. Down in the reserves. I says, "I got to get out of this place." So, I put in for a transfer right away. It took two years to get out of that place. They put me into Six Engine and it was the best thing that ever happened to me.

When I walked into Twenty-seven, you had a hook and ladder and you had an engine, two engines. We were a two-piece company. We're one and three with a two-piece company. That gives you one hanger and a captain to put a fire out, two drivers, a wagon and a pumper. And you had a gig. I went in the kitchen and the guys are all drinking coffee, small dog. I was nervous, real nervous, they ribbed the young guys back in them days.

When I first came on the job, the first thing in the morning, you test your gear. You test your stuff. I was helping one guy. I says, "Can I help you with that, Mike?" And he goes, "Get lost you flunky." So, I said, "Alright. That's the way it's going to be." It wasn't busy in that house at all. There was very little to do in there. What do we do? We sit around here and watch people play cards. It was a long, long day, I'll tell you that. The clock didn't move. But then I found out later, so and so died, the wall caved in on him. So, I knew that it's for real.

Of course, I knew nothing when I went to Six Engine. I didn't know the first thing about putting a fire out. At Twenty-seven, we had mostly brush fires and car fires and stuff like that. It's not that the guys didn't have balls, they did. But we never had any fires. And they had such old-fashioned ways of doing things. We had a fire one time in a two-story frame and the captain said, "Let's get the roof ladder." We put the roof ladder up to a one-story building next door. And then he says, "Go down and get the stick." They had a wooden stick and they put hose straps around it. You'd strap the hose, the deuce and a half to the stick. And he'd tell us to shoot the water in the window which was insane. But that's how he taught us.

I knew that was wrong because these guys up in the window are saying, "Shut that stupid thing down." So, it was time to make a move out of there. When I first went up there, I wasn't even in the door fifteen minutes and we got a job over on Central Avenue. Greeley was the captain in Six Engine. I ripped the inch and a half out of the bed and I just dropped it on the ground. The captain says, "That's not how we do it up here. Flip that thing and put it on your shoulder next time. Look, it's all tangled up now. Now stretch it out." I knew nothing, right. Had to be told everything. And it took a little while, but then things fell into place.

T. Grehl: I walked into Twenty-seven Engine/Four Truck Down Neck on Elm Road. Never really having spent any time Down Neck, I was totally lost. As a matter of fact, I was there a month and a guy knocked on the back door. I opened the door. He wanted directions for Hanover Street. So, I said, "I don't know. Let me get one of the men who have been here. I've only been here a month." So, the guy got it. He opened the door. He said, "You're standing right on Hanover Street." I had no knowledge of Down Neck at all, no knowledge. But that's where I walked into on August 31, 1971.

I walked into the firehouse in red, white, and blue sneakers and white pants. Captain Lardiere was sitting there waiting for me, my first captain. Told me, "Have a cup of coffee kid, relax. I'll show you the firehouse in a minute or two." The bell hit, it was a real good old garbage junk fire with a lot of tires and my white pants became black. I took a lot of heat for that for years. My red, white, and blue sneakers I tried to save. The white pants, I just threw them away. There's no way of saving anything from a tire fire. Needless to say, bright white pants didn't make it. We were down there all day. Actually, it was a very good way of starting. It took off the edge. I didn't meet anybody who walked in the firehouse other than Lardiere. Probably said hello to one or two people, nervous as can be, not knowing what to expect. The fire, and it wasn't a fire that was dangerous. It was just picking up tires and move this, do that. It was a lot of buggy lugging, a lot of manual work, but nothing dangerous, not a house fire, nothing like that.

Then everybody came over. We had red helmets at the time. You stuck out like a sore thumb. So, here's a new kid with white pants that are now black and a red helmet on. Everybody kind of came over and talked to you. "Hey, hey you're the new kid. Welcome." It was really good. It really broke the ice. It was different than just sitting there waiting for the old-fashioned senior guy to really like snarl at you. You couldn't talk to the senior guy in the house. That has changed a lot. That really has. The senior guy still holds something, but he's not like you can't talk to him. Don't talk to that senior guy. You had a buffer. Like the guy who came on before you, even if it was ten years before you, was your buffer. He would introduce you to the senior guy.

Now, today when you walk into the firehouse, most guys come up and they introduce themselves. Welcome aboard. It was a little different then. They were a little stand-offish, but not for long, after you got to know them. The same thing with the captain. He introduced himself. I'll show you around. But it was always, "Yes, Cap. No, Cap. Can I go across the street?"

In Four Truck, we never really had anything major down there. We had Chestnut Street and Orchard Street, but we were always either the last due truck or the second alarm up there. It was a slow company. That's why I was trying to get a transfer out. I was twenty-two. I wanted to do something. I guess my father was a little over protective of certain spots that openings were coming up. That was probably one of the reasons I didn't transfer. Certain places were kind of like blocked. I guess my father was looking out for me.

On May 7, '72, I lost my captain, Captain Lardiere, up on Orchard Street. We pulled up. Second alarm again, it was just a block or two the other side of McCarter Highway, in fact we parked on McCarter Highway. It was a very, very foggy night, rainy night. All the smoke was lying down and the Chief told us over the radio to stand by. So, Lardiere decided to walk up to the fire and see what was going on. I was twenty-two, twenty-three at the time, just wanted to do anything. I had a hook. I started walking up behind him. He told me, "Stay here." I said, "Nah, I'll walk up with you, see what you're going to do." Well, we walked around the corner and like I said you couldn't see a lot because the smoke was hanging down. We started to walk into the building and somebody yelled for a hook. "I got it." He says, "No, no, no, I got it. You go get a hook." "No, no, no get inside. I got it. Let me do something. I've been waiting for a fire forever. Let me do something." "No," he says, "I got it. Go get another hook off of Five Truck." Five Truck was right there. I walked down and I couldn't reach the hook from the side I was on. So, I walked around the truck because it was on the other side of the truck, grabbed the hook, walked back in front of the building and the building collapsed. He died along with Schoemer and LaTorre at that fire. That's something I'll never forget, obviously. To this day I believe he saved my life because he took my hook.

When the building collapsed, it just came down. Everybody knew everybody was buried. Everybody just started digging. Looking for people. Schoemer's brother was buried also and he got out. He had burns on the back. Pretty deep burns on the back. We were there. The Battalion Chief sent us right back to quarters because they apparently saw where Lardiere was and saw the collapse. He was killed instantly. His back was shattered. So, they said, just get out of here because we know you guys are screwed up mentally. It was early evening because we got back to the firehouse before nine o'clock. Every single night exactly at nine o'clock Lardiere's wife would call, exactly. And he would leave the card game and go answer the phone. Well, the phone was ringing. The pay phone was ringing at nine o'clock. Nobody would go near the phone and answer it. We just sat around and obviously we didn't have grief counseling or any of that counseling, but there were a lot of people who came down. Made sure we were all right. That was traumatic.

Romano: First day I got assigned to Truck Five on the third tour. They sent us to the firehouse. I didn't even have a helmet. I had to borrow somebody's helmet. At that time, we used the leather helmets which are fitted to your head. And who's ever helmet I borrowed for the day, of course didn't fit correctly. That was my introduction to the fire department. My first night on the job I walked into the kitchen at Five Truck not knowing a soul. It was the change of tours third tour/fourth tour. We were relieving the fourth tour. And the first thing they told me was, "Oh, you're going on detail to Ten Truck for two nights." There was no provision for while you're the rookie; you're the probationary; you have to be in a house with a captain. That didn't exist. You were the rookie; you took the detail. You're going on detail. The first thing I was on detail to Ten Truck on the third tour. Ten o'clock in the evening, the whole crew is drunk. This is my introduction to the fire department. Two nights in Ten Truck, they had no captain. Nothing of consequence happened except a move up to Irvington in a hail storm. And at that time, they had one of the old Pirsch hook and ladders, no bucket seats, open cab, and you hung on the side of the ladder. We drove to Irvington from Bergen Street in a hail storm, sleet storm, whatever you call it, freezing rain. By the time we got to Irvington I was just a solid block of ice. That was my second night in the firehouse.

Burkhardt: My first assignment was actually a nightmare. We first went into the field after the guys got killed on Pennington and Orchard. They got banged up and deaths were involved. When I got assigned, I wanted to go to Twenty Engine.

But Bruce Morgan, because he had some college before that, he went to Six Engine and there was an opening in Six Engine. Nobody wanted to go to Six Engine and work with the captain there. He wasn't too popular, so I put in for Six Engine. The transfer list comes out, I get sent down to One Truck on the third tour. I wanted to go to Six Engine on the fourth tour. I didn't want to go to One Truck because my brother was in One Engine on the third tour. I told my father, "I don't want to go to Mulberry Street." And he didn't want me going there because he didn't want to lose two kids. So, we went up, talked to the Director at the time who was Caufield. Caufield couldn't make a move one way or the other and said, "No, stay there. They're not going to be in the building at the same time." I tell my father, "You're going to the same box. One guy's on the hose, the other guy's on the truck." I'm not big on truck work anyway. So, we try to get ahold of the councilman for the West Ward which was Mike Bottone. Called him, Mr. Bottone. Meet me at Eighteenth Avenue. We went to Eighteenth Avenue, walked in. He talked to Caufield, come out, "You go to Springfield Avenue tomorrow." Memo came out. I went to Six Engine on the fourth tour and I stayed there until I got promoted.

R. Stoffers: My first fire was me and George on the roof, the first roof job and there was no saw. We were using axes because it was a peaked two and a half story. He'd start chopping, get tired, and we'd leap frog each other trying to put the holes in and vent it. The very next day we both showed up at work with a hundred and four fevers and Frankie Calvetti sent us both home. But that was the standard. That's how we operated.

Rosamilia: As a cadet, we were in the firehouse mainly at night. They never let us stay too late. They would do two nights. We would work with the same crew for two nights in a row. But it would be from six until eleven in the evening. We were greeted carefully and differently. Some fellows were really warm with you and some captains were happy to have you and others couldn't wait for you to get out of their firehouse. But most of the guys, they were okay. Felt so welcomed.

When we went from cadet to firefighter, now you're in, now you're a fireman and now you're in a whole different situation. Because it was only me and Bruce Morgan, it was summertime, and there happened to be two spots open at Six Engine on the second and the fourth tour and they stuck us right there. So, they even let us stay together kind of that way. Which was really pretty nice. The old timers were getting beat up and they're leaving so there's openings.

The city really wasn't that busy in the '50s, but then the '60's got crazy, by '70s you started seeing that. There were some fellows that were there for quite a while. Maybe even went to those places when it wasn't so busy and they were still there. So, they were working there for a long time and then little by little younger guys started coming in.

Morgan: One of our first fires when Kevin Burkhardt came over to Six Engine, we had a fire in the third floor, Magnolia Street. We had a ton of kids we were pulling out of this building like crazy. We were in position to stretch a line into the building. So, we did our job. We stretched it in and in the process, we were pulling kids out and just pumping them down the steps to guys. It was like an old fire brigade where the guys were passing the buckets to each other and dumping them on the fire. We were passing kids down the stairs like that. And there was supposed to be a woman that was still on the third floor that we were going to go after. We were told not to, go down and mask up and that's what we did. We were under the impression that the person who told us not to go after the woman was going to do it. He never did it. We ended up finding her, actually Billy Quirk found her later on in the back room. That was my first death at a fire. But what makes it stick in my mind was Kevin and I were going to go in for her and we were told not to do it. Both he and I always felt that had we done it right then and there, she probably would have been alive. As a result of not doing it right then and there, she wasn't. We went back to the building I'd say about seven or eight times that night and we were stoned, abused. That was another side of the fire department that I hadn't seen up until that point in time and wasn't prepared for.

Coale: I came on with Jimmy Langenbach. He and I were in the same company. When we walked in, the first day in the firehouse, we were told, "You guys are going to sit here all day and listen to the alarms." They showed us how you book them. You had to write in every alarm that came in throughout the whole city. You would write down the time, the station, and who went. Now you had to keep track of which companies are in and which companies are out because nobody's telling you, you went. You were in charge. You were the house watch. You were actually in charge of that firehouse. We would sit there for weeks at a time just booking everything and learning the alarms and the bell system.

Langenbach: I went over to Park Avenue for a little while, Seven Truck and then a guy in Five Truck wanted to get out of Five Truck. So, I swapped with him. I went to Five Truck. I was in Seven Truck for a couple of months. Then I left out of there and I went over to Five Truck.

It was the best time. I never had so much fun as I had with those guys. Captain Cassidy was pretty strict about nine o'clock we do our housework. And we'd always go out and do some kind of a drill. Either in the house or we'd go somewhere and do something, always one of the two days, but the rest of the time was just fun and games.

At first, I didn't eat with them. Five Truck and Twelve Engine ate together. I wasn't allowed to eat with them for I bet it was a couple of months, until I proved myself. I used to brown bag it. Brown bag it and sit in Five Truck or sit where ever and eat. And they would go in next door and eat, but I wasn't allowed until finally Red Conlon said it was okay. That I could eat with them. But it's just the way it was. You had to make your bones like it was in the mob or something. You kind of appreciated it because once you finally got that, "Okay, kid. Red says you can eat with us now." Woah, man. I'm really here.

Of course, everybody thinks I'm the red ass kid. Especially working on Belmont Avenue. All those guys were legends on this job. The Veseys and the Hooters, all those guys were tremendous firemen in their time, the things that they did. Chuck Deutch and those guys, the things that they did. There was a lot of respect and with the respect is a lot of good-natured kidding, ribbing, from them.

I remember; we had a fire. Shimph was our Captain. We had five people piled up in the hallway, dead. They tried to get out the door, couldn't get out the door. And the fire is behind them and Shimph is yelling at us, "Fuck them, fuck them, get to the fire, get to the fire." We're thinking, "How can this guy be so cold?" But he was right. We aren't going to do anything for them, so we're climbing over dead people to get to the fire. We had a fire on Pennsylvania Avenue. A nickel, dime fire, two guys die in it. We were sitting down having dinner, having beef stew, I'll never forget that, having beef stew, go to the fire, find two guys, drag them out, do CPR all the way to the bus, get them on the bus. They both die. Get back to the firehouse and now we're bitching and moaning that the beef stew is cold. That we have to re-heat the beef stew. We didn't have microwaves then. Forgot all about the two dead guys. We get back to the firehouse and bitch about you're soaking wet and your beef stew is cold.

Milford Avenue, I almost died in a fire. I'll never forget that. I was in Five Truck again and we caught a job. It was a three-story frame. Fire was on the first and second floor. We didn't have our aerial ladder. The aerial was broken. I was tillering, get off and we see a guy walking in the third-floor window with the fire behind him, so we threw a thirty-five foot. Go up there. I get up the ladder and I try to reach the guy. Now he flopped half way out the window. It was snowing. It was cold. Reach in and try to grab him and I can't move him. Can't move him. I'm getting pissed, so I finally jumped inside the room. I took my mask and put it on him. What it was when he flopped out the window his feet hooked under the radiator. So, I can't lift him out. I have to take his feet out. So, we finally get the guy out, get him down. Cassidy comes up, they put another thirty-five-foot ladder up. Cassidy comes up and he hands me a booster line because now the fire's in the room with me and all this time I didn't have the mask on. So, I'm standing there looking at the booster. I'm looking at the fire, looking at the booster. I'm saying, "I know they go together, but I don't know what this is for. I know what that is and I'm pretty sure, but." I remember this like it was yesterday. Making that kind of like decision process. I know what this is. So, I finally said, "Fuck this." I threw the thing down and went back down the ladder. Well, by the time I got to the bottom, I passed out. I stopped breathing there. Johnny Fagan threw me in the chief's gig, took me to Barnabas. I stopped breathing again and then I was there for a couple of days. I had burnt my throat, inside my lungs. But that was an interesting fire.

Brownlee: I had absolutely no idea what to expect when I walked into Avon Avenue. The truck at the time was one and four. And the engine with me was one and three. John Kossakowski had just left and I took his spot. And Bill Heilman had just left and nobody took his spot. So, the truck had Bernie Snyder, Georgie Caswell, Johnny Spada, and Pat Tansey. Cliff Titcomb was the captain and then about two months later Bob Langevin came and made them one and five. Then Banahan came to Eighteen a few months after that. He was on the cadet program. So, when he came into the firehouse, he came into Eighteen. He was only there for a little while and then they put him in the ambulance program. Then Carl got promoted and it was me and Jose.

Blum's Department Store was still on the corner of Twelfth Street and Springfield Avenue. That was my first two bagger. Blum's Department Store. My first death was on Fabian Place, right across the street from the Spider Lounge. The mother was in the Spider Lounge drinking and the baby was in the crib dead. My captain grabbed me and said come over here and look at this because you're going to see a lot of it. I had to go take a look at the baby in the crib. Looked like a little chicken cooked. That was my first death on the job.

Carter: I went to Eleven Engine and proceeded to not have a working fire for like a month. At the time they were doing around 1800 runs and I was ready. Now that I was full-fledged, I'm on the team, let me go to fires. Nothing happened for about a month. Then I was working for one of the guys on the third tour and I caught my first on the job fire on Hudson Street between Orange and Sussex. It was like a duplex fire on one side and that's where I bumped into my old classmate Vinny Ladd, literally. He was pulling the ceiling and I walked through the door. He gave a yank with the hook and hit me in the stomach and knocked me back out the door.

Then I found a hook laying against the wall and something needed to be pulled. Brian Ewing was with Three Truck on the third tour at the time. I figured, "Well, I'll pull." And I hear this voice, "Get your fucking mitts off my fucking hook you big lug." That was Brian. I met him for the first time.

They shut down Engine Two, Twenty, and Seven all at the same time. I guess that was like December of '74 going into January of '75. What that did to Eleven Engine was we went nuts on runs. We went from like 1,100 to 2,500. And we would go all the way over to Springfield Avenue where we never went. We were at fires down at the Third Battalion, which I guess was preparing us for the way things are today. That was back in the days when there was a Third Deputy. We used to have three deputies and five battalions on duty. And then we had what, twenty-five engines, twelve hook and ladders, two tact squads that replaced the salvage company, and the fire boat had a full crew.

About that same time, 1975, we had a move up. Eleven didn't move up much, but Eleven had a move up to Irvington. Irvington had a big fire and Bob Miller was in the Fourth Battalion at the time. So, they sent Eleven and Nine Truck and another engine. We're up in Irvington and there's nothing there. There's nothing there to make coffee with or anything, so now we're getting a little steamed. You woke us up and we can't have coffee. We can't have any libation because we're out of town. So, I forget who it was, broke open the Irvington coffee locker. We broke in and bear in mind you have like two engines and a truck and the battalion, then the Arson Squad rolls over. They want to see what's going on.

So, now we get a card game going. In Irvington Civic Center main fire station, we broke open their coffee locker. We're drinking coffee, smoking, playing cards, dumping the ashes on the floor, and one off-duty Irvington guy comes in for the recall. He looks through the door and here's total, complete pandemonium, chaos, arguments, cards, guys throwing stuff all over the place. Turns around and walks out of the firehouse, leaves. So, we don't go to a fire that night. We had caught one before we left Newark. Didn't catch anything in Irvington and we're rolling back down Central Avenue when a box comes in for Summer Avenue somewhere down about Crane, Wood, down in the old first ward. Deputy Three, Chief Magnusson gets on the scene. He says he has a three story, ordinary construction warehouse on fire going stem to stern.

We're just cresting the hill by Eleven. We're going to stop and back in and he hits for the second. We knew we should have been on the first, but we were out of town at Irvington. So, we just keep rolling past the firehouse and as soon as we come past the big apartment house on Central Avenue there at Eighth Street there's this giant glow in the sky. Down we roll. It was a real big warehouse. I guess it spread to a couple of buildings on either side and the only point is it was the big fire after Irvington. Big fire after the debauchery in Irvington.

J.P. Ryan: My first assignment was One Engine. Actually, the first thing I ran into in the firehouse was Deputy Chief Joe McLaughlin. I'm walking into the side door of One Truck and I'm carrying all my gear. I'm brand new. I'm very nervous and I couldn't really see where I was going. Deputy Chief McLaughlin was standing at his normal position, pulling his mail out of his mail slot and I bumped right into him. Darn near knocked him over and sure got blasted for that, but we became great friends after that, no problem.

My career in One Engine was not too long. I went to the Tact Squad and we went to every fire in the city. We could average four or five fires in the daytime and easily that at nighttime. We had a lot of work, but it was good work. We learned the trade well. We learned how to operate at large and small fires.

So, I started in One Engine, but I didn't care for it because there was not much going on there. From One Engine I went to Twenty Engine, which turned into the Tact Squad. Then in 1976 there were layoffs. I was bounced out of the Tact Squad to Fifteen Engine for two days, two nights. And from there an opportunity came for to me to go to Eleven Engine. I stayed with Eleven Engine and Eleven Truck for eighteen years. That was at Central Avenue and South Ninth Street.

Early years, my first fire. My first fire was in the third sub-basement of Bamberger's. I'm going down in an elevator and there's smoke pouring up this elevator. I'm thinking to myself, "There's no windows here. There're no windows to jump out of. When I get down there, there's no windows." We put the fire out. It was okay. It wasn't a big deal. But I remember that clear thought. "There's no way to get out of this place."

Luxton: I went to Six Engine straight from the Academy. The captain was Mike Marillo, who had taken Bobby Miller's spot. Then it was Billy Costigan, Paul Adams, Mike Kelly, Gerry Rosamilia, and I was the fifth guy. We were one and five. We had just gotten the one and five. I was the fifth man. I probably bounced somebody to get there. I don't know how that worked. Jimmy Nolan was good friends with Joe Redden and I know he said something to Redden. "Yeah, put the kid in Six Engine." It was interesting. It was nice. The very first night in the firehouse, I know I got on the back end of the truck at five o'clock at night. We went out, went from one fire to another, didn't get back to the firehouse, no dinner, nothing, until two o'clock in the morning. Chief McGrory came around. Felix

Cardillo was driving him. He said "You're not supposed to be here. I need a detail to Twenty-nine Engine and it's you." So, I got packed up to Twenty-nine Engine for a week. Carrol Henderson was up there and John Higginson, I was on the back step with him. I forget the other guys. I did my first week there. Then I came back to Six Engine and Costigan.

That first night there were two or three signal elevens. It was a blur. You sort of followed in Costigan's footsteps. He just disappeared. You were aware he has to be at the end of this line someplace. You're going through and there's fire all around you. Aren't they supposed to put this fire out? "Come on kid, let's go." It was interesting. He was a good fireman.

Pignato: The firehouse I walked into was on Central Avenue. I didn't know a person in the place. I walked in there and I was okay. It was a pretty good bunch of guys. The second day, I had Wesley Yale and myself. We were both sent to the same tour from the same academy class, we were detailed to Vailsburg. We got to see a whole complete opposite side of the fire department. All the old guys were up there. All they wanted to know was if we could fix their cars for them. Sure enough, every time they needed their cars fixed, we got detailed up there.

You live in a place, you kind of get used to it. You get used to the rats and the cockroaches crawling all over your bed and your clothes and your personal stuff. The building falling down around you. There was asbestos and a winter without heat living in a sleeping bag. You get used to it. Until you leave that spot, you don't know any difference. When I went on detail, all the firehouses were in just about the same kind of shape so it was the same. The guys were the same. We went to a lot of fires, so I enjoyed it. Some guys cooked. Some guys didn't cook. Sometimes the guys would start cooking and they get a bug up their butt and stop cooking. So, you can't plan on anything. You fended for yourself or sometimes you were in on the meal or you didn't cook for six months. That was a strange house to be in. There was no set pattern for anything. Including anybody being here who was supposed to be there. In the six years I was in that firehouse, I can count on one hand how many time the full crew was there, both companies had everybody there. You were pretty well cloistered in one spot.

My first real fire had to be on Dickerson and Third. It was a two and a half story frame. We put the aerial ladder up to the top window to ventilate the window. There were supposed to be kids trapped in there. I threw my tank on and climbed up there. I got my hook stuck in the blinds while I was taking out the window and I couldn't get it out. I'm trying to get my hook unstuck and all of the sudden the blinds sucked in, which is classic sign of a backdraft. There's an explosion or a poof. I look in the alleyway to my right. The flames blew the windows out the side of the house from where I was. Jumped six feet across the alley way and started the next house on fire.

The fire came out from underneath me. I'm trying to get down this ladder. I get hooked on a wire, probably a telephone wire. My tank gets stuck on a wire. I'm trying to get out of this wire. The fire is starting to come up by the ladder. I final got myself out and I climb down.

I see all these guys from Eleven Engine lying on the side walk. They're burnt or hurt. What happened was as I was popping the windows up there. All the guys were trying to get in the front door. They busted in the front door. It was so hot the lock was melted. They got in there. Back then they had the Macks and they only had a three-hundred-gallon tank. Seven Engine was the second due engine. Fifteen had to come from the other side. Meanwhile the engine driver is trying to hook up to the hydrant. He hooks up to the hydrant, but the little pentagon on top was gone. Somebody had sawed the brass thing off there. I remember him banging on the hydrant with a maul, a sledge hammer. He's trying to crack the bonnet. If he cracked the bonnet, he can open it up with a Stillson wrench. The next hydrant was all the way off out on Central Avenue. It was just so far away.

They had gone in there as far as they could with six hundred gallons. They ran out of water. The air they had introduced into this building, now fed the fire.

Now they had no water. It blew back at them. That's when it blew out the side windows and started to burn them. They came tumbling back out. To add a little spice to this, there were two boys in there yelling for help. They died in the fire. They didn't die from the smoke condition. They were cooked, burned alive. I heard some noises, but at the time I didn't know what it was.

It was rather new to me, seeing the guys get burnt. I never saw firemen burnt before. I got little burns myself as a volunteer, but nothing like this. One guy's hand was burnt up. Other guys were trying to make it into the building. They got a supply. Somebody was back-stretching all the way back to Central Avenue, a couple of blocks, because they couldn't find a hydrant in that area. The kids were left home alone. That was one of the many fires I've been to where they leave the kids home alone. That was my first fire.

One day we had a spare truck, Ward LaFrance. Get a school box that morning. Pull up and the fenders fell off. Embarrassed in front of all these kids, all these people coming out of the school. We got some quarter inch rope and we tied them up to the lights. Call up Empire Street and see the welder. We go down there and the welder welds them back on. We were there like two, three hours. Get back to quarters and we see the Tact Squad. I wave at the guys there because one of the guys I car pool with. They were doing a hydrant inspection. Then I heard "Working fire send the box! Send a second alarm!" Out we go. We get a block from the fire, a gigantic fire, and the truck dies. The captain says, "Grab a tool. Go up there. And I'll assign you to work with different companies." So, I get sent to work with Six Engine. They're right in front of this building. At that time this fire was so hot the horns of the cars were blasting. The horns had been melted and fused and the switches were making contact. They were across the street.

Picture the sight of the fire, a five-story brick on fire almost a city-block long. Fire out of every window. We had just gone by this building on the way back from Empire Street. I'm with Six Engine. I said, "Captain, I'm here to work with you." The captain says, "I want to move my engine out of here. It's starting to burn up.

We're going to put a piece of three inch in there." Sort of like a feed line, because he had stretched in. He had his deck gun working. Now, when I went on the one side of the truck, I got soaking wet from the spray of the deck gun. When I went on the other side of the engine, I was instantly dry. That's how much radiant heat there was. I felt myself burning.

Went over to help the fellow make the connection, because they had just moved the engine out of there. I'm making the connection with the guy. I'm trying to get this thing lined up and make the connection. He looks up. His eyes get about as big as saucers and his mouth drops open. I see he's jumping up to his feet and I follow his stare. Here comes five stories of wall towards us. We run. There are two photographers from newspapers who were on the other side of the street. We grab them and throw them behind the other eight-story building across the street just as the wall came down.

If that captain hadn't moved that engine, the guys there would have all been crushed. We'd all have been crushed. If he hadn't seen what was going on, we all would have probably been killed right there. We took a line up the eight-story building. If you ever think of looking into hell or looking into a volcano, that's what it looked like. I looked over the edge of that eight-story building, looked down, the thermal updraft almost blew my helmet off.

The two best rescues I've ever seen were from fellows of Eleven. One was Eleven Engine; one was Eleven Truck. We had this one piece of junk, Ward LaFrance spare. It was there when I came on duty. I started it up. Box comes in later on. I try to start the thing up. It wouldn't start. I'm pulling all these wires. Finally, I get it started. Meanwhile Engine Eleven is calling a working fire. I have to drive to Orange Street. I finally get this piece of junk to Orange Street, right in front of the building.

There's supposed to be a kid trapped up on the third floor. I jumped on there, I pulled up the aerial ladder. The throttle wasn't working. If I was smarter or more experienced with this, I would have grabbed somebody and just told him to step on the gas pedal. It would have gone up faster. That aerial ladder was slow, so slow. Finally, Harry Tokanos got tired of waiting, throws a ground ladder up. Climbs up the fire escape. Goes all the way up there. People are pointing. Goes into the bedroom. Comes out with a baby. Steps between two windows and just at that moment it explodes. Just like in the movie "Backdraft." It blew out the two windows. Here he is sitting there with this baby.

The other rescue was Jules Banks. Jules was a big, tough guy, professional bowler, ex-marine. Very strong, tough. We worked pretty well together, even though we argued. I always drove, he tillered. He liked the way I drove. So, that's the way it worked. We worked on the roof together. He was a lot stronger than I was and it worked out well. Good relationship. We had a job in the middle of the night. You could see the flames coming out into the middle of the street, blowing out of the top windows in front of the house. The engine's doing their thing. There was a little boy outside the building, fully dressed at three o'clock in the morning. I said, "You live here?" He goes, "Yeah." I says, "What are you doing outside?" He says, "My sisters dressed me." "Where are they at?" "They're in that bedroom up there." "Why aren't they coming out?" He says, "I don't know why they ain't coming out." Probably they went back in for something.

Where we were, there was no shot with the aerial ladder. There was no way to get to it to the building. So, I said, "Let's throw the ladder." So, Jules and I grab the ladder. It's raining. There's a fence right there. We put the thing up to the window ledge. It's like teetering. The ladder was kind of short. Just made the window ledge. We were sinking into the muck, so I had to anchor the ladder down. I'm holding the ladder down. He climbs up the ladder and jumps into the window. I try to follow him. I'm climbing up the ladder. Now it's sinking into the mud more. Now it's teetering on the fence. It starts to slide down the side of the building. I grab onto the ledge and try to pull myself up. I can't get myself inside the window. Jules is there. He has three bodies with him. He's carrying three bodies. He yells something to me. I can't hold on any more. I free fall down a story. I drop down into the mud and I went to the back of the building.

Meanwhile, he's coming down the stairs with these two girls he found, two teenagers. He's out of breath. We start CPR on them. The other guys started helping. He finally gets his breath. He says, "There's another girl. Did you get her?" I says, "No, I fell out the window. I couldn't hold on any more." So, it turned out that the engine company went up there and they found the other girl and brought her down. All three girls died. We got commendations for this.

Connell: I went to Five Engine for my first five and a half years. I was assigned to Five on the initial transfer list leaving the Academy, but I wanted to be a truck man. I was kind of disappointed I was going to an engine company. A twist of fate is Harry Halpin was going to Two Truck and he wanted to be an engine man. We talked it over. We were going to do a mutual swap. We went to see Chief Tartus, who was assigned to the Academy at the time, and Chief Tartus more or less talked me into going to Five Engine. So, I went to Five Engine and Harry Halpin went to Two Truck.

Five was one and five the first month I was there. Abernathy Mason was still assigned to the company and a month after I got there he was pulled out, went to EMS. The entire crew were old timers. My Captain was Captain Buonincontri, Firefighter John Farrell, who later became my Captain for a short period of time, Firefighter Charlie Alaimo, Abernathy Mason. A short while later George Alfano came down.

It took me six months to get my first real fire. Most of the guys I came on with had two or three the first night they worked, but it took me about six months to get to my first working fire. We weren't really drilling or getting any work. If you have a brush fire or a car fire, I don't consider them work. Basically, that was it. And we had a lot of dump fires at that time. I spent many nights down at the dumps watching the blue, orange, and green flames come out and the pretty colored smokes. We'd all be sitting around eating our sandwiches all full of all kinds of chemicals and stuff. Sitting in the smoke streams and smell the pretty fumes. There was no such thing as Haz-mat at that time.

The first year I was there we did 835 runs. The year I left to go to High Street, we just missed a thousand runs. During the layoffs I was assigned to EMS riding out of Thirteen Engine. I rode with Steve Roberts, who was a cadet, and a fireman who later ended up at Four Truck, Kovacs. I was basically a millstone around the neck. Since I did not live in the city, I didn't know where I was going. So, I was useless driving. I had no EMT training other than basic first aid training down here one day. I had no first aid training. So, I was useless in the back. I was useless. I spent six weeks there. Wrote many a report requesting a transfer to anyplace, every place.

Finally, after six weeks they transferred me up to Nine Truck. I replaced Jack Maloney. He went to the Rescue Squad. I was up there for approximately two months. Loved it and I was doing my best to stay up there. After two months, they brought Jack Maloney back and the fire department was starting to phase out some of the ambulance drivers. I asked Jack Maloney if he wanted to swap with me. I stay in Nine Truck and he could come to Five Engine. See, he was an older gentleman and everything else. And he more or less laughed at me and told me to get the hell out. The funny part about this is about three and a half years later, right after I left Five Engine and went to Two Truck, Jack Maloney transferred down to Five Engine and took my spot in Five Engine.

The day Newark Slip went up, I was assigned to Nine Truck, between my EMS career and returning to Five Engine. We didn't go there. We went to Chadwick Avenue and we had four houses going when we pulled up. Chief Joe Miller from the Fifth Battalion was the battalion chief in charge. He pulled up basically the same time Nine Truck did and he called for a second alarm. They told him, "Well, we have companies coming in. Once they come here, we'll dispatch them to you." We raised the aerial to the roof of a two-story building and me and

Tony Miedler went up there. We're cutting the roof. I think that's the hottest I've ever been outside of a building on that roof. And all around us I'm watching the tar boiling on the edges of the roof and the black smoke getting thicker. I keep on tapping Tony on the shoulder. I said, "Tone, not for nothing. We shouldn't be here. Tone we shouldn't be here." He goes, "That's all right, this cut, one more cut." Then I look and the roof is starting to flash. We threw the K -12 down and we just both got off the roof and the whole roof lit up.

We went down and my knees were shaking. I remember a Battalion Chief pulling up on the scene of a job and asking what companies responding. He had a roof fire going. The operator told him he had Truck Twelve. He said, "What engine company?" "No engine company. You have Truck Twelve." The city was stripped. Everybody was committed to these different jobs going throughout the city, mainly High Street.

I had one early experience that showed the mentality of firemen. Again, I was in Five Engine. I was only on the job for a year and a half, if that and we got called for a fire watch. When we got there, it was the remains of I guess what was once a one-story factory. We have our lines set up and we're in a black neighborhood. These two women come out and they slam a card table down behind us and then they walk away. A couple of minutes later they come out with sandwiches and ice tea and everything else, feeding us. We all looked around at each other and we were all afraid to be the first one to bite into or drink anything because we didn't have the trust of them and we're not used to people being nice to us when we were in that section of town. It was my stupidity at that time. The one thing I remember the most, how stupid I was not trusting the people. Somebody doing something nice for you and not having any dealing with the number of black people I do now. Learning to judge each one individually. The suspicion everybody had, even the guys who had been on for a while. The suspicion everybody had of these people trying to be nice to us.

Langevin: My first and only assignment was Ladder Company Nine, Avon Avenue. It was very busy. When I was appointed, the two years prior to that had been the busiest time in the Newark Fire Department up until then. I reported to Avon Avenue on a Thursday day shift. We hit for the cycle. We had a three oh eight, a three oh nine, a signal eleven, and we also had a deuce my first day in the firehouse. My second day in the firehouse, the following day, Friday, I had my first death. I guess I was prepared to face it, but really that soon. It was a young child.

Back then the fire load was tremendous. You'd come to work on a night tour. It didn't matter what night of the week. The weekends were even worse, but you were probably guaranteed two possibly three jobs a night, guaranteed. When I was assigned, I was not a driver right away. The way I learned how to drive was I would drive back from the alarms. I'd just get the feel of it and everything. And I didn't know the streets either. I had to learn them. So, that's how I learned how to drive, was driving back from alarms. I guess I was in the company about four months and back then we drove by the month. We drove a whole month. I think it was my first night of my first month that I was driving, my first run. It turned out to be a three-alarm fire and I didn't know what the hell to do. The captain was giving me orders. I'm trying to do this. I'm trying to do that. But the fire went out.

Shortly after we got rid of the snorkel, we acquired the first rear mount aerial apparatus in the city. We had a working fire on the corner of Clinton Avenue and South Eighteenth Street and my Captain was still Captain Titcomb. We had a person hanging out the window, third floor window in the rear. It was only an alleyway. I was driving and he wanted me to put the stick up and he was climbing while I was putting the stick up. In the meantime, the kid had jumped. This kid was about ten years old, eleven years old. By that time Cliff was at the tip of the aerial and caught him in mid-air. Probably the greatest grab I ever saw. The kid climbed down the ladder by himself. That was the greatest grab I ever saw.

Perdon: I went to Four Truck on the fourth tour. Jimmy Jennings was in my class. He was also put there. He was in Twenty-seven Engine. We had Kupko and Cerami. They were on a different tour. Billy McCarthy, he came in with the next class. He was put there. So anyway, we were all Down Neck guys. They had the openings in the house at that time, which I always thought was a mistake. Putting new kids in a slow company.

The drills I did were because when we first got on the captain wanted to make sure that the new guys could do at least the basics. I'm in a truck company. He wanted to make sure you could go up the aerial so he extended it straight up. You had to climb up to the top, hook in, work the pipe, basics After that nothing, absolutely nothing. That's all a given for the area. Guys are down there for a reason. And they worked the same with the drills and everything. If you had the right captain, a younger captain, it's different. But my captain was an old man already. Other than that, we used to pray for getting move ups. We got them.

We caught a nice job up in the Fourth Battalion, but our whole company was embarrassed by Frankie Mastroeni. He was driving the chief at that time. Now we're going, we have to go open the roof. Four Truck is Four Truck. So, we're going to the roof to open up. Now I'm like third and we had the two experienced guys up there. They're staying right there. They're not moving because it was so smoky and everything. We're on this aerial. So, Frankie Mastroeni comes up. He's the chief's driver. Comes up, "All right, get out of the way." Just comes up, goes by us, climbs onto the roof, starts to open it up. I just followed him. I said, "All right." I just followed him. Walked past the other guys from Four Truck, but that was Four Truck. Frankie did all the work. He embarrassed the whole company. Well, maybe the older guys didn't get embarrassed, but I know I felt a little soggy

I put in for Six Engine immediately. I just waited and waited. The first time around with the opening, I lost out to someone who probably had less time than me, but was a little bit better connected. I was fortunate to be put in Seventeen

Engine. I got my first exposure to a working captain. He actually worked at a fire and then from there I got to Six Engine.

I was laid off, but it was just a matter of waiting to get back on. For me it was a short time. That's because I was a resident. You had to be a resident to be put back on CETA. I came back to Seventeen and it was good. Career wise it was the best thing to happen to me, staying at Seventeen Engine. I didn't want to stay there, but I was like a brand-new guy going up there. I might as well have been coming right out of the Academy for all the experience you get Down Neck, which was none. But I remember going there. Billy Brownlee was there. We were in the Academy together. Brock was my captain. Joe Donahue was there and Sammy Cauca.

But I remember, the first fire I caught we were first due. They said, "All right, here's the tip." So, I took it and just feeling the heat for the first time, I hit the wall. I honestly hit the wall. From that day I've never looked back. I was so embarrassed. I apologized to everybody after that, but there was real heat. Twelve Engine came out of nowhere from another direction and just blew by me. I see them through the door. I was so embarrassed for myself and the whole company. I apologized which probably was a good thing because I remember after that everything just got better. But just the experience, even after I had like a year and change on, you'd think I would have been beyond that point. It was brand new.

But you were surrounded by tremendous people as far as I'm concerned and they just made the whole thing easier. Five Truck, Twelve Engine, I mean Eighteen Engine had good people. And they took care of you. Frank Franco, Joe McCarthy. They made the whole thing easier. Seventeen was still on the slower end. They were still probably considered more of an outlying company. They still weren't core, center core. It was a ton busier than where I was at. I'm going to say around 1700, around there, 1500 runs a year.

Then I transferred to Six Engine. It was a whole new ball game. It really was. I mean the captain was better. It was a whole new ballgame. I mean over in

Seventeen, anything you caught it was yours. But over at Six, now you're fighting for the tip. Everything got better. Everything was amplified, the number of runs, the number of fires, and the fight for the tip. Now you're trying to make deals. If it's on your side you get it. If it's on my side it's mine.

I walked in. There was Birdman (Kevin Burkhardt), Bruce Morgan, Billy Weber, Jimmy Cody was the captain, and John Scofield was driving Chief Jan Taucsh.

From Seventeen to Six Engine, a lot more aggressive. That was another learning experience for me from Seventeen to Six. You find out you didn't take yourself to the limit yet. There's a whole new limit here. The bar was raised and sometimes you just stood there and took it. But the bar was raised when you went there and that's why you went there.

Banta: When I came out of the Academy, I was assigned to Engine One on Mulberry Street. I came in through the back door. You didn't come in through the front door. The first thing that anybody ever said to me as I walked through the kitchen door, I was told by the captain of the company sitting at the table, "Kid, don't put your gear down, you're not going to be here very long." Which told me I was going to be the guy on detail. And that's where I was. I was detailed out my first day in. They sent me to Engine Nineteen to start with on Frelinghuysen Avenue. I walked in the door at Engine Nineteen at eight o'clock and the first thing the guy in Nineteen Engine said was, "Hey kid, you know how to do the book watch?" And I said, "Yes I do." And he said, "Okay, well then you have the watch."

About fifteen minutes later the telephone rings in the firehouse and it's the chief telling the guy, send the new kid from One Engine over to Two Engine. So, I packed up my gear again and I went all the way back across the city to Engine Two on Center Street. I spent my first day in Two Engine which was one of the best days I ever had in the firehouse. John Hoffman was the captain. Dennis

Brophy was a fireman. Leo Brochu and Digger O'Neil were out on sick leave at the time. By ten o'clock I was feeling no pain and when I went home that night at six o'clock, my girlfriend said to me, "You're drunk." And I said, "I sure am, but I am going to love this job."

I was there for about ten months. In January of '75, I transferred to Ten Engine on Astor Street. One Engine was a downtown company, not a lot of fires, really not a lot of runs. Weeknights the night tours were pretty slow. What we usually had were false alarms down at the end of Orchard Street, Chestnut Street. My whole time in One Engine, in those ten, eleven months I was there, I don't think I had more than six or eight fires the whole time I was there. But I do remember the first fire I had.

It was on Orchard Street right off of Chestnut and it was about three o'clock in the morning. It was in May. We came down the street and we had a two-and-a-half-inch hand line up to the second floor, through the apartment, out a bathroom window, onto a small porch roof. The fire was in the building to our right. Because the roof was so small, I was the only one that was out there. The captain was actually standing in the bathtub in the window encouraging me. And I thought to myself, "It's three or four o'clock in the morning. Here I am on Orchard Street in the city of Newark with the heat and the smoke beating my face. What am I doing on this job?" And I came back from the fire that morning and I thought for sure I'm going to quit this job.

I remember my first fire in Ten Engine was at Broad and South Street. I believe the name of the place was the Savoy. It was like a transient hotel. We had a pretty good fire on the second or third floor in several of the rooms. It was a vacant building at the time. And I remember being in the hallway, going down the hallway with my captain. He was teaching me how to use an inch and half line, how to work with it and all that because it was my first fire with him. I remember the embers coming down on the back of my coat because I didn't get my collar up high enough. And getting burned all across the back of my neck. That was my first fire experience in Astor Street.

Killeen: Instead of coming in days, I came in at night. I asked Chief Miller, Bobby Miller, if I could come in at night, because it was a Friday night. He said, "Yeah come on in." So, I came in and that was it. I started that night. Instead of taking the two days off and coming in the next Wednesday, I came in that night. I didn't want to miss that Friday, Saturday night in the hot spot.

I met the guys, was told what not to do. This is where you put your gear. That's where you sleep. I'm wearing my collar pins. I had the collar pins. I came in with the hat, tie, collar pins. I was working that night. I walk in. The first thing I'm told. Get the hat and the tie and those collar pins off, put them away, put them on your dress uniform. Paul Hauser was driving. Billy Heilman was the acting captain, and I'm on the back step and that was it. This is it. I'm on the back step, in a busy house, in a hot house, and here I am. My first night, I'm on the back by myself. The captain was out injured. Georgie Feely was injured. A couple of guys were banged up. They were gone and that was it.

We caught a couple of fires. There weren't like any like gigantic fires we were at all night. We were going in and out, in and out all night. I believe we had about ten runs, around there. I was almost clueless. Being a buff is one thing, but now you end up putting a line in your hand and you're told to do something. You're looking for fire. I had no idea how to stop and listen for the fire. How to feel for it. I didn't know how the buildings were laid out. There are so many things that you pick up as you go along that when you first walk in you don't realize. You go in and now it's black and you know you're waiting for somebody to grab you by the ass and take you in further. And that's what it was. We're stretching booster and inch-and-a-half. That's what we were stretching that night. Anything to beat the fire. I got a discrete pass then to stay alive the for night there. And the second night was pretty much the same.

My first real fire I remember being spun around in corners and kicked. I'm not sure what happened. I know this was not the way to do it. I'm doing something wrong here. I think Twenty Engine was taking advantage of me at the time. It was the new kid being in the way. And at the time I had nobody to show me how to do it, to be honest. I'm brand new on the job and I don't want to do anything to mess it up. I've got the same thing everybody does. It was a good fire on Magnolia and it seemed to be a big building. And we go there. I was pretty much tossed around, spun around on a stair landing. Guys were going around me. We're stretching a two-and-a-half. It was a big open area and they wanted two-and-a-half. We had a lot of fire there.

I got trampled on, kicked, molested going up the stairs. I didn't know what to do at the time. I was just like baffled. I wasn't up to speed and after that I became more up to speed. I became more aggressive. I was too nice. I didn't understand this is my fire. I wanted to say, "Oh you want this, oh, okay fine."

Camasta: They sent me to Engine Ten. My God, what's in Engine Ten? Nobody goes there. Nobody was ever sent to Engine Ten for I don't know how many years. I was the only one. I drew Engine Ten. I rode past it. It looked like a garage. I said, "My God what am I going to do. It's not a firehouse." At graduation I said to my father, "Dad this is my firehouse." And he sees no front lawn, no driveway. You barely got a sidewalk and a door. The windows are all painted over and have plywood over them. And I says, "Well, we'll give it a whirl." And that's what I walked into. But it was fun.

I remember one fire that Captain McGrath got himself up on the second floor and the stairs gave way. And Five Truck pulled him out the side window with the aerial. And it looked really dramatic because this whole window was nothing but fire and he came out of it. I was driving at the time, so it looked really good to me because I was a couple hundred feet away. I could just see his profile or shadow come out of a window on to the aerial. But what it was, it was the casing around the window that was burning there. He was basically in good shape. It looked a lot more dramatic than it was. That was one of my earlier fires driving. And I remember stretching into that fire. When we wrapped the hydrant, it didn't take. So as opposed to having five lengths behind me when I got out of the cab, there was one length laying there. And fortunately, Leon White, Auxiliary Captain White, who was called bicycle Charlie at the time, helped me hand stretch back. That was a two bagger up on the hill.

Bisogna: Right out of the Academy I went to Twenty Engine. I got lucky. I think they sent me there because I jumped out of the tower into the net that was there. Me and Clinton Miller both jumped from the second floor. If I had to go to the top floor, I would have bit my tongue. Nobody went to the top floor. They thought we were nuts to go out the second. A bunch of guys went out the first-floor window, no big deal. The second-floor window, that hurt a little bit when you hit. Me and Clinton did that and we both got sent to Twenty Engine as a pair. I don't know why.

My father, being on the job at the time said, "Are you sure you want to go there?" I said, "Dad, let the chip fall where they want." He said, "Well, that place has a reputation as a party house." I said, "I don't know any different. I'll go. If that's where they're sending, I'll go." I walked in the door and it was the United States Fire Department. It wasn't the city of Newark.

Tony Giorgio was the captain. It was a two-piece company. It had a hose wagon, a pumper, a first line pumper, an older house wagon. Double bay, single door, a little house watch room on the side, a sitting room with a drain in the floor, which was good when we cleaned it with a booster line. Bunch of lockers and a big table and a little kitchen off to the side where they made gourmet meals. Sometimes we had shrimp parmesan. When I got on the job, I weighed 145 and in about five years I was pushing 190. I was single. Most of the time I was eating there.

They had a good mix of guys. Teddy Holod, I hooked up with there and a lot of good friends too. We had Christmas parties with Five Truck and Six Engine. In the summer times we had picnics, not just one. We had a couple of picnics and always a Christmas party. Frank McCrone was Santa and they did it up. They really had a lot of families, the kids got involved with mothers, wives, whatever. Mine wasn't a mother at the time. But it was good because you got to not only work with the guys, you got to hang out with them and become friends with guys in different firehouses too. They were always tight with Five Truck and Six Engine because they always rode to the same boxes together, same crew of guys all the time. Racing each other to the fires. I thought I was in heaven. It was a lot of fun. You'd go to work and you'd laugh all day long, play handball. It was a great job. You couldn't ask for anything else. We were one and five at Twenty Engine with two pieces when I first walked in. Me and Clinton made them one and five.

I think my first night we caught a back porch job and at first it was the back porch and then about two hours later it had the whole house. The drill was they gave it a warning. Got the back porch going and then they would burn the whole house down. They lit the back porch and we went through the first floor because it seemed like it was inside. Three or four hours later, they had the whole second and third floor going. This is my first night on the job. I think I might have had two days there. I definitely started on a day and that was my first night, two working fires. I thought it was great. I was having a good time. I enjoyed it. These guys even though they were fast and they liked to rush in, they weren't crazy.

We would have a working fire I would say, my tour, let's say three a month. When I say a working fire, a house fire. We had car fires, apartment fires, small stuff all the time. Mattress fires, you had that all the time, garbage, dumpsters, two or three of those a night. A dumpster, a car fire, you were always going in and out the door. I would say five, six, seven, ten runs a night at that point in Twenty Engine with probably three good house fires a month.

Partridge: Well, my first assignment's an interesting story. At the time I came on the job the Newark Fire Department had just taken over EMS. The city EMS was a disaster at the time. They had basically just ambulance drivers, that's it. They had some EMTs working for them, but most of them were just people off the street. Apparently, there were some people in the fire department who came up with a brain storm that the fire department should take over EMS. It would be good for the fire department. It would be good for EMS, but mainly it would be good for them because they would get promoted. And at the time the show Emergency was very big and paramedics were just kind of making their first appearance in the country, different places. L.A. was probably in the forefront of that. But there was a battalion chief and there were several captains and there were several firemen who thought they could each jump up a step. They were on a promotion list or whatever. And they got this through. The city gave EMS to the fire department.

So, we had a brand-new deputy chief, four new battalion chiefs, a number of captains. And the way they got some of the firefighters to come in was to say, "You're going to get extra money." Eventually you'd be paramedics. You're going to get extra pay. So, these guys went into the program and like many cities, it didn't turn out the way it was forecast to be. So, it wasn't long before the guys who had originally volunteered for EMS wanted to get out. The question was, "How do we make that happen? How do we get them out?" Well, we take recruits from the Academy. We tell them they're going to work in EMS.

As soon as that rumor hit us in the Academy, that some of us were going to be going to EMS, I instantly knew I would be one. Because I had nobody on the job, with no relatives, I had no hook. I didn't live in the city. I just knew I was going to be one. That's what happened. I wound up working in EMS until I could get out. I forget how long I was there. It wasn't a year even. I was angry, upset, heartbroken, all kinds of negative emotions about working there. But a lot of people took me on the side and said, "Stick it out, kid. You will get out of it and then you will be a Newark firefighter. Just stick it out."

It was hard, but I stuck it out. There were a couple of guys who did quit the job and went other places. I could have done that too. My number came up in a couple of the other cities that I had checked off on the application. But I really wanted to stay in Newark, so somehow, I stuck it out.

EMS was a horror show. By that time, it was all low morale. They only had, four, maybe five ambulances. Now this covers the entire city of Newark. We're in the middle of the war years and it's only a few years after the riots. It was mayhem, just mayhem. A completely inadequate number of ambulances to cover the city. And there was no type of triage or calls or trying to separate out runs that we shouldn't have been going on. It was just, if somebody called for an ambulance, they'd get one. It would be routine that runs would be backed up for twenty minutes or an hour. They had ambulances in One Engine, Thirteen Engine, Seventeen Engine, and the Burg. Seventeen Engine was the worst. They were actually doing 17,000 runs a year.

People gave me bad advice on how to get out of EMS. What did I know? One captain said, "Well, you have to be firm. You have to write a report saying you demand to be released from EMS. That will get their attention and make them listen." What do I know?

So, I'd send in reports like this and transfer request like that. None of that worked, but one day I talked to the chief's driver. Chief Redden was Chief of Department at the time and I talked to his driver. He was the only one who steered me straight. And he said, "Look, request an appointment with the boss." Go up there and ask a favor, basically. That's what I did. I went up. I had an audience with Chief Redden which was like going to see God. I'm completely in awe of the man. I'm a twenty-year-old kid. Brand new on the job. He listened to what I had to say and he let me out. He put me in Nine Engine on the third tour.

I didn't know them. Redden put me there I guess as an extra gift. It would have been enough to let me out of EMS and put me anywhere, but he actually picked out a great spot because at the time Nine Engine was like number two on work and number three on runs or something like that. A very busy place. The lower Third Battalion was really on fire at that point. We were into the war years and Nine Engine was a high morale place. They had good bosses there and they had good firefighters there.

I had Joe Ricca for a captain. Which was another gift. He had been the youngest captain on the job. I think he broke his brother Angelo's record who had previously been the youngest captain on the job. I worked with some great guys, Bob DeFroscia, Bob Catalano, Kevin Dowd. It was a really, really great outfit. And the Third Battalion was in there. Jimmy Raymond was the battalion chief and Andy Pappalardo was the aide. We had a very, very good house and I enjoyed it a lot. I was kind of overawed. I felt like, well, here you are, you finally made the big time. Now you're in a real firehouse in a real city. And I was plain scared because all I wanted to do was measure up and be able to do the job. I just wanted these guys to think well of me and to think I was somebody they could make into something. I was very, very nervous about walking in there.

But I felt welcomed when I got there. The transfer order came out on a Friday or something like that and it was effective the following week, And the third tour was actually working in the interim before the effective date. So, I had actually gone down, walked in, and introduced myself. I'm the new kid that's coming next week and I think they thought that was a good idea. They seemed to appreciate that. And then when I got there, they were very, very welcoming. Joe Ricca was very big on training and drills, very, very big. Probably you'd be hard pressed to have a better captain to break you in as a new firefighter.

Ricca: I got assigned to Seventeen Engine on the first tour. I walked in and I saw Captain Hughes. Bernie Snyder was sitting down reading an Oklahoma (a fire service textbook) and I think Mike Lawless was upstairs and Pat Tansey was walking around. I'm trying to remember my first day there. I walked in with my badge and my handmade name tag on. Captain Hughes says, "There's a little bit of a problem, Ron." I said, "What's that?" "There's a little problem going on between the crew of Nine Truck and their captain."

I got sent to Nine Truck, but I was assigned to Seventeen Engine. Bobbo Miller at the time was in charge of the Fourth Battalion. So, he set things up the way he wanted to and that's where I started. I stayed in Nine Truck until I got laid off with that first group of guys who got laid off.

First day in the firehouse, the first run, I was sitting on the Snorkel, which Nine Truck had then. Tony Peters is the door man because there's no automatic door closers. He comes running up to the rig to get back on it after he shut the door. I took his helmet, handed it to him, hit him in the face, his glasses flew off, fell on the ground, and the tandem rear wheels ran them over. That was my first greeting for Tony. I thought about it afterwards. I don't know if I ever offered to pay for them or not.

From the first fire with the windows breaking, the sound of the saw, the hose whipping against the walls, it was just exhilarating. I couldn't put it into words if I tried to describe it because I've tried to describe it to people and they just can never get it. A person would have to physically live it, to appreciate what you're saying.

We had a fire on Nineteenth Street. I was on the job a few months. George Caswell impressed upon me, when you're searching, if it feels like a person, make sure it's not a dog and you go yelling crazy. I think it was Nineteenth Street, I crawled into this one room. There was a family. The father was on top of the mother and the mother was on top of the baby. All three of them died, but they each protected each other. And the first thing I felt was dog, I thought, to my left. Later on, I felt the bodies, I felt the arms. It was my first time, I started screaming. The first thing when the guys came in is they went to the dog. And I heard somebody say, "Hey, J O, it's the dog." Then they realize the people were next to them. The dog had died first.

I was one of the first ten who got hired back from the layoff because I lived in the city. I never got a notice. My brother Angelo calls me up one day. He says, "Ron, did you get called?" I says, "For what?" He said, "To come back." I said, "No." I called Monday morning at nine o'clock to Chief O'Beirne. Chief O'Beirne said, "Ricca, you're supposed to be here. You're getting re-hired." I remember throwing on some clothes, not even washing, taking the Thirteen Broad down to City Hall, ran back into City Hall, and got re-sworn in. I came back under CETA, but I was one of the first groups to come back from that lay off.

Sammy Cauca was just leaving Five Truck. Ray Frost had caught a change of tour job with me. They talked about it and Frankie Calvetti gave me a call and asked me if I'd like to come to Five Truck. And that's how I ended up there with Chief Carragher. Chief Carragher had asked me previously, before I got laid off, if I wanted the spot. But I didn't want to cause friction with Captain Titcomb because I was a new guy and didn't want to rock the boat. But I wanted to go to Five Truck because my brother Angelo went there in '57 and since '57 there's been one of us on Belmont Avenue.

So, I went to Five Truck on Third tour when I came back. Frankie Calvetti is the captain. Kenny Miller. Pete Romano, Ray Frost, and Ray Stoffers, and myself. We're one and five. This was after I was brought back. Certain companies rode heavy. Chief Carragher believed in riding his trucks heavy. A lot of times the engine would get a detail before we would because he wanted the trucks heavy. I remember for a short period of time with Teddy Holod riding with us, one and six. Didn't last a long time, but there was short period. Did a lot of damage when it came to truck work. It was like riding in with two truck companies. You had a good captain that worked, Frankie. He split us up, taught us a whole lot. I was teamed up with Ray Stoffers for probably the whole time I was at Five Truck. When we went for the roof, me and him always ended up together.

Straile: My first assignment out of the Academy, they put us onto something new that they had started. It was called like on the job training. They sent all nine of us to different tact squads. I got assigned to Tach One, tour one on Prince Street which used to be the old Twenty Engine. And we were there for several months. It was a very good learning experience because in the Tact Squad you did engine work and you did truck work. One day the captain might say, "Alright, you're in charge of the hose, you're going to do the line today." Or, "Grab a pike pole or an axe, you're a truck man today." We would go as additional help to a signal eleven or better because we went to every working fire in the city. We would go and do either truck work, engine work, or it was combination. You got turns doing them both. So, we learned a lot in the OJT program that they had. That was my first assignment.

How did they react when I walked in? Well, you hear stories, you see movies and stuff of different things with how they react and treat rookie firemen. Here I am the new red ass walking in the firehouse. And when I walk in, I'm carrying my bag with all my gear and everything. And there's ten or fifteen guys in the kitchen because it was a change of tour. I was going in on a night shift, my first one. I got to the doorway and there's like this bunch of guys. "Hold it right there. Who are you?" Told them who I was. They yell upstairs, "Cap, come down. The new guy's here." Now I figure they're going to mess with me, so I'm standing there and I'm standing there. They come and they say, "Get the book, get the book." I say, "Oh, now they're going to beat me with a book." They get the book and they're standing next to me. They open the book; it had to be a foot and a half wide and two feet long. They open the book to a page, standing next to me with it, and they're all yelling "Bully, Bully." What the hell, I'm looking at the book now. It's a book, The United States Presidents. And the president's picture they got is the picture of Teddy Roosevelt. At that time, I wore glasses, had hair and I looked exactly like Teddy Roosevelt's picture, so the name Bully stuck for my entire career.

They did not know me. It's just that they hit it. The way I walked in. They were a wild bunch of guys. I don't know where they came up with that. If they saw a picture of me before I got there and put it together. I don't know. All I know is I thought I was going to get beat with a book. That name stuck. They called me Bully from '74 until the day I retired.

I was welcomed. Yes. It was a great welcome. They were a great bunch of guys. My captain was Tony Giorgio, Senior. It was a good bunch of guys I worked with. It was a good learning experience with that On-the-Job Training because we were there several months before we went to a field assignment to an engine or a truck company. So, you learned a lot in both aspects of the job. It was on the job training.

Gesualdo: First assignment was Twenty-nine Engine out of the Academy and I think I was here for two days and came back for the nights. Then I was detailed. After that it just a matter of coming back here for maybe two days, going somewhere else for two nights, two days, coming back. Covered the whole Fourth Battalion, which I think was a good thing. Got to see all the firehouses, meet all the guys. It was probably I took a liking to this house because there were older guys here. I was thirty years old at the time. Most of us had been in the service and they were all kind of mature and it was an excellent captain, Jimmy Kearny. So, I figured I could learn a lot from him and still be with people in my age group as opposed to being in a house with younger guys. It was comfortable; coming here was very comfortable.

We were averaging between 2000 and 2400 runs the first probably four or five years that I was here. That's when we had the Kretchner Homes and we were there quite a bit. There were a lot of second alarms. We responded to a lot of second alarm fires. But it was busy. You'd find yourself out a couple of times a night in wet clothing. I can remember very vividly back then because your hands used to freeze around the bar on the back step when you came back from the second one at two o'clock in the morning. You had to peel your hands off the bar.

When I walked in initially, it was a nice welcome. I think they appreciated having an older individual too. Seeing as that they were all up there in age, not old but older. And having somebody with a background at least with the military and the other firefighting thing. Just having somebody being genuinely interested in and anxious. I don't remember any flak for anybody. I guess maybe, if there was a heat merchant at the time it would have been George Jorda, but he's all noise, all bark and no bite. I found that out. I'd say the only one that was a little tougher than him on a detail anyway, not in this house, would have been Bill Quirk over at Five Truck. He turned out be a sweetheart. We got really close after a while, but he was a character. He put you through the grinder when you first got there, but other than that nobody ever made any threats or anything. It was all verbal comments, abuse. I mean I learned how to handle that. It was not a problem, but I think with most of these guys, you find out later on, you just go right back at them and they calm down and they get to know that you're not going to listen to all their bullshit for the rest of your career. But it was very comfortable walking in here.

My first fire was right around where the theater is now on Springfield Avenue, right near Six Engine. I believe it was our second night and it was a four-story frame, which there weren't too many of at the time. We got there. I'm really not sure if we were last due on the first or first due on the second, but we were there pretty quick because they banged the second alarm immediately. It had to be the first alarm now that I think about it, because there wasn't much water on the fire. It was fire just blowing out every window. To me it was just like, wow, this shit burns. In England we never saw anything like that because everything was brick and stone. To see this four-story structure just totally engulf and the thing that stuck in my head at that point was that I remember twelve people died in that fire and I believe eight of them were children, four adults. Three days later coming back on our day shift, you think you'd block it out of your head and all that, boom here it comes back again. Three days later we had to go back to the scene because they were still sifting through the debris for body parts and bodies. The Arson Squad was there. I remember Bob Radecke and I guess Nardone were there. They were bagging and tagging parts as we uncovered them. That's when it really sunk in that twelve people died in this structure. I was like, "Do I want to do this for another twenty-four years." But that was my first fire.

The other one that was memorable, stuck in my head was a situation on a detail at Seventeen Engine. We're first due and I was a very aggressive kind of guy. I wanted to take the line in and I got up there and we operated, had water, no problem. It was a HUD sealed building, so I tried pushing the plywood off the windows, but couldn't do it because of the two by fours. I remember puncturing my hand because there was a nail sticking through it and I had the Fireball gloves on. I didn't pay much attention at the time, but it was a pretty good gash. All I remember is being steamed to death up there and thinking where the hell is everybody. Who's my backup guy here. Only to find out later on that Jimmy Edgers, who was a firefighter at Seventeen Engine, ex-boxer, bouncer, that kind of guy. He was holding everybody back. Telling everybody, "It's all right, we got it." And thinking to myself, "Yes, we have it. I have it." I remember that only because it was a funny story I would tell everybody. Here's a guy holding everybody back. That's the way it was back in those days. Nobody wanted anybody jumping on their fire. That was the other memorable fire.

J. Prachar: I was roving for approximately six months. We all got assigned tours. And I got assigned to the fourth tour. But I was injured in the Academy, so I had a three-week stint at light duty working five days a week at Special Service. I would have never traded that experience for the world because at the time Special Service was pretty well loaded with people. It was actually a regular crew. They had a captain per tour. They had guys working tours, four, five guys per tour. They had a fully staffed hose shop, mask shop, ladder shop, supply room. The whole bit, it was a big operation. And a lot of the guys down there were old timers. A lot of them were World War II vets. I just loved hanging out with these guys because they were great. These guys carried their balls in wheel barrels. They lived through a war. They came on the fire department. Went through the riots, it was great.

Then after three weeks, I was fit for duty on the fourth tour. And fortunately, most of my time on the fourth tour was spent in the first and fourth battalions. So, whatever work there was, I was going to be able to catch it. I did the circuit. I was Eleven Engine, Eleven Truck, Seven Engine, Three Truck, Twelve Engine, Five Truck, Ten, Seventeen, Nine Truck, Eighteen, Twenty-nine, Ten Truck, out there in Tela Viv, the outer limits.

After I did my three weeks of light duty, I finally made it out to the field and I went to Twelve Engine on the fourth tour. Twelve Engine and Five Truck were side by side. Two separate buildings, but basically a dual company, double house. My uncle was in Five Truck. When I was a senior in high school, I rode with Five Truck as a senior project. So, I knew pretty much everybody there before I even came on. I was assigned to Twelve Engine. I was there for two weeks. We didn't do a damn thing.

We went out a lot, caught garbage fires, stuff like that, nothing major. My last night there, I was going to be going to Eighteen Engine my next day trick. Last night there we caught a working fire. First fire I had since I got burnt in the academy. And I didn't realize how badly getting burnt in the academy affected me until my head crossed the stairway up to the third floor. As I crossed the floor level of the third floor and I'm getting a little higher up and it's getting a little hotter, I froze. Just for a second, I froze because I felt that heat and it's exactly like when I fried my ears and my neck. I froze for a second. And in the back of my head it said, "This is it. You either keep going and finish this up or you turn around and head down those stairs and walk out the door of the firehouse and find another job." I kept going and I was scared to death. I don't think I was ever more scared in my life up until that point because I knew what had happened to me a month previous.

And I was working with Richie Kilty, who was a hell of a fireman. Wayne Rosetti was there and I knew I could count on those guys. It was a good job. It was a two-and-a-half story frame; fire was going good on the third floor. It was hot. It was smoky. Made it through. Finished it up and said, "You know what? I can do this." So, that was my first working fire and I knew when I got through it I could do it.

But one of the funniest things that happened to me while we're roving is I was assigned to either Eighteen Engine or Nine Truck. I think it was Eighteen Engine. And I have bad eyes. I went and got clips for my MSA mask because we used the MSA masks back then. I don't know if I got it from Special Service or ordered it from Absolute Fire Equipment or whoever, but I had the clips. I went to my Optometrist. He made up lens for it and it could fit right into the face piece. So even though when it's smoky you can't see anyway, there're times when it's not that smoky, you still need the mask. I had the glasses on. I could see.

So, I believe I was assigned to Eighteen Engine. I put my clip onto my face piece and then somebody from Nine Truck had to go somewhere. I think it was Joe McCarthy. Like it was typical of the fire department then and now, somebody's got to go somewhere, you take the body from somebody that's riding heavy. You send them over there. Oh, I'm the rover. So, I go from Eighteen to Nine Truck. I moved my stuff over to Nine Truck. I take my clip. I put it into the face piece I'm using. Joe comes back. I go back to Eighteen Engine. I forget to take my glasses with me.

As luck would have it, we catch a fire. That was my first fire with a tip and I was working with Mike Lalor, Mike let me take the tip. Nice and calm. Good job, good working fire. Two rooms on the first floor of the house. We went in the backdoor. We knocked the crap out of it. Mike was reassuring, "Go ahead, keep working the line. That's it." It was great. Fire's knocked down. We're all chewing the shit. Guys are ventilating, overhauling, this that and the other thing. And poor

Joe McCarthy's still standing there with his mask on because he thinks it's smoky. He can't see anything.

And somebody says to him, "Joe, why are you still wearing your mask." He says, "It's still smoky in here. I can't see." They said, "It's clear as a bell." He takes his mask off. There's my eyeglass clip in there. He couldn't see. Guilty as charged. Got a good laugh out of that one. I was afraid he was going to kill me, but afterwards it was pretty funny. That was probably the funniest thing that happen while I was roving.

Bounced around, caught some good work. Rode with the Tact Squad. Rode with Seven Engine, Central Avenue. I remember riding with the Tact Squad with Captain Joe Hopkins. And there was a fire down at the Farmers' Market Down Neck. So, we ride from South Orange and Prince in the bread truck with the air horn hooked to the air tank. I think Mikey Martino was driving. We go all the way down to the Farmers' Market and had the first line in the building. You know, you can tell stories about stuff like that, but until you live it yourself you never believe it. I knew then what I'd been told, "Stay in the busy companies kid."

First permanent assignment was Seventeen Engine on the fourth tour *Mit unter sea kommander* Eddie Brock. First words out of his mouth when I walked in the door at Seventeen Engine, his newly assigned kid is, "Great another young punk I got to work with." Because in the crew was Billy Brownlee, Frank Dugan, Jimmy Edger, and I replaced Sammy Cauca. Sammy Cauca left and went down to Fourteen Engine. So, I guess Frank Dugan and Billy Brownlee were considered the other punks. That started a rather interesting relationship with Captain Brock. Eddie had done his time and was ready to just kind of take it easy a little bit and we were a little too aggressive for him. Me, Frank, and Billy got yelled at a lot, going places we weren't supposed to go because the captain wasn't with us.

Mitchell: I was roving, Down Neck. It was horrible. I got to wash my car a lot. I roved for six months down there. I think I saw two fires. And the guys down there didn't do much. They said, "We don't go in there." I just couldn't wait to get uptown to a busy company.

When I finally got assigned, it was to Ten Engine. Ten Engine was in a bad neighborhood, a drug neighborhood, but the people were great. I mean they were like friendly to us all the time. You knew everybody in the neighborhood. Couldn't leave your car running outside or it'll be gone. But I mean basically, the neighbors were good. It was like the drugs you had to worry about. Most of the guys in there were on the job quite a few years because it was a busy company. They liked the company. I guess I had three older guys with the captain, Jimmy Wilson. Frank Public, Jimmy Collins, and Tony Ventola were middle aged. I was the young guy. And I stayed there until I got an opportunity to go to a younger group of guys which was Four Engine. I learned a lot there. Tony Ventola was a good fireman. Learned a lot from him.

We had a lot of first due jobs in that area. That was a busy area at that time. And there were enough fires that I was able to get a lot of tip time, a lot of work time. Where you know a lot of houses you wouldn't get that because mostly the older guys would want the tip. But there we had enough work that I was able to get it. Especially since the older guys didn't really want it.

Daly: I was in the worst place you could be, Down Neck. They put me Down Neck and it was like telling me, cut your head off. You don't want to be down here. I realized I didn't want to be there. I was at Truck Eight, Engine Five, Engine Twenty-seven. That's where I caught my first job. It was on New York and Napoleon. It happened a month in and that was my first death also. Then they shipped me one night down to Thirty-two. I thought I was going to pull my hair out. A box comes in. Two o'clock in the morning, a five box. I figure a five box, I'm going out. I'm coming out of the bunkroom and I'm walking out and one of the guys goes, "We don't get that." And I looked at him and I said, "You don't get five boxes?" And he goes, "See that sign? When that blows up, we get that." They had all the oil tankers and everything down there. And that's what he told me. I just shook my head and I said to myself, "That's it. I'm getting out of here." I go to see the chief, he's Chief White, Battalion Five. I went up to him practically on my hands and knees. "Get me the hell out of there." And that's when he put me at Twenty-seven for a couple of months. We used to rove, but you're staying there. He put me at Twenty-seven and that's where I caught the New York and Napoleon fire.

It was our first day in and there was a guy on the fifth floor in a wheel chair and that's when he passed. I was in there trying to get in the room. I couldn't believe people brought furniture out before they brought him out. I had to climb over TVs and dressers and stuff. I tried to get into his room. I had to move mattresses, dressers, pass him in his room. I look over and see the guy. I'm going to get him and poof the room lit up. He was dead like that. The guys from Twenty-seven were worried about me. They pulled me out because we had to get out of there. There's a guy in there, but behind him we had fire coming down the stairs. We had to bail out quick. Davy Jones was trying to get through, laddering a window. He was off duty. He couldn't get to him. But that was my first real fire and after the fire they commented on how calm I was. Most rookies are hyperventilating. I kind of liked it. It's kind of fun. But that was my first assignment, roving Down Neck and then after the summer they sent us back to the Academy.

Zieser: After the Academy, we were roving. And I was roving on the fourth tour at that time. I spent my whole career working on the third tour, but I was on the fourth tour. I went right to Ten Truck. Frank Franco was my captain. I did get some of the new guy stuff, but they treated me really good. I remember being nervous like getting my turnout gear on and the captain said, "Take it easy as you put on your stuff." We went on our first run and I'm over there like fumbling putting my boots on. He's got his shoes tied there. And he just pulls the one sting so the shoe comes off and the other shoe. And he's pushing into his boots, like a gentleman. In a quick manner, but not like racing like you think you would. "Hey, kid, this is how you do it. Take it easy, just don't be so nervous." I think I learned a lot just going out on that first run with him. Like, don't rush out the door. Think about where you're going. Think about what you're doing. You can put your gear on. Don't go running to the rig where you're going to slip and fall on the way there. Then you're no good to anybody.

So, that first run I think I learned a lot. If you remember at that time, it was always one of the guy's jobs to close the door to the firehouse. We didn't have the remote at the time, but we did have an electric door opener. So, someone would open the door, but you would have to wait there until the rig got out and it was emphasized. If it was emphasized once it was emphasized a thousand times. Wait until the rig gets out before you push the button because every-once-in-a-while someone pushed the button early and there would be some damage to the door. The captain would have to write. No captain wanted to do that, so they emphasized, wait until the rig's out. Then you would run up to the apparatus, get on it, and go to the incident.

Chief DeTroia was a friend of our family. We lived in Vailsburg. He was involved with my family, Knights of Columbus and things like that. So, I'm working at Ten Truck. He puts me there. I wound up working there about six weeks. But I got out of there. He wanted to keep me there because he had to fill a spot. I got him on the side, I said, "Chief, this is too slow for me." Because here are all my peers going to fires and I'm in Ten Truck which is a slower company even at the time. And I wasn't going to fires. He said, "Well I didn't know that you weren't happy here." I wanted to make it clear; the captain was great; the firemen were great; everyone treated me real nice; it's just the work load is what I wanted to get away from. After that, the whole time I was in either Twelve Engine and Five Truck or Eighteen Engine and Nine Truck. He kept me there the whole time. The one time he even let me drive him one or two nights, I got my chops busted a lot. "What do you know kid?" They said, "You're driving the chief, who are you? What are you a wise guy? Driving the chief." I don't know why he picked me, but I know that we knew him from Vailsburg. I didn't know him really well, but there was a relationship there.

Of course, I'm Artie's son or more so my uncle Joe was the Fifth Battalion Chief. So, more people kind of knew Uncle Joe. "Oh, are you Joe's son?" "No, I'm Artie's son." They knew both my father and uncle, but you're always somebody's son. So, you always want to kind of prove yourself, that you're your own man. They both had great reputations that I wanted to emulate.

Hopkins: The first day we had to show up at Six Engine with the deputy and he told you where to go. On the third tour, that was Chief Kinnear. I went to Seven Engine. I walked in the door and half the first tour was there because it was early. And I knew Rocco Piegaro was there, Hettinger was there. I knew those guys from my father. And a couple of other guys were there. Gerry Knight and Ralph Horning were there. They were all first tour guys.

I walk in the door. The phone rings. Chief Melody was on tour three then. He said, "Go up to Eleven Engine." They were short. I went up to Eleven Engine and I spent a couple days there. And then they bounced you around from there. I guess I was up there for a vacation which consisted of probably about two weeks. I went from there to - - - I think I worked in every firehouse except Nine Engine when we roved. That was the only firehouse I didn't work in. Worked in Thirty-two Engine for a couple of days. Worked everywhere. They stuck you everywhere, but mainly uptown.

You walked in and basically everybody's talking. They're not really paying too much attention and you sort of got to say, "Hey, I'm here." And you're here. Rocco Piegaro, who I've known since birth, was around. He's over by the stove cooking the night's meal; the first tour was coming back in that night. He was making meatballs and sausage and stuff like that. So, I walked over and I was talking to him mainly. Then Chief Melody, who I knew over years too, before I came on the job. He comes walking up, "Mark, you got to go up to Eleven Engine." So, basically, I really didn't get to talk to anybody at Seven Engine. When I went to Eleven Engine, they had no captain. Tommy McGovern was the captain. He was on vacation. You had Mike Cawley, Mike Coale, and me. So, they were one and two. Back then they had the Mack. So, you're on the back step. I'm on the back step by myself. I was the new guy and I was on the back step by myself. So, they told me just bend your knees and hit the button and hang on. That's all he said.

I absolutely felt welcome. Yeah, there were no problems. Mike Coale, he's a real good guy. Still friends with him today. Poor Mike Cawley, he passed away, but they were great. No problem. The truck, they had Gorman who I have known since we were kids. Richie Pedimone was there. Meeker was the captain. Who else was there? Georgie Orlando was also on the engine, but he wasn't there. He was detailed to the truck that day. So, they were one and three. We were one and two.

Sandella: We were roving. My first night in the firehouse I went over to Park Avenue. Second tour on Park Avenue and I walked in, met the guys, great bunch of guys, Sammy Pappalardo and Captain Zizza were there. Captain Caine was also there. It was a good first experience. I had a fire, caught a fire my first night. I think I was assigned to the truck and of course Sam Pappalardo, he grabbed me, stay close to me and I did. He showed me a few things. It was a good experience, a good first night. I was welcomed.

The old timers were great. Some of them were legends. You looked at them and you heard stories about them. They were all good guys, all World War II veterans, Korean War Veterans. Some of them were older Vietnam guys. But I liked those old timers. They were the best guys. They were fantastic. They just had a way about them, those people. And I got a kick out of them, loved spending time with them and talking. They taught me a lot. Learned a lot talking to those guys.

After I went to Fifteen Engine on Park Avenue, the next shift, I went to Nine Engine. And then after that, the first day, I went to Six Engine. Six Engine had the deputy. Report to the deputy to be assigned. The company was out. He said, "Stay here for today." I stayed there that day and I never left, for seventeen years. Six Engine was a busy place. The projects were filled to the max. Right across the street you had that bar. Behind the firehouse there were some walk-ups occupied for the most part. And it was just a lot of activity going on there.

We had a real good fire on Sayre Street my first winter. It was very cold. You guys relieved us. It was a three-story brick, a big brick building. Apartments on both sides of the stairway going up. I remember it was top to bottom going good. The Tact Squad was there. They were very close by on Prince Street at the time. I was fairly new and it was pretty amazing. Dick Tiffany had the tip and there was just no stopping him. He was going, putting everything out in sight. I remember going up the stairs and fumbling and breaking and coming down. It was pretty interesting. It was vented pretty good. I mean, it wasn't really a tough thing with heat or anything. But it was all just the disruption. But I always remember that fire. It was pretty intense and I was new and it had an impact on me because I was new. I had never really experienced anything like that before in my life. It was a good job. It was a good fire and I remember coming out and going into the Tact Squad van to keep warm. We just sat in there to keep warm. Yeah, that's one that stuck with me.

Witte: I was nervous when you first walked in. Nervous, what do they expect, what do I have to do. New to the job. You're, "What's this? How am I going to perform? Am I going to do the job?" All those concerns were in there. I walked into Ladder Six on the first tour. I got to see Hollywood Phil. That was my first introduction, walking in, seeing this guy walking back from sunbathing in the back. Cut off shorts, sunglasses, flip-flops, and a beach chair. "Hey kid, how you doing?" It was, "You're the new kid. You're here." Then there was another guy I didn't know, who was a probie there. When I saw him, he had a big stomach; he looked like a fifteen-year vet. He was laying on a lounge, knocked out. It wasn't until I got on the rig, that I noticed there's another probie here. It was him.

I bounced around over the summer. I remember I did Ladder Six for about two weeks. I don't remember how long it took me, but I walked over to the chief and asked, "Can I get a busy company?" I was moved. Got me out and I bounced around. I remember going to Five Engine. In fact, I liked Five Engine. I was going to stay there. It was a good bunch of guys. That was my first real fire where we had jumpers.

They parked the rig. I got off on one side, came around and there are two people on the ground. I watched the one fireman, the guy who was on the back, step over them, grab the hose, step over them, and go inside. I just looked at him, "Okay I'll followed him." Later on, he tells us, "There's nothing more we could have done for them. They're already out of the building. You got to go inside see who else in there we can save." So, it's an impression.

Brown: My first impression of the job was initially, shock. Things I saw were shocking. Some things were very grotesque, like the first bodies. And the smell of flesh burning, what you smelled. And plenty of things that happened like, I went out on a first aid emergency, girl told me she was pregnant. Went into the apartment, we looked around, the woman is in labor, and we see twelve tall cans of Colt 45 sitting out on the dining room table. The girl was drunk and she pissed on herself, made like her water broke.

The first fire I went to. I was riding Twenty-nine Engine. Al Brand was my captain. And it was so funny because it was what we called a chicken shit fire, but I went running up the stairs, lost my helmet, tripped over the hose, fell down the stairs. Al Brand picked me up. I fell down again. He said, "Calm down, son, we're going to get the job done." It was good though because I couldn't sleep in the firehouse. And when I got that fire, it got better.

Then we had the electrical warehouse. Three alarm fire, about two o'clock in the morning. Me and Richie Reddick are at Twenty-nine Engine. We got that on the third alarm. We took a two-and-a-half and tried to go into that building. And my picture is on the cover of Firehouse magazine. That's why I remember it. Bobby Frey and all the guys at Twenty-nine were telling me, that was me on the cover of Firehouse magazine. And I said, "No, that's not me." And they said, "Well, you're the only probie in the company with a new coat and new boots, it's got to be you." That was funny.

Kormash: Out of the Academy I went straight to Seventeen. It was the shakeup. They got caught doing something before that, so out of my class, me, Pauly Cox, Ray Fallone, Gary Palmerson, might have been one or two other guys went there on all four different tours spread out. But it was all basically because of what happened there.

Dennis Robbins was the captain. He was just transferred there. Harold MacIntosh was there. He was transferred in there. There was a lot of firemen that were on the job that were transferred in there because of the shake up too. On other tours you had Jack Hurle, John Fedash, Eli Savarese. But my crew was Dennis Robbins was the captain, Bernie Snyder, Florent Natale, Harold MacIntosh, and me. When I walked in, I felt welcomed. We were all pretty new. You'd see the first tour; you'd see the third tour; and they were all new. Jack Hurle was over there too. The first tour, the second tour, the third tour was fine, no problem. The fourth tour, all of them were alright.

I walked into that firehouse and my first impression was it was a dirty place. I mean dirt looked like it hadn't been cleaned in like twenty, thirty years. Filthy, I mean absolutely filthy, run down, dilapidated. There's a diesel pump in the kitchen. Dog hairs, floors looked like they haven't been cleaned in twenty years. Pretty messed up. You got used to it quick though.

When I first came on, I couldn't believe the number of fires that were happening. I read the newspapers enough prior to coming on. Very few fires were even printed in the paper. Then I later found out that to a degree Newark was sanitizing stuff to try to build its reputation back up. That the newspapers were controlled to a degree, but the number of fires was unbelievable.

The most memorable fires I worked was that rash of fires in May of '80, that twenty-four hours. I was working for Pauly Cox. It started on the first tour that night. I remember we had two earlier fires then we ended up going Down Neck to Lexington Street until eight in the morning. We went from Lexington back to Seventeen Engine to change shifts. I immediately went from there to I think Ali or Eighteenth and I ended up on Clay Street later. Clay Street by McCarter Highway over there by the concrete joint along 280. But I don't know how many fires I went to in that thing. They're all listed in that one article that was in Firehouse Magazine. I worked at the whole thing. Just the luck of the draw. I got the whole mother lode.

Reiss: I was really excited to be there. I was at Engine Seven, tour one. They were a busy company which I was very happy with. I didn't get stuck Down Neck or somewhere where it was slow. Truck Three was still there at the time and also Battalion One. So, there were a lot of people there. I think they were pretty excited to get a new guy. I don't know if they were not expecting one; I'm not sure what happened. George Werdann had been there before me and he had just retired. He had actually been at Engine Seven since before I was born. So, he spent his entire career there and then I came in and replaced him. So, I was the third man. There were only three firefighters and one captain in Engine Seven at the time.

I had been as an auxiliary at Engine Nine for about two years before I came on the job. So, I was kind of used to what was happening in the firehouse, how the firehouses worked and things like that. But Engine Nine's a one company house and at the time Engine Seven was a two company, so there were a lot more people around, a lot more hustle and bustle. And it was a chief's house so you have to be a little more on your toes than in some of the other houses.

I felt very welcomed. They were very happy to see me. The two firemen that were assigned to Engine Seven at the time were not cracker-jack firemen let's say. And they were very happy that they had a new guy, a gung-ho guy. The chief explained about two years later. I was looking to move to Truck Eleven and the battalion chief said to me, "You can't go." And I said, "Why not?" He said, "Because if I lose you, I lose the whole company. I'll have nobody else to bring a line into the building." So, he said, "Listen, I'm going to retire in one year. If stay for one more year, I'll guarantee you that you can go to Truck Eleven then. If you stay here then I can keep the company. If you leave, I'm not sure what's going to happen with this company." So, I stayed.

When I was first in Engine Seven taking a line down the hallway, I was looking around at some of these people in other companies and I'm saying, "These guys are good. These guys are really good. I'm going to have to be on my game to even stay with them." I always felt that I had to work really hard just to make sure I fit in with the group. They were encouraging and they were always helping me.

I think the first month I drove, May, 1980, the number seems to stick in my mind that we had thirty working fires that month. So, almost one a day. The first night I drove, I walked into the firehouse five o'clock to relieve Tony Giorgio, young Tony. The bells are ringing as I'm walking in. And he says casually, "What'd you say Tom? How you doing? I think you're going to get that. There are companies out." I said, "Okay." So, I walk in and I get my gear off the hook. And sure enough, we're first due at a factory on Seventh Avenue and High Street. So, we go down there. We're down there until midnight. We have our dinner at midnight for half an hour. Then we go to a three bagger Down Neck. So, we were out the entire night except for half an hour that we were in quarters eating our dinner at midnight. That was the first night I drove.

1980s: The Height, Then Easing

Caufield: When I reported to dispatch, I wasn't unwelcomed. I think part of my problem was my name. I mean, the boss's name is Caufield and here comes a guy named Caufield. Are they planting him over here to find out what we're doing? I think I broke that pretty quickly though. I think they pretty much figured that out. First of all, some of the guys knew my dad because we had some World War IIers up there. We had light duty firefighters, not just operators, and they knew my dad. They liked my dad. Not that they disliked my uncle, but he was the boss. It's a whole different thing. And I don't think it took me long for them to understand that I didn't go to Fire Headquarters on my days off. Headquarters was in City Hall.

They used to do a unique thing with us. They used to put us on straight days for a couple weeks. And that allowed the other guys to meet me because they all worked days sometime during those two weeks. And so, I got to work with each of them. We could meet each other, figure each other out a little bit. And then I ended up on Chief Al Lasso's tour. He was my chief operator when I came on. And then Clarence Austin, myself. Joe Mueller, he was an old, very hard of hearing operator. He was a light duty firefighter. I loved him dearly, but he was deaf.

We always used to tell him, "Joe you ought to do something about those ears." He came in a week after he retired. I think he was doing some paperwork on the second floor. And he came up to see us. He had two new hearing aids he could work with. He said, "I got them." "You should have gotten them when you were here."

I don't know how my tour felt about me, but I was good with them. Within a couple, three weeks we were getting along fine. We were eating together. At that time dispatch was in Room 421 in City Hall. We were up there for years. It was like working in the museum. It was absolutely beautiful. It was like working in a museum and it worked. It worked very well.

F. Bellina: This is something I'll never forget. I walked into Five Engine. When I walked in, there was somebody sitting in front of the firehouse. Black firefighter, his name was Charlie Bishop. He was there. I can picture him now, he was leaning in between the column of the two doors, on a chair leaning back at seven thirty in the morning. I didn't think anything of it, but now I can tell you I know why he was leaning and he's sitting in front of the firehouse. So, I go into the firehouse. He goes, "Yeah, just go in." He followed me in. "Put your stuff down. Go introduce yourself to the captain."

I walked in and they started to bust my chops, like they had all this time on the job. Now in the Academy they told me, if you have any deficiencies, if you're not comfortable with something, let the captain know. So, I got to get things out now. Told the captain that I was afraid of heights. I have an issue with heights. He proceeded to bust my chops with that. Telling me he's going to get Ladder Eight up here. I'm going to the top of the aerial and all this stuff. They were busting my chops, but they were get-overs and I didn't realize it.

It turns out that Charlie Bishop told me, "These guys don't like me cause I'm black." And he became a friend of mine. He said to me, "You got to get out of here. I know you're roving, but you got to get out of here. Don't listen to them." When I caught the first fire on Elm Street with them, Charlie was behind me. Charlie was there. Charlie was from Seventeen Engine. There was a big mishap at Seventeen Engine, they flushed him out of there. He was just in the mix. They got rid of all four tours there. Caufield got rid of the whole house. Switched the whole house around and that's how he wound up down there. But it was true. When Charlie would leave the room, they were making racial comments and Charlie knew. He didn't care. You couldn't say anything to him. He just didn't care that they were doing that. He goes, "They're doing the same thing with you. You know, when you leave the room, they're ripping you up. You got to get out if here."

I moved to Six Engine and felt welcomed. I felt there was no pressure because the pressure was the job. The pressure was what we were going to do that day and that night. So, it was basically easy for you guys because all you had to say was, "No, he's not going to work out. Or yes, he's going to work out." So, I knew I was welcome. You have an opportunity. That's how I felt. After I realized it wasn't Five Engine. After I realize where I was at and what was expected of me and I had to make a decision on my own that I want to participate with this. It was easy. It was easy. Because you're either going to fall into place or get the hell out.

I remember my first fire with Five Engine and how Charlie was backing me up and letting me take a line in. I actually felt the difference. My first fire at Six Engine with you guys giving me the tip after it was knocked down and asking me to do certain things. I remember being on top of a mattress and shooting water into a mirror. The reflection of the apparatus outside was red and I thought it was fire. Kevin said, "Okay, shut the line down. You're splashing everybody here. It's a mirror." I have a lot of memories, but I like to think about the funny ones. I don't want to think about any bad things. There's a lot of bad things that went on, the deaths. I don't want to get into that, just funny ones.

Wapples: My first assignment after the four-week period which I came on the job, I went to Seven Engine. And when I went to Seven Engine, Captain Rydzewski was my captain. And Chief McCormack was the battalion chief. I remember that first fire that I had. It was a fire where we had a run down on West Market Street in an abandoned building. And the first floor was on fire, the ground level, a store front. We went in there. I didn't know what was going on. I just went in and followed the captain. They knocked down the fire. Because I was just there watching, I didn't know what was happening. It was an experience. It wasn't really scary. It was scary going in initially, but once when I got in and saw what was going on and the feeling of being in fire and the actual phase of firefighting, then a little bit of the jitters and apprehensiveness was relieved. And later on, that same night we caught a two alarm down on 611 High Street. The electricity had gone out. And the fire must have been on the fourteenth floor. So, we had to walk up. That was an experience.

So, the first night that I wind up going into the firehouse, I experienced a lot. And I found out then that you don't just take this job for granted, after seeing guys from Eleven Engine at 611 High. They were just sitting on steps, just worn out from walking up the steps. So, I could imagine at that time how it would be going into the fire to fight the fire. I believe the following night, my second night at Seven Engine, we caught a signal eleven which we were second, maybe third due at, but the fire was so intense. It was a third-floor fire, a brick structure. And the fire was going really good. It was going up through the roof. So, we went in. We went in to make the third floor. And as we were going in, by this time I was still a little apprehensive, but we were going in and it just so happened I was working with Captain Rydzewski. It was Gene Brenner, some other guy, I forget who exactly that was, and myself. Gene was pumping. The captain, he was on the tip and the other gentleman was on the tip and I was following these two guys. And it so happened that they wind up going in with the line and as they went in with the line, I was right behind them.

And somehow, they wind up coming out and I was still in there. As they were coming out, I spun around a couple of times by them passing by me and hitting me I wind up spinning around. And I didn't know to go forward, backwards. I didn't know which way I was after being turned. How we wound up being lost in the shuffle I really don't know, but they backed out. I was still in there. And I said, "Well, let me think. They said don't panic in such a situation. What you do is just think about the situation." And as I thought about it, I said, "Well, one thing Carl Duerr said, you follow the male coupling in and you go back the female way. Either you put it in or you take it out. So, I wound up following the line and I wound up going toward the engine. As I was going toward the engine, I came out. Chief McCormack was in the hallway. He asked me where was my crew. I told the chief, "I don't know." And I had my shield on the helmet, probationary firefighter. And

I'm looking at him. I don't know where my crew is. He told me to just wait in the hallway. He'll find out where they were. So, I felt a little awkward being in that position at that time. Come to find out, the captain and the other guy that was with us wound up going to the floor above. By that time, they came back downstairs. We regrouped and I regained the composure. Everything was in place, okay.

After going back to the Academy, I was sent to Nineteen Engine. I had a captain down there. I'm not going to say that I idolized this individual. But I came back, worked at Nineteen Engine for eight months. And I felt cheated being in Nineteen Engine. All the other guys who I came on the job with were up on the hill. And I had a desire to go in fire and fight fire and learn the job. So that I could be in a situation when the next test came around that I could use the firefighting experience along with the book knowledge and know what I was doing. I felt as though that's what I had wanted, the hands-on experience. But I ended up in a house where the captain was very lax. When we did get a fire, he didn't even want to go to the fire. So, I had to do something about that. After being there for eight months, I put in for a transfer. I used to have guys come down to the firehouse from Nine Truck, Eighteen Engine and through talking to these guys I found out there was an opening. So, I put in my papers to go up on the hill, up to Nine Truck. I stayed up there for about four years and gained a lot of experience there, a lot.

E. Griffith: I actually ended up at Truck Six, Thirteen Engine like when I roved around. And I worked with some great captains. Tommy McGovern was a captain in Rescue, got to work with him. My battalion chief was Rich Bitter. That was funny because the first time I met him I was standing there. You had to line up when the chief came into quarters. They said, "Look, it's Walter Matthau." I looked over and I go, "Oh, my God, he does look like Walter Matthau." I'm not saying it out loud. I'm saying it to myself. And I started to laugh. It just came out. He immediately walked down the line to me, probably seven guys away. He comes up. Now he's really looking in my face and he has a stern grin. He looked at me and he said, "What's your problem?" I said, "Nothing sir." He says, "Then why are you laughing?" I said, "I'd rather not say." He said, "You're just a dumb shit, aren't you?" I said, "Yeah, yeah, that's probably the case, yes." And he's going, "I want to know why you're laughing." I said, "I think it's better left unsaid. I really do." Then he just walked away. Then afterwards it was Captain Jones, Lowell Jones was the captain and he said, "What were you laughing at?" And I said, "Actually, somebody said he looked like Walter Matthau." He laughed and said it was a great answer.

Maybe he would have laughed about it too, but you're a new guy. I learned the hard way. Everybody said keep your ears open and your mouth shut and there were times when my mouth got me in a lot of trouble. But it's all good because I learned from it.

You think you know because you went to the Academy and you think you know, but that's the thing because you didn't know. So, they taught me how to use a mask. I feel I can use a mask. My first fire, my days with Thirteen Engine, I was with Richie Guliani. He was the captain at Thirteen Engine and he goes, "Okay, kid, now get the mask on." And I go, "Yeah, I got the mask on. Look at that. I got it on." We had the don use switch then and the whole bit. Then we go into the building. The first floor wasn't bad. The fire's on the second floor. A little smoky but not bad, but I don't have it on and then all of the sudden we go up the stairs and I start to cough a little bit. He says, "Hey you want to muzzle up kid." And I muzzle up and then we go up there and he goes, "You hold on to my coat." And I said, "What the hell did I get myself into." I felt like I was being dragged along. That there was this organized, insane chaos. Now you're feeling heat. There are cinders coming down. You can't see. Guys are yelling, screaming, cursing and he's going, "You got my coat?" And I'm going, "Yeah, I got your coat." And he's yelling at the tip guy. They're going, "You see that?" And I'm going, "See what?" I'm looking around and I can't see a thing. I see smoke. There are bits and pieces. It was crazy. And then the steam and the heat, and I go "Holy shit, this is for real.

This is no joke." You need to go and take care of the fire. You just don't get the feeling on the inside. We were sent out of the Academy early because our class was so large. So, after basic training, half of us went into the field and half stay in the Academy to finish the training. We hadn't gotten the live burns yet. That wasn't for another four weeks, but here I am going in, getting dragged in.

So that was it and at that time it was still pretty busy. You caught fires, especially the third battalion there. That whole area was going. You always got something. After that I said, "Okay, yes, we got to look at this in a little bit different way and start paying attention to things." Ask a question about something. The guys were always very nice. They explained that to you. But I was like the cog in the wheel. They needed me like a hole in the head because I knew absolutely nothing.

The next time I went to the truck, Lowell Jones actually gave me the book *Fire Tactics and Principles* by Clark and he had a paper clip on it. He gave it to me and Lawrence Webb was with me. He gave us the book and said, "Read this." It was a night. He said, "Read this. I'm going to give you a test on it before dinner." I looked at him and I said, "What are you crazy? What is that all about?" Give me a test? They didn't tell me about this. So, I read the chapter. It was really about ground ladders and placements and all that. He gave a test and we ate dinner and he graded it and come out. He said, "The reason I did this is because I have you. I don't know what you know. So, by doing that at least I can go and start explaining stuff to you." I thought that was really good.

Nasta: My first day I reported was Thanksgiving Day, 1984. My first assignment was Engine Twenty-Six with Captain Eddie McCarthy up in Vailsburg. I was there one day. I worked that Thanksgiving and the next day I was moved to Truck Eleven with Bobby Carter. Basically, the whole time I stayed out in the field, I stayed with Truck Eleven. A couple of nights they moved me to Engine Seven. I was the roving guy, so they needed to move me, but I pretty much spent the majority of those couple of months in Eleven Truck. When I walked in on Thanksgiving Day, it kind of surprised me, they're drinking beer which was like, "Holy cow, this is like really happening." Had a great Thanksgiving dinner. It was a ten-hour day. I think they had one run that day. And I think it was for an electrical short. That was my first run on the Newark Fire Department. Then I went home and had Thanksgiving dinner with my family.

The next day I went to Eleven Truck and what surprised me again was the culture in the firehouse. I was naïve to that. That was something they never taught in the Academy. They never taught you what the real firehouse was like. They taught you to count bells and all that stuff. I got to say, Bobby Carter was a great guy to work for. It's the day after a holiday. Everybody likes to cruise through those days, just kind of answer the alarms, but at ten o'clock we're out there. He took me out drilling. Started showing me stuff. You know at the Academy you don't get the opportunity to do a lot of truck work. So, we went to a couple of abandoned structures and he showed me how to pull ceilings and where to look for hidden fire. And I appreciated that. Becoming a captain later on, you realize that this is what we do to our subordinates and it's the Newark Fire Department tradition as well as the fire service. But I learned a lot under him.

My first really good fire I went with Eleven Truck. It was a good job on Warren Street. I'll never forget it. I think the medical research building stands there now. It was a three-story brick. We had a rescue problem. I get off the truck. The battalion chief is Chief Meeker. Seven Engine was there in seconds because it's right, literally, behind the firehouse. And I remember Bobby Carter turning to me. He says, "Sit in the truck. I don't have time to deal with you right now." That was all he said and he ran into this building. I just listened. Well, lo and behold, they rescued probably I think around seven people. Billy Murnane and Six Engine rescued a bunch of people. Eleven Truck rescued a bunch of people. And tragically four people were killed in that fire.

So, after things settled down, Bobby came back out, he brought me inside. There was still some burning, but the rescues were over so now he had time to deal with me. I understood exactly why he gave me that initial order at that exact second, as new as I was. We went back in and I got to see my first fire deaths which were at my first fire. It was amazing never being used to those type of conditions of the way that fire went. The people for security reasons had the windows boarded from the inside. And you were literally able to see their nail marks in the plywood. They were trying to claw their way out of the room that they died in. Killed the whole family. And that's how my career started. That was my first fire.

I was saying to myself, alright we got that one under our belt. A couple weeks later working with Seven Engine, we had a fire in a two-story frame right next door to the Red Flame Lounge on Bergen Street. It was right behind Six's quarters. And three people died in that one. I started talking to guys I came on the job with, "Wow, is this going to be every time I go out the door?" That's how I started in the first couple of weeks of my career, that type of tragedy. I'm like wow. That was it. That was shocking.

No matter what firehouse I walked into when I was roving and it was pretty much only the Burg, Eleven Truck, and Seven Engine. That was pretty much my roving. Every company I stayed with until I got my permanent assignment, every firehouse was welcoming, very helpful, willing to train you. They expected you to step up. They didn't baby you. We were told in the Academy, go in there. Don't be the last guy to get up when it's time to do housework and don't be afraid to do dishes and get involved in cooking meals. I guess that's kind of the tradition and I know for a fact that it still goes on today. Those are the good parts.

Weidele: I went to Avon Avenue with another fireman, Bobby Testa. We both came into the same house the first day. First day you came in. You're all nervous you're scared. You don't know how the guys are going to look at you. But they opened their arms and greeted us. I had guys like Pat Durkin, Mike Lalor, Frank

Franco, Vinny Kuhn, Herbie Volkert. My first chief was Chief DeTroia, real solid guy, all business, no joking around. They took us in. Showed us stuff and they're still my friends to this day. A lot of those have retired, but they're still friends of mine.

When I first came on my first day, they had a big fire on Twenty-first Street in Irvington. We went to that. My first day, they said, "Put your gear on we're going to a fire." I had Pat Durkin, Vinny Kuhn, and Herbie Volkert and I was the brand-new guy. We pulled up, two buildings going good. Report of people trapped. People were screaming and they said, "Grab the line." I was the second man on the line, pulling it up there. When we got in there, there was so much fire, they moved me back to the third guy on the line. So, I was pulling and I'm struggling behind these guys. Felt like someone was pulling me. I'm pulling the line, fighting my way up. We finally put the fire out on the third floor, we broke the windows out, we ventilated. When we looked back, I had a small kid's bicycle, my foot went through the spokes and I dragged it from the front. I thought something was wrong man. Maybe I won't be a good fireman because I can't do it. But I dragged the bicycle, clothes, coach pillows, everything. All the guys that were there were laughing that I dragged this bicycle through. That was my first fire ever and I was like wow. It was crazy. I didn't even feel it on my boot.

Arce: I first went in to Engine Six. I worked there for a couple of months and then I did Eleven on Central Avenue for a couple of months. I think that was back and forth between those two companies for the first year. And then they assigned me to Engine Seven. And then I did fifteen years at Engine Seven.

We were very busy. I mean if you came in early, seven o'clock in the morning, you're going to a fire in progress. Or to relieve somebody. You were in fires constantly. You would come in to a fire. And you were dreading the nights because you were up all night. You'd see the moon come out. I mean at five o'clock in the morning. Fires were burning like crazy. And it was like that constantly. We were so happy. We were very, very busy, doing 3000, 4000 runs in a year. You're talking about twenty, thirty runs a day easily.

I was a little nervous when I first walked into the firehouse really not knowing anybody. Young and you do like the job, but it was like, I guess being nervous. Some of the guys made me feel welcome. But I didn't get to talk to a lot of guys my first couple of weeks getting used to coming to the firehouse, getting used to the guys, that's hard. They expect stuff from you, but you haven't a clue. So, they had to change that. Then just jumping into the field, wow. I had no training what so ever, no experience of anything. Just two weeks in the Academy then you jump into the field, fighting fires.

We did close to 4000 runs in that time which was a lot of runs. And we had the projects. How many times you go to the projects? Twelve, thirteen stories, you walk up, no working elevators. You know you do that five times a day, it's incredible, incredible.

Johnson: It was actually pretty busy. The city was in transition, especially in the North Ward. It was burning up there by what is now NJIT, that was burning, by School Street. I roved for approximately two years. I didn't have a captain when I first came on the job.

I was in the Fifth Battalion. I was assigned. I went from Engine Fourteen, Engine Twenty-seven I stayed. I stayed at Engine Five. Chief Pierce actually had me assigned to Engine Five. I was there with Bobby Clarke, John Aquino, and a couple of other guys that I don't recall their names. But I was assigned to Five Engine and I stayed there for three or four years.

DeCuester: I was assigned to Seven Truck, but there was no captain at Seven Truck, so I spent some time at Nine Engine with Owen Donnelly. That's a gentleman there, Owen. Chief Sandra-din was there. It was a lot of car fires. Nine

Engine was famous for the car fires for a long time. Then I went to Park Avenue and Tony Connell was the captain there.

I was welcomed in the firehouse. The house was good. It was John Salvato, Joe Purcell, Captain Kirkland. A good bunch of guys basically. I was taken in under the tutelage of Sam Pappalardo, I did a lot of roof work.

At first it wasn't busy and then I was getting to do the down watch and sometimes did some stupid mistakes. But then they had the fire where Jimmy Murry passed away at the Prudential Building. I think I was upset because it really wasn't that far away, but everybody in the city was there except us. But then when work did come it got more and more. I did a lot of roof work with Sammy. Park Avenue got a whole lot busier.

They had the articulated bucket at Six Truck and they would never put that up. We had a tiller and I'd be in the back tillering. And you could see Six Truck waving like we had to put the ladder up. So, one time we got a big like paper towel box and taped it to the end of our aerial and we'd drive up and down in front of Six Truck.

I remember one of my first fires was somewhere between Park Avenue and Orange Street on the corner somewhere there. The fire was knocked down, but there was real heavy smoke in the living room. And across the living room was Sam Pappalardo. And all I remember is him lighting up a cigarette and I smoked, but I mean the only thing you could see was the light from the cigarette when he inhaled. And then he would go "ah", like this is the greatest thing. I said, "No, there's no way I'm doing this."

The mutual aid fires are sometimes a problem. Going into other towns. We had a problem. We were on the roof and it reminded me of the movie, *War of the Worlds*. Remember when that thing comes into the room and looks. Well, they had that telescoping thing and we were up on the roof and this comes up. I'm like "Holy, shit. If they put the water on, someone's getting blown off the roof here." So, we nearly get into fisticuffs there.

Giordano: I went through the Academy by myself the first time I went through because I had to sue the city to get on the job. Spent about six weeks there learning what basics I could as an individual. Then I went to Bergen and Lehigh. They gave me a pillow case and bed sheets, my badge number was on it and they said, "Son, you're going to Bergen and Lehigh and you're starting on Monday."

Well, it's funny. When they told me "You're going to be assigned to Bergen and Lehigh." That's in Newark? I was from the North Ward. I had never been past that part of the city in my life. So, as most of us tried to do, I went there days. Walked in and introduced myself. I'm not sure what they thought. All they know is I'm coming to work the next day. And it was very good. I met the greatest people and mentors. It was very interesting. I met so many old school guys that were still left and just overall great guys. It's a second family. So, I told them I'd be coming in the next day. It's funny. I lived the closest, fifteen miles, cross town Newark. I would probably be the one getting to work late at eight o'clock, only ten to eight. Usually, guys want you there fifteen to a half hour early for relief, but my Captain Gesualdo would say, "Only you."

I was on Twenty-nine Engine. They said you're hanging on the back of somebody's coat. I'm going to say my first one or two fires I was literally hanging on the back of somebody's coat. My first fire was right around the corner from Bergen and Lehigh. It was a simple mattress fire in a bedroom and back then everybody used the same face piece. You had to wash it out before the shift. You didn't have a personal one. And my first fire was literally fifty yards from the firehouse. I went to get my air tank. As soon as I got in there, my air tank started running out of air and I wind up going out. Everybody was busy at the fire. By the time I got myself together to go back in with another tank, it was pretty much over. It was a mattress fire in a bed. I wasn't that happy because I really checked mine every day. When the fire happened, somebody else was a little more aggressive than me. They just grabbed the first one they could grab. I picked the next tank that was on there and nobody had checked it. It was low on air. That's the way it goes.

Things got better. My second fire was over in the Central Ward near where Eleven Engine, Eleven Truck were over on Central Avenue. It was a big apartment building. And I'm going to say things progressed from there. We had started to do more drilling and other things. Just started to get more acclimated to how things work. It was a three-alarm fire and it's so real when you're sitting there and you're brand new. Lights and sirens are going off and you're on your way to your first fire. It was so exciting. A month on the job and you're going out to a working fire. You know when you get there, you're going to work.

I got to Bergen and Lehigh in early December and I was only there a few shifts. And then Marcus Reddick died on New Year's Eve in the Ironbound.

I went to work on January second. They said I was the last person hired and the first transferred. They sent me from Bergen and Lehigh to Five Engine with Deputy Two and I went to work there with Chief Griggs and his driver Fred Charpentier. I remained there until the class went back into the Academy. The class came in. I left Five Engine and went and finished the course with a whole group of great guys.

Lee: I end up at Nine Engine with a great group of guys. My captain was Kenny Marcell. He's an outstanding captain. And I had senior firefighters with me at the time who all became officers themselves. I learnt a lot in that seven-week period. The majority of my roving time I was at Nine Engine and I spent maybe one or two days at Engine Fifteen. As a probie, I was already told, you should be seen and not heard. So, I followed that as soon as I came in. I kept my mouth closed and I did what needed to be done with the senior guys. I was welcomed. I had no issues coming in. Like I said they were a great group of guys. It was a busy company. We caught fires and the good thing was the fires started off small like an outside fire then a vehicle fire then a small apartment fire and then one of the last fires I had was a two-alarm fire with rescues before I went back to the Academy so it developed nicely.

Sorace: My first assignment was Ladder Six or back then it was Truck Six on Mount Prospect Avenue. I was assigned to Truck Six on the first tour. I guess it was known back then for being an average company. Of course, it wasn't the busiest like Truck Eleven or Truck Nine, Truck Five. They did running. Truck Six wasn't getting a lot of fires, but my first couple of weeks there, we ended up having almost a multiple alarm fire every night. Because Broadway and Halleck were burning, the Branch Brook Park skating rink burned. They were getting a decent number of fires the first couple of weeks there.

I was very much welcomed there. Truck Six was there and Engine Thirteen was there. And they're very hospitable. They're all happy to see me. I had Myles McDonald as my official first captain over there. I think he might have been detailed there, assigned there for a period because of Five Truck. He was at Five Truck and I think they moved him up there for a while. So, everybody there just took a great liking to each other and everything worked out.

Back then I don't remember any timeframe before we could start driving. And it was almost a couple of weeks on the department when they allowed me to drive. I showed an interest in it and they allowed me to get my credentials at the time. And then you had to get certified in either like the truck or the engine. The Snorkel was our main truck, but then when that broke down, we got an old spare and back then it was a tiller. And then when that broke down, we ended up getting Truck Eleven's rear-mount ladder when they got a new truck. So, I'll say in the first couple of months, I was able to get certified to drive and operate the Snorkel and the tiller front and back.

When I was over at Mount Prospect Avenue, Myles was our captain there and everything was great. But I wanted to get to a busier engine company. I was trying to get to Engine Six. When I was in the Third Battalion there wasn't any opening in Engine Six, so I would take all the out of house details. Usually, the details were two days or two nights or a vacation pick. The captain at Nine Engine was Kenny Marcell. I got detailed to Nine Engine, and everything was great there. All the firemen, they all got along and again we did all our drills and everything. So, Captain Marcell at the time wanted me to try to put in to go to Engine Nine. He didn't have any openings, but he anticipated one. Then I'd end up at Park Avenue, at Truck Seven or Fifteen. I was taking all these details to Rescue One and Truck One because that was the Third Battalion. Still, I enjoyed every minute at Truck Six, but eventually I ended up transferring over to the engine. So, I transferred from Six Truck to Engine Thirteen. I was there a couple of months and then finally an opening came up at Engine Six and I went to Engine Six. I finally got over there on the first tour. And it was a young crew. We had myself, Sylvester Lee, Johnny Griggs, and Kevin Killeen was our acting officer all the time because we were all brand new on the job, the three of us.

Capt. Masters: I got out of the Academy and went to Four Truck on the first tour with Andy Marcell for a few weeks. Andy was a class act. Worked with my dad at Eleven Truck. You see I had that privilege. The chief back then was Joe Miller. Andy Marcell was his driver. Andy Petracto, he was from up on the hill and a few other good guys. They knew my dad. So, I had like a little advantage because they knew me. They knew me when I was a kid, so for me I just did what my dad said. Just keep your mouth shut. Do as you're told and just listen and learn, listen and learn and go out drilling and that was it. It was a little intimidating going to your first fire because you knew you wanted to be steered in the right direction. All you had to do was listen to the senior guy. And they would never steer you wrong. They would tease you or bust your chops a little on the fire apparatus floor or in the house, but on the fire ground it was all business. I felt welcomed. I was Tony's son. I heard that a lot. I'm Tony's kid, Tony Masters' kid. "Oh, he's a great cook. Can you cook?" I said, "Oh, yeah." That's how my twenty-seven years cooking on the job happened. And I couldn't be happier. Everybody enjoyed my meals.

One of the first fires I had was on Frelinghuysen Avenue going toward Elizabeth, I forget the cross street. It was a Chinese restaurant in the middle of the day. And I went home very upset that day. It went to a second alarm because there was a forcible entry problem and there were immigrant Chinese guys stuck on the second floor. What happened was we had trouble getting in the front and the back, finally they made entry. The fire was going really good on the first floor. They baked to death like an oven because of the tin roofs. And later on, the Arson Squad came out with a duffle bag full of money with the proceeds from the restaurant. And that's what they did with the new immigrants. They locked them in, leave them at work. I remember going home, explaining to my dad and I was very upset over that one. I think three people died.

I was down at Four Truck for about a month and then graduation for the second class of '86 came. I put in for Park Avenue on the fourth tour because I was ill advised by the Witte brothers to put in papers in the Academy specifying what tour and all that. And I had my ass reamed out by Captain Duerr and Chief Freda for putting in transfer papers while in the Academy. I ended up at Twenty-eight Engine for a couple of months with Carl Schnering, another classmate of mine. And then we kept hounding Chief Gaynor. He was the Third Battalion, second tour. Finally, after enough hounding, they put Carl at Seven Engine on the second tour and me at Truck Seven, tour two. After going to Park Avenue, I would float between Seven Truck and Fifteen Engine. Whoever was shorthanded, so I got a little bit of engine under my belt which was nice, but mainly I stayed a truck guy at Seven Truck.

Seven did maybe 2500 runs and a lot of working fires. We rebuilt the whole of the North Ward, Broadway, Oriental, all of them. A lot of jobs back then. You're young and you got a lot of good experience. No fire is ever the same, some are accidental, but a lot of them were set in abandoned buildings. We had one fire; we just came back from a big fire in the Burg in a supermarket. And we're all cleaning up and then about two, two-thirty in the morning we hear banging on the doors.

Tony Connell was my captain and John Salvato was Fifteen Engine's acting captain. People are screaming. We just opened the doors. On Fifth Street there were two three-family houses fully involved.

When we pulled up there, people were grabbing us because they knew people were in there. We lost a couple of people that night. But we found out the cause of that fire was it was a drug house. They were using drugs and the chemicals involved. So, it ended up being three houses total. I ended up calling a second because my captain was being pulled out of the cab because there were people trapped. I screamed like a banty, he said, although I knew that.

We tried to get into the main fire building, but even though we were like a block away, you couldn't get in. There was too much fire around and we just went to two and a half. The truck had a two and a half, The engine had a two and a half, plus the deck pipe, plus an inch and three-quarter on the exposure. Everybody just manned the hoses and surrounded it because there was really too much fire. Then with the exposures, the second alarm companies maintained them. All in all, it worked out. I know we lost two houses fully and then half of one.

Goetchius: On my first night in the field, after spending a week in the Academy, I went to the Deputy's on Springfield Avenue. And he assigned me temporarily to Central Avenue. He had to show me on a map where to go from Springfield Avenue to Central Avenue and Nineth Street. That was an interesting night. There was a bang on the overhead door and a couple of shots were fired right outside the firehouse. All the firemen leapt out and I just followed along. I'm watching the firemen work on this poor guy that just got shot. And then looking down and seeing a three- or four-year-old kid looking at this body getting worked on. At the time *Hill Street Blues* was on TV. I felt I was in a *Hill Street Blues* episode watching this poor kid watch this guy get worked on.

I was at Central Avenue in the truck for two weeks. Then they transferred we over to Seven Engine for a temporary deal. They switched Imre Szigeti, his brother

Tom, and myself from Seven Engine to Eleven Truck, so we had a little cross training going on. It just so happened when I was in the truck, we hardly turned a wheel those two weeks.

At Seven Engine, I caught my first fire with Dennis Cogan and Mike Miggins. He was a fireman there. He was there temporarily. I caught a fire on Broad Street and Clark in an old retirement house. It was shocking to see these guys were stretching the hose actually into the building next door, seeing the fire going right next door. And these guys setting up the hose and then they're lighting up a cigarette like there's nothing going on.

Seven Engine was my first permanent assignment. I was there for I would say five years. And I was there when they switched us down to Mulberry Street. But for the first four or five years, they were probably some of the busiest we ever had. Anything from car fires to structure fires, giant factory fires and we were all over the place. Seven Engine being centrally located, we would get Down Neck and we were uptown, downtown, all over the place. I guess that's where I got my most experience.

We had Captain Dennis Cogan as the captain and Ray Wallace was our senior fireman. And there were three probationary firefighters, myself, Thomas Szegti, and Louis Orlando. We all came on the same time. It was pretty interesting, three new guys on the job working in the same company. We got to learn from a real good captain, Dennis Cogan. And we had Chief Meeker there with Al Plaugic. We really didn't do a lot of training back then. It was more like hands on. It would be more like on the scene. This is the way you do certain things. You should know this. You should know that from the Training Academy. Remember this, remember that. That was pretty much training back then.

Ch. Centanni: Everybody thinks they have their juice and their moves, so at the time John Sandella lived next door to me on Garside Street. So, I had always talked to him about where I'm going. I believed I was going to Park Avenue, to

Ladder Seven. John Salvato was there who was a neighborhood friend of our family. My friend Billy George came on the job with me, wanted me to go to Nine Engine. We were going to work together. I wanted to tiller. So, I had told John, could you help me out and make some calls. "Yeah, no problem. No problem." I come out of the Academy roving and they put me in Six Engine. And the funny story with that was Carl Duerr is reading the names off and he goes, "Okay I got this guy's going here, this guy's going here. Centanni, f-ing hero, Six Engine. I don't know who you know." And I was kind of surprised. I'm like, "No, I'm going the Seven Truck." We've got these room rules set up.

I showed up in the firehouse and I saw John Sandella a couple of days later. He's like, "You're going to be here for a little while. If you don't like it, let me know." And you know, I think I spent over my career between captain and firefighter, about seventeen years there. It was the best experience of my life. If I could say it Neal, I actually went to your spot and I worked with some phenomenal people, Kevin Killeen, Frank Bellina, Scott Gerow. John Kramer was my first captain. And we were fairly busy at the time, so active. It was unbelievable, an unbelievable experience. So, my first assignment was Engine Six, tour one on Springfield Avenue.

I can remember my first day like it was my first kiss or my first baseball game. I showed up with the collar pins on and shoes and a tie and I had a brown bag with a cold cut sandwich in it for lunch. I stopped at the corner store on Garside. I got my sandwich. Frank Bellina asked me what was in the bag. Then he took the bag and threw it in the garbage. Said we'll take care of lunch later. And he told me to remove all that silly non-sense I was wearing. They gave me a broom and he said, "Let's start doing housework." And as I thought it was a little rough then, I was really greeted warmly and brought right into the fold and treated great. Made you feel like part of the family, within a few days I felt like I was there forever.

I believe it was Keven Killeen, shortly after that, started calling me young boy. And I was like, "Why are you calling me young boy?" And young boy morphed to young-in and young boy and that's the way it was called on the loud speaker. "Young boy you got a phone call." That kind of stuck with me for a while because I guess I wasn't even twenty yet when I came on. So, I was the youngest kid there. And that was it. I was young boy.

One night we had a fire on Sixteenth Avenue and Twelfth Street I believe. Big three-story frame tenement building. It was a hybrid building, there was some construction, modification made to a real old building. They did some work on it. We wind up pulling up and black smoke is pushing out everywhere, joint's rolling. We were first due. Stairs are all burning. I wound up on the third floor with the tip. Mark Hopkins is backing me up. I can't get off the landing. The cockloft's going and apartments on both sides are going. I'm just trying to hold it. "Hold up. Young boy, hold up. We got another line coming up." Seven Engine was going to bring another line up because Eighteen was on the second floor. He says, "Just hold up, man, we got it. Don't go any further." And everything just suddenly got quiet and silent. Instead of the stairs collapsing, the entire landing collapsed, all three landings.

What we found out later was when they changed the configuration of the building and fixed it, they put a stairway in the middle of the building. All they did was face nail it and hang all the beams. There was no hanging out or overlap of the joists. So, it was setup for failure. So, everything collapsed and I'm on the third floor with the tip. I kind of knew something was wrong, but I thought I was just going to be falling to the next landing. The hose started pulling me. I was burning inside my thighs and my ears were burning. I just said, I'm going with this. I had that come to Jesus moment. I knew I'm in trouble here. I wasn't staying where I was because I knew I was in more trouble. Everybody was gone somehow and I wanted to be with them.

So, it wound up being the entire three landings and stairwell collapsed. Pretty much buried Billy Murnane and those guys underneath it. Mark falls on one side of the piles. Seven Engine dives back into the second floor. Artie Zieser always says, "Because I saw legs dangling, we got to get another line back up there. Somebody's trapped up there. The next thing, we stick our head out and the hose is zipping by and some bodies are going by." I had a couple of options here, not that I had any will in it. You actually can see a mark on my head. I hit my head on the way down. Which is probably a good thing because I must have gotten knocked out. I land right next to Mark Hopkins on a pile of debris. If I land a little bit more to the right, I'm impaled on all of the railing spindles. A little bit more to the left, I go into the basement and probably break my back. Mark said, the only thing he was waiting for after all the debris stopped was for me to come down and land on him and crush him. So, unbelievable. Everybody's scurrying to get us out. I think I tore the ligaments in my ankles. We're in the hospital all night. Who's burnt and scratched? I had blood in my urine from getting banged around. But the most important thing is that next morning Richie thought it was appropriate for us to all go out and celebrate that we were still alive. So, we went to the Playpen on Fourteenth Avenue, there's a little bar there.

Because the businesses are open. By the time we got out of the hospital and everybody got their paper work it was probably twelve o'clock. And I don't think we made it out of there until it got dark. I'm on crutches, who's got the thing wrapped around their head. And we talked about how that could have been really different. And that was probably one of the two- or three-times Chief Dunn ever yelled at us. He was furious because he was asking us to come out. You know, old school bosses had their twenty-minute rule and we weren't getting it. We weren't making it. The joint's rolling. What he sees outside, we don't see inside. And he's doing the radio thing. You know, "Six I need out of there, back down. We're going to hit it with big water." And Rickie's going, "We got it. Give us another minute. We got it. Give us another minute. We got it." "John, you got it?" "I got it. Just get me another line. I got it."

So, we're playing the game. We got it. We got it. And the next thing is two companies almost get killed and he wasn't happy. He wasn't happy. He gives us the riot act. I was back in work probably after two shifts, driving the chief with an air cast on my leg. Limping around and George who was the chief's driver, jumped over to Six just so I could come back. Because I didn't want to stay home or miss anything. So, I'm driving and he had a meeting with us. "You got kids, you got two little kids. I'm with them all the time." At the time I had two kids. "With your wife I go to parties. I'm not burying anybody. I'm too far in my career." Yelling at us. "If I tell you to come out, you come out." And six months later we did the same thing on Kinney Street and we had to rescue Bobby Rommiehs and Seven Engine out of the windows. Floors are leaning inside and they're hanging on window sills, freezing cold night. He wasn't happy then either. So, we had a little run where he yelled at us a couple of times. But yeah, it could have been a career changing experience for any one of us.

N Bellina: My first day in Truck One, I walk in and the only guy that was sitting in the kitchen was Deputy Chief Kinnear. I don't know why he was there, but he was there. I came in and he introduced himself. I told him my name and everything and he said, "Good Luck. Stay safe, and you're going to love this job. It's the best job in the world." And then other guys came. Joe Battaglia was the captain there at the time and he came down. He came in because the first tour was coming in. And then all the guys came in, Gerry Lardiere, Steve Marusiak, and Tom Farley were there. When I got out of the Academy the second time, I came back there, the first fire I had was the rolling rink in Branch Brook Park. That's where they thought that Tom Farley had a heart attack. He went out and I was left with Gerry Lardiere, Steve Marusiak, and myself and the captain.

I was welcomed. Joe Battaglia was dynamite. After I was introduced to all the guys that were there and there's a lot of people in this kitchen, the third tour was getting off. So, they came down. Joe Doughert, Mike Popik, Billy Burkhardt, and the captain was Ed Connolly. And it was like, wow. What's going on? Everybody introduced themselves. There's a lot of joking around about being new. But they were all laughing and everything. They made me feel comfortable. I didn't know what to expect. What am I going to do? Because I had heard rumors about things and at the time you're reading books, Report from Company 82, 10,000 Alarms, all those books from FDNY.

When I knew I was going to One Truck, that was the assignment, I'm like, "One Truck? Why am I going to One Truck?" My brother Frank said, "Shut up. Just go to One Truck." I had a good time for the two years that I was there.

We really didn't do anything at that first fire I had. My first fire I went to the rolling rink. We operated a two-and-a-half at that fire. When I came on, we were getting a lot of fires at 140 Thomas Street, that factory. They always had a lot of plastics stored in it because they made hairdryers back then. You could use a truck there because the ladder had to go to a window. There was a lot of pulling on the inside because of a lot of this plastic stuff that was on fire. And they had a lot of cars that they were pulling in the back and setting them on fire. So, there's a lot of pulling, just pulling things apart so you can get water on it. That's a little different than a fire in a building where you're pulling walls and ceilings. Stuff in a factory is a little different. Especially if you get something with recycling with the paper we used to get, those big bales of paper. That was crazy. That was a lot of work. Especially if you didn't have a truck to pull this stuff out. That could burn for days. But the truck work could really be tiring. You're walking out of there, "Okay, I can't move my arms."

Alexander I: My first assignment was Truck Company Five on the third tour. My very first night in the firehouse I had a chance to greet my captain and meet my guys. We talked for maybe about two hours and the bells just started going off. That night two hours into my shift, we caught my first job which was a three alarm. I'll never forget. It was on South Eighth Street. It was just unfortunate to see what I saw that night. We actually lost a family. I'll never forget, my captain actually grabbed me. He said, "Listen, come on in. You need to see this because you got another twenty-five years to go. We're not going to hide you from this." That was when I had my first opportunity to see burnt bodies. It bothered me a little, but again like I said I thought my captain was one of the greatest people I'd ever met in my life. He talked me through it and it just helped me prepare to go on the rest of my career, understand what I got involved with.

Walking into the firehouse was probably my biggest game. I played sports a lot and you'd have this nervousness sometimes, but that was my biggest game. In 1987, I never thought walking into the firehouse that I would be walking into a firehouse that consisted of all Caucasians. That in itself took me for a loop, but I walked in very nervous. At the time I was like twenty-four years old. And I just went in with the knowhow from what my parents taught me. You don't have to be better than anybody. You do your best. So, I just went in with that mind frame and I really got to know a lot of guys and I found out that the fire department is a family.

But I didn't feel welcomed because of the way I was approached. There was still some racism at that time. Seeing twelve guys sitting at the table and all Caucasian, the one guy, the first thing he said to me was, "Hey sonny, do you like white guys?" And I'm like, whoa. He just blew me away. Like how do I answer that? My response to him was, "I have nothing against them." And as soon as I said that my captain, Tommy McDonnell, walked right up to me. He put his arm around me and said, "Come with me." He took me out to the apparatus floor and he explained, "You have to excuse guys like that, but this is what you're going to deal with here. But my tour, I don't allow some of the things that these guys get away with." So, at that point it made me a little bit more at ease and I said, "You know what, okay now I know what I got to deal with."

A. Maresca: My first spot was Eleven Engine. I took Damian Emerick's spot after he had the accident. It was busy. It wasn't as busy as in the past from what I understood, but we were busy. I forget how many runs we were doing at the time.

I kept track of it for a while. We caught a lot of fires. Not quite like the early '80s or late 70s.

I was excited about going into the firehouse. It was something I looked forward to all my life, but I really didn't know what to expect. It ended up being the greatest job that I ever did. The guys that I worked with when I first came on taught me everything. John Muoio, John Riker, he taught me how to pump. I never realized the guys kept their gear hung up right out on the rig. I had no clue coming in. These guys took me under their wing and they really taught me. And it was a nice atmosphere.

I was there a couple of years and then I had an opportunity to go to Six Engine which was the busiest house at the time. Growing up, my father had always talked very highly of George Perdon, Kevin Burkhardt, and Kevin Flannagan. And when the opportunity came to work with them, I jumped at it because that was like my idol. So, I went to Six Engine for a couple years.

One of the most memorable fires I went to was Ricoh Chemical. A real nasty fire and actually my father was in charge. He was the deputy and I was with the Squad. He sent us to go to this back generator. And he knew it was bad at the time. They ended up taking about twenty guys to the hospital. I remember talking to my father years later. He said Ricoh Chemical came up to him in the spring and they asked how the hell you put this fire out. Even he didn't notice how bad it was at the time. And that was one of the biggest, nastiest fires that I can remember. And then we had another fire on McCarter Highway. It was a warehouse that burnt down. It was from the Civil War. It was a Civil War hospital and then they converted it into a warehouse. I just remember it melting the cars across McCarter Highway. There was a car dealership on the other side. And it melted the cars in the dealership.

DeLeon: At Eight Engine I did feel welcomed. When I started making the hill, not as much. The difference was they want to see you do the job. And they're going to care. They're going to give you a hard time. But as soon as you start to show that you're there to do the job, you're there to learn, they back off.

And in the beginning, I used to get there about a quarter to six. I'm used to my old job. Yeah, fifteen, ten before and you're good. Until I learned that, no that's not good enough, try to get there an hour before. Get to know what happened, what's broken. Get your equipment, check your stuff, get yourself ready. Because if you walk in so late, it's going to happen that you're caught off guard. That fire's going to come in.

And sure enough, my first day, no more than ten, fifteen minutes after six, we caught a fire on Adams Street, auto body shop. And my captain was Eugene Anderson, but he was on vacation. I had Chris Della Santi and Jeff Alaimo and myself at Eight Engine. Which I didn't want. I wanted to go up the hill like everybody else. But hey, you got to start somewhere, so here in my head I'm thinking, "Okay, day one, fifteen minutes into it. This is it. I'm going to be a one dayer, I'm going to be in the paper tomorrow, big explosion, tanks, fireman killed." And I thought, "Ut-oh, maybe this is not such a good idea." But after that I felt more confident. The next day the next shift said, "Hey kid, you're a jinx. We've been really quiet here for a long time and we like it that way." I was on the third tour. That's how I started. I think I took Eddy Dunham's place when he got promoted. I ended up in that spot.

The two guys I had in the beginning; one was transferred there; he was at Four Engine. He got transferred there because he got in trouble. He was on strike two as far as getting caught for drugs. I didn't know that. And the other guy was Jeff Alaimo. He also was on strike two because he had trouble with substance abuse. So, those were my two guys. It was oh and three. It was no officer for officer. None of that stuff at that time, acting captain. Chris was the acting captain when we caught that job on the first day. I thought the world of them because, hey, they had the experience. I'm a rookie, got to do what they tell me to do. But those were my execs.

But Captain Anderson was great because he would go to the apparatus, pick up all the appliances, throw them on the table and say, "Okay, what's this Al? What is it for? How do you connect it?" Other times he would take something from the engine and say, "Okay, this is what we're going to do with it." And we would go out there and drill. But I would be a little over aggressive because he was two guys behind me on the line and I was driving that line. I guess I had so much strength at that time. I was twenty-seven. He would be like, slow down, slow down. I'm throwing the hose line around. But he was definitely there to show me how to work the engine, the pumping. And we had the hard suction hose. We worked with the foam. I thought it was hook up to a hydrant, get water, comes out the hose. Put the fire out. Put it back and you're done. And all that in between, friction loss and pressures, I had no idea. How to prime the pump if you're going to do hard suction. I didn't know all that stuff. So, I picked up a lot, a lot from the captain, a lot.

I remember after I got certified my first week pumping. Owen Donnelly worked for Gene Anderson. We caught a fire on Clover and Ferry, first due. They stretched the line and went up to the second floor to start working. We didn't have personal portable radios at the time. So, you had to go hook up to the hydrant. I was busy doing that. Owen came down and he's furious at me. "What are you doing? I asked for water." "Cap, I didn't hear you. I was hooking up to the hydrant. I was getting water for you." So, I didn't open the line. I didn't open the Mattydale. That's what he wanted. He wanted those couple minutes while I hook up. Didn't know that. Another lesson learned. So, after a year and a half and a few experiences I ended up going to One Truck on the second tour. I stayed in One Truck; I believe a couple of years.

Taylor: I absolutely felt welcomed when I walked into the firehouse. I walked into Nineteen Engine, tour four. I stayed there three years. Then I went to Truck Ten. Stayed there eighteen years then I was having some medical problems and I ended up retiring out of Special Service.

The old timers greeted me, you and Chief Freda. Then I went to Bergen Street and met all those guys who broke me in. Henry Carr was alive then. Joe McCarthy was alive. Not only Bergen Street where I was. When I started being eligible for overtime and had the opportunity to go around the city or you meet guys in your battalion at fires or at rackets. There was just a wonderful camaraderie.

Al Brand was my first captain. Me, him, and Angel Rivera. So, we mostly rode one and two until we got another guy later on. But Nineteen didn't get a lot of first due work, so I wasn't getting the experience like some of the guys I came on with. That's why I transferred to Truck Ten. To learn the job a little better.

Capt. Griggs: First assigned to Six. I got lucky. I was on the first tour at Engine Six. I was working with Sylvester Lee who was a fireman. Chief Killeen who was a fireman at the time. And there was a young fireman by the name of Jeff Lukawski. He was there. We were a relatively young crew. Outside of Kevin Killeen, Sylvester Lee had me by two years. Jeff Lukawski had me by two. They came on together. After that Mike Sorace came. He had me by two. He came on in '86. And then eventually Mike Gilroy came on, we were in the same class together, '88. We were a relatively young crew and then Patty Doherty came on board. That was great because he had the Twenty Engine experience. He came from Ladder Seven at the time, from the fourth tour. He was a great officer.

And I remember Jeff introduced me to the engine. We were going over the engine on the apron. I had a cup of coffee in my hand because that's the first thing everybody says, go get a cup of coffee. That's what I did, but I didn't have my uniform on yet. It was still early. He introduced me to the engine and was going over the engine because he was the chauffer that day. I think maybe twenty minutes into my shift, we caught a fire on either Bruce or Bedford Street. We were looking east and said, "We got a job." Because we had a heavy smoke condition. We ended up having a fire first thing in the morning. And then we preceded to have two other fires.

I think the third tour came in that night to relieve us. I started on the morning shift. And one of the old veterans there, George Pianka, must have seen the shock on my face. He pulled me aside and said, "Take it easy. It's not normally like this every day." I think he thought I was ready to throw the towel in that first day. But my head was reeling.

At the time, we were doing at least 3000 runs a year. Walking into the firehouse was a little tough. I remember a lot of people were nice to you, but there were a lot of people that didn't want to be bothered with you either. It took a while to break the ice. It's just the way it was, so I had to just take it easy and do my job and eventually people came around.

Pat came on about a year later. I didn't have a captain my first year. Kevin Killeen did the only acting my first year. So, it was a little tough that first year. Getting acclimated, but it was a good thing. And Kevin ended up getting hurt. He was out for a while, so I saw a lot of overtime captains, a lot of the older fellows. That's how I ended up with meeting Patty Doherty for the first time. He caught a couple of overtimes then. He liked it and that was my introduction to my first captain. I got lucky. I mean I met everybody. I met all the great guys. Captain Nanartowicz, Captain Bobcheck, Captain Haran from Ladder Eleven. So, I met like great, great people. So, it was a good experience to get to meet people. I was a new kid, so you're sucking up stuff like a sponge, so it was good. And then I ended up with Patty which was perfect because we had a young crew at the time and he was able to get us together.

Greene: My first assignment was Engine Five and I went there for about ten minutes before they told me, as soon as I go there, that I was being detailed to Engine Twenty-seven. So, I went to Engine Twenty-seven and I don't know how long I was down there before I went back to Engine Five. That was a couple of months. I felt very welcome when I came into the firehouse.

When I went to Engine Twenty-seven which was actually my first assignment, we were one and three. And Captain Ruane who was really a great guy. I really liked him. He was very instrumental in giving me a positive outlook about the department. Quite a gentleman. So, I went from Five to Twenty-seven to Five. Chief Carragher was the Deputy and I just remember him saying that, "Dave, you know, I think you'd be a good fireman. You'll never learn enough down here. You need to go up on the hill." I just looked for an open spot. I saw that they had one in Ladder Eleven, so I put in my papers for that spot. It just so happened that Chief Calvetti came through, He might have been like acting Deputy Chief or something like that and he said, "Oh, you're the kid who wants to come up to Ladder Eleven." And I said, "Yeah, they're really a bunch of nice guys." He said, "I got an opening in Engine Seven, too. Do you want the engine or the ladder?" Well, I had never even been on a ladder so I said, "Probably the engine. I've never been assigned to a ladder." He said, "Yeah. You'll really like that. You'll really like them. We got two young guys up there, Anthony Austin and Orlando Arce. You'll really like them." So, he said, "Why don't you put in your papers for them?" And I did. I was on the next transfer list for that, for Engine Seven.

The first fire I had was the first day on the job. We had a small kitchen fire. I think we were second due. I walked in there with my officer. He didn't have his mask on, so I didn't put mine on. I was choking, but he wasn't. I don't know what the secret was. I was new. The fire had been kind of knocked down and they were just overhauling. They gave me the tip and I did some additional overhauling. But I just recall that. I'm in there coughing and the fire had been knocked down, but these guys were just like standing around like it was clear. I had virgin lungs or something.

Then later that afternoon we had a fire on West Kinney Street and we weren't on the first alarm. We were actually on the second alarm. It was an apartment building. I think it was a four or five story brick apartment building. I knew the building. It had been abandoned. I mean I passed by it. And I couldn't believe that you could put that much water on a fire and it not go out. It seemed like they had it from every angle possible and it was not going out. It was amazing.

Sperli: I went to Fifteen Engine on Park Avenue. Captain Robert Lehman, was my captain on the first tour. The captain on the ladder was Jeffery Rudden. On the engine I had James Warren. Hiram Acevedo who just transferred from Mount Prospect Avenue, I think Engine Thirteen. That was in September, in December we got another new firefighter, Artie Ciampi. It made us one and four. And on the ladder truck there was Jimmy Headen, Milton Baskett, Gunther Albino, and Glen Bagley.

My first day the captain went over the boundaries for the battalion and described how you could just differentiate the boxes. Then he showed me the boundary where thirty-one boxes were, thirty-two, thirty-three, thirty-four, thirty-five. And he told me anytime a box came in the city, I had to go to the cards and pull the card up. We didn't have running books then. We had these cards and each box number was four digits. We would go, pull the card and see which companies were due on the box. So, he told me every box that came in, I would go and pull that card until I had the box system down pat. And he told me he didn't want me going up at night. He wanted me to stay on the book with the guy at least the first couple of nights until I had it down pat which is what I did.

My second night in, we had a first due fire. It was a signal eleven in a four-story brick. Someone lit a fire at the bottom of the stairs. I just remember it was about five-thirty or six at night. We had just come in to start the night shift. They send the box out. At this time, I'm slowly getting dressed on the rig as we're going; they had this bench seat. And the one guy says to me, "There's smoke. There's smoke. You better get dressed quicker." I didn't know how close this was. I wasn't too familiar with the streets yet. And it was pretty close. It was only like five blocks. So, I hurried up. I put everything on. We rushed in there with a line and we ended up knocking it out pretty quick. That was my first fire. It was my second night in. And it was a rude awakening. But I loved it.

Then my first night on the house watch was in November and we had fourteen buildings on fire in the middle of the night. So, they said that I was cursed. And sure enough, over time, many of the nights I was on the book I kept guys up with me at the fires. So, that did hold true. That was my first night on the book and we ended up having my biggest fire of my career.

That was over in the Fourth Battalion, Johnson Avenue, West Alpine, Irvine Turner Boulevard. It was a windswept night and the wind just whipped around. It was blowing the embers everywhere. Couldn't believe it. There was low water pressure and before you know it, there were fourteen buildings involved all said and done.

The wind was really fierce. I remember while I was on the book there was a two-alarm fire earlier in the evening down at the old farmers' Down Neck. And I remember I was looking out the window when I was listening to the fire. It was maybe around one, one-thirty in the morning. And the wind was blowing so fierce that the garbage cans were rolling down the street. So, now I'm on the book. I ran out to chase the garbage cans to bring them back and put them in the alley where they were a little bit more sheltered. Then this fire came in. Deputy Two is coming up and he said, "We have an apartment building about two blocks away on fire, transmit the box for that." That went to a second alarm, so Engine Fifteen went. I guess combined it was like a fourth alarm.

I remember pulling up and we stretched our whole hose bed and connected in with Engine Nine. They're far away on Clinton Avenue. The embers were just blowing across the street. It was just landing on roofs of other buildings. There were people on this little two and a half story frame where we parked the rig a couple of houses down from there. They were watching on the porch. When it was all said and done and I was going back to the rig, I looked over and there was nothing left of that house but that porch and a chimney standing. The whole house was burned down. So, it's kind of sad, but it was fierce. It was fierce mother nature.

The water pressure was horrible. We went into one house and we actually used a pot and water from the sink to hit hot spots around the windows. We ended up shutting down some lines and we got one line working. It was a two and a half and we used that for a while in combination with Engine Nine. And that's pretty much what we did. Then we went down the road to one of the apartment buildings. Engine Eight which was in service at the time and the one side of the rig was all melted. I guess as the building was burning the radiant heat had burned it up. We worked at that apartment building for a while with an inch-and-three-quarters.

Fires were coming pretty quickly back then even in the Third Battalion. I learned quick. Engine Nine was first due at most of the fires in the Third Battalion. And they didn't like to stretch. Fifteen, being second due most of the time on a lot of the thirty-one boxes where the fires were, ended up stretching in a lot. So, I learned very quickly.

Alvarez: My first assignment was Fifteen Engine on the fourth tour. At that time the captain was out for the first three months. There were acting captains. He was out on an injury, so I didn't have a captain for the first three months I was on the job.

They were very nice to me when I walked in. What I found out later, the reason I ended up at Fifteen Engine was one of the captains had a little self-interest involved. He went to the Academy and he scouted out somebody that he thought he would like that spoke English and Spanish. Because he had a girlfriend or a fiancé at the time from the Dominican Republic. And he didn't speak Spanish and she didn't speak English. He wanted somebody young that would basically put up with what he asked me to do which was very, very awkward. But a young guy in a new job, you don't want to disappoint anybody. You really don't want to say anything against it. He used to call her and I was his interpreter between him and her having conversations. So, that's the reason I ended up at Fifteen Engine. He needed somebody who spoke Spanish and English to interpret between him and his girlfriend. I did that for several months and that part, that was very uncomfortable for me.

In the firehouse there was never any animosity or any problems. I never had any issues with any of the guys in the firehouse, but they were killing each other. And I thought one day they were going to kill each other. Two times they went at each other with knives in the kitchen. There were arguments. There were chairs thrown across the room breaking against walls because guys would duck. When I came on, I was about a hundred and forty pounds. All the guys were big guys. I remember one guy was six-six. He had to be about two-eighty. I think they started at about two-forty, so here are all these guys that are much bigger than me. They outweighed me by a hundred pounds.

I was like, man, if they ever turn on me for whatever reason, I'm a dead little guy here. I just didn't like the atmosphere. I really didn't feel endangered at all. I just thought like, well if they turn on me, but I knew that I wasn't going to piss-off anybody else. I felt I'm pretty easy going, but I just didn't like being in that atmosphere compared to the atmosphere that I came from when I used to hang out at Eight Engine before I got on the job. That bond and that friendship that I wanted, that I expected from this job. To go over there to see them, it was a totally different world. So, I was there for a short time and I managed to transfer out in the next transfer list.

At the very beginning at Fifteen, a couple of times we went out, they tried to teach me how to pump. They did have me practice driving. And actually, the acting captain took a lot of interest in me for that. At that time, you didn't have to wait a year. Now you have to wait six months before you get behind the wheel and year before you can go and test to get your certification to drive to an incident and be a pump operator. At that time, there were no rules so I got behind the wheel right away. I had driven off road dump trucks and heavy equipment, so I took to the fire engine very easily. I drove very well. And I was always a car geek anyway, so driving was my thing. I learned how to pump right away, I'm mechanically inclined so I got it. I studied a few notes someone gave me, so after two weeks, they brought me back to the Academy and I took the test for pump operator. And I got certified in under three weeks. I was a pump operator. Where now it's a year and it's this whole process and everything.

After that it was pretty much very laid back. Then when my captain got there three months later, he did a couple of drills and it was just carefree and laid back. When I got transferred, the only opening was Eight Engine where I used to go visit. So, I got transferred over there. It was a very slow house. It was all older guys. So, basically like we did nothing. And at that time also, the afternoon was nap time. They called it nap time. After lunch everybody took a nap. And it was like everybody disappeared. You were there alone. That was the day. That was pretty much the day at the time. So, then you prepared to go home, because you went home at six o'clock when your relief came in. So, the guys woke up from their nap, had some coffee, a little conversation. And then you went home.

I was at Eight Engine a little under a year. It's not where I wanted to be. I wanted to catch some action, so I transferred from there, I transferred to Seventeen Engine. And I was there with two guys I was in the Academy with. I saw fires at Fifteen Engine. That was pretty good. At least one guaranteed car fire every day, minimum. One guaranteed car fire every day shift and every night shift, at least one. And then house fires, I'd say like once a tour. And then at Eight Engine, two fires and it was just a different world. How the captain did things, the captain I had there. I remember one of the fires we caught was on Patterson Street. We were one and three. There was a guy that was ready to retire. He was driving. There was another guy who had substance abuse problems. He was a drinker, amongst other things, so he wasn't that alert. And then the captain just wasn't really into the job, so he stayed outside. He waited downstairs and I took the line up by myself and took care of the fire myself before the second engine arrive. At least the captain had the driver give me water when I needed it. We had no radios. It was kind of count six, seven and charge the line. The fire was on the third floor. I brought the line up all by myself. Back then I was young. I came back down and the captain goes "Did you get it?" And I said, "Yeah, yeah, it's pretty much out." And that's how it worked. He said, "Okay, good job." But when I got to Seventeen Engine, that's when we were really rocking and rolling.

Cordasco: I went to Fourteen Engine and had heard a lot of stories about the tour I was going to. So, I was a little apprehensive about that. I actually gave them the name of the "brain dead crew." I had Benny Ricciardi, Tommy Bouticarus, Rick Camba, and eventually Willy "the ram" Ward. Actually, he was the best fireman out of the four of them. He just had a drug issue on the side. But he would actually look to teach me at least because the other ones I would get nothing. I actually had Boots there for a while and then he went down to Four Truck because he and Benny Ricciardi had incidents. And then Willie Ward left because him and Benny Ricciardi had incidents. And then at one time it was just Rich Camba, myself, and Benny.

I knew a few of the guys who worked in the house and I was warned about Benny. I guess, in retrospect it actually worked out that it was me instead of somebody else who was more level headed, because my first first-due fire with him, Felix Cardillo was working overtime with us. We actually had an auto body shop on Mulberry Street and Kinney, fully involve when we pull up. So, Felix was getting a line to the door. I wasn't going to take it in because I was on the other side. He said, "Matty I want you to get it." And he was going to get the hydrant with the driver and he assumed Benny was coming with me. So, I go into the fire and I'm going in and I turn around and there's nobody. We're first due and there's nobody with me. After I knock down the fire, I don't know what to do next.

So, Ten Engine with Captain Reiss, John Nepa, and Ray Adams which is a very good crew, I wound up learning a lot from them when we had other fires. I see them come in and they're going, "Oh, there's more fire." There's a turn around, but I didn't know what to do. It was a turn-around more into the building and I followed them in. And then Benny comes and says, "I was making sure the roll down door didn't close on you." Because we went in a loading dock. After it's knocked down, he's saying, "Alright, let's hit these hot spots here." And I say, "Hey Cap, what happened?" "I was watching the door."

And then what happened is I finally got a good captain and then the crew started to change. Actually, later on I was with a good crew. I got Bobby Tittel. Who is aces. Who taught me a lot. Excellent fireman, excellent captain. Tittel was like night and day. So, I finally wound up getting a good captain. Things improved. So, luckily it was only a year with Benny.

Daniels: I wind up getting the Rescue Squad. They tell me report to Lafayette Street, where the firehouse was, 188 Lafayette Street. So, I get down there. My first day, I know I'm in Rescue, but I'm sitting in the truck. And I sit there. They told us, "Show up with your tie on and your bell cap on and I did it. And Mike Daly and John Wielgomas and Captain Luxton was the captain, too. And it was I think Carmen Fallone. And they're looking at me. I sit just for a minute. "So, kid, what's your name? What are you over here for?" And they looked at me like I was a stranger walking in, which I was, but I had the uniform on. Look at me sit there for about a half hour because I showed up at about six forty-five. They said be there an hour and I didn't want to be late. I'm sitting up there with my hat on. "First of all, take that stupid hat off your head. And the tie." Okay. He says, "Where are you supposed to be at? Where are you assigned?" "I'm assigned here." I didn't know it was a double house. So, I'm sitting on the Truck side. So, about a half hour later he says, "Where are you supposed to be at?" "Rescue." "Oh, that's next door. Go next door." That was funny. That was my first day walking into the firehouse. I'll never forget that. It was amazing.

From day one, I walked in, there were the only two people there. The captain wasn't even there. So, it was only them sitting in the kitchen. The captain might have been someplace else in the house. I introduced myself and those two were there. They were both firemen at the time. It wasn't pleasant. I felt initially as if I've invaded their space. That's how I felt. Eventually the captain comes down and I introduced myself. They give me a bunk. They give me a locker. I'm taking all of this in and I'm just looking and taking everything in. I just want to do my best. I'm not thinking they didn't like me. They didn't know who I was. Eventually I get my bunk and they start filling me in. This is the Rescue Squad, "You stick with the captain." That's what I heard. You stick with the captain. That's all I heard. A few days of that.

They never really did embrace me to be honest with you. It was rough and I used to speak to one of the other guys who was at Rescue, Phil Norman. He used to sit down and talk to me. He kind of took a personal interest in me. And let me know we had some issues in the fire department and he kind of helped me through it. And then I also used to go across to the Truck side and that's where I met Larry Berfet, Wesley Taylor, Brian Kirkland. I went over there because I didn't know anybody even on my tour. Nobody cared to kind of open up. My first assignment when I first got to them was to learn the truck. But I couldn't really do anything because I didn't know anything.

And so, I had to learn everything and learn all the compartments. I was diligent about that. They used to test me to see if I knew. I knew where everything on that little truck was. Although I didn't know how to use it. I knew where everything was and I tried my best to just present myself the best I can. But even now, they never took to me. They never took me in like I would take in a probationary firefighter. Now I got to tell you and I'm not trying to say anything negative. I got to tell you that outside the firehouse at fires I did what they told me to do. I stayed with the captain.

I learned a lot by observation because they didn't really teach me. I learned and I like to learn. I watched how they did things. I watched how they operated. I watched what they would do. I would never be behind. If they ran into a building, I don't care how smokey, how much it was burning, I was right there with them. I would work my tail off. One thing I was taught, even in the Academy, never give your tool up. If you give your tool up, you're useless. That's what they taught us and so even in that situation I would never give my tool up. I was always the one who would say, I'll do it. I'll pull. So, I began to build my reputation and my confidence on the job. Not with the people I worked with, but with the rest of the department. And there were guys, older guys, white guys as well that said, "Hey, kid get over here, let me teach you something."

I was getting it from other people. I wasn't getting it a lot from the guys that I was working with. Nothing I did. They just didn't want me there. As a matter of fact, they said to me that I shouldn't be there. So, I would sit there and they would talk about everybody and everything in front of me. And say things like you shouldn't be here. No new kid out of the Academy should be here. They should spend at least two years in this company and two years in that company before they come to Rescue. Right, Okay, fine, but I'm here.

I would sit at the table. Listen and not talk. I did all that. Right, I took it seriously. My desire was not to be in a situation where I would cause complications or act like I know it all. My desire was to learn. I just listened and I was determined that I would learn. That's what happened. I'd like to say it was great, but no they didn't accept me at first.

That went on until I actually asked for a transfer. So, I was with them for the first two years, maybe going on three years. I said, "Captain, with all due respect, I think I would prefer to transfer out." And I told him why I preferred to transfer out. I didn't tell him the real reason. I just told him I think it would be better if I looked for other experiences. But I could take the guys rubbing it in and not accepting me, but as a captain I felt that he as a captain should have guarded me from a lot of that and taken it in. But unfortunately, he valued their opinions and their positions more than he care about me. I felt he wasn't going to be that role model for me and he wasn't going to be the guy to teach me this job and make me feel accepted. So, I put my papers in. I went to Rescue on the fourth tour.

I remember the first job that I got in the Rescue. It was off of Broad Street, those little townhouses off of Broad Street. Right there going behind Technology High, right behind there. And we caught an apartment building, a four-story apartment building. Now of course my captain said stick with me. This is like the first two weeks on the job. Then I caught a fire in an apartment building off of Frelinghuysen Avenue. They pulled a lady out, but she didn't live. Then the next big fire that we got was that next day down here off of Broad Street. We go up and he puts his stuff on. He doesn't put a mask on. Now I'm thinking he's going to say mask up, nah he just goes right in. I got fresh lungs, so as soon as I hit this little haze of smoke I'm coughing. While I'm coughing, I go and mask up. I look around and he's gone. But he said stay with him. So, the chief says, "Who are you?" I said, "Probationary firefighter Daniels." He says, "You go to him. Go to the floor above the fire, and you guys do a search."

I go with this truck guy. We go up. Because I can't be in there by myself, I go up and we do a search and I get down the hallway and I'm starting to do the search and the guy turns around to me and he says, "You know how to get out of here?" And I say, "What? You don't know how to get out of here? What?" So, I do everything you guys taught me. I planted my shoulder back on the wall. I paid attention when I was going out and I led us all the way back out. This is my first real fire. I led us out. I get to the staircase and he goes, "You alright kid? You alright?" "Yeah, man, I'm okay, I'm okay, really." And we go out, but at that point I knew that I could do the job.

LaPenta: I was assigned to Engine Nine on the first tour. My captain was Kenny Marcell. I had firefighter Jimmy Titcomb, firefighter Bobby Tittel, and

Andy Truskowski. Mendola was the battalion chief, Battalion Three and the driver was Danny Cappola. So, that was my crew when I came on the job.

I had met Kenny Marcell. My mom at the time was working for a retired Newark fireman, Tommy DeLuca. She ran his business. Kenny used to come in all the time. So, I kind of knew Kenny and we talked and we talked. Kenny got me to go to Nine Engine from the Academy. Because he met me prior to that and we talked a lot. So, he said, you're a nice guy. You want to get into the job. You want to learn so he took me in. He told the guys that I was coming. So, it was probably a little easier for me. But I still got harassed like everybody else.

I was very excited when I walked into the door at Nine Engine. I was like, "Okay, now it's for real." When you're going through the Academy, you don't really get that firehouse atmosphere. But when you walk into the door and the off coming tour is there. And guys are calling you red ass. "Who's this red ass?" "Hey, how are you doing?" "Hi I'm probie Steve LaPenta." And guys look at you and don't say anything. You know what's it's like. But I was excited.

It actually was pretty funny because Chief Bob Shimph was the Third Battalion chief because Chief Mendola had hernia surgery. He didn't say anything to me. He didn't look at me. The guys made me raise my hand in the kitchen to speak. Stuff like that, kind of like friendly ball breaking, a little bit. Shimph wouldn't look at me. He won't say anything. He would be like, "Tell the probie to pass me the sugar."

My first night in the firehouse I had a rip-roaring fire. I was like, "Oh my God, like here I'm in the firehouse three hours and I'm on like North Fifth Street in a three-story brick." You can't even see the building there's so much smoke. And Captain Marcell says, "Stay with me kid." No kidding. Obviously, it went alright. That's really where you get your training, in the field.

And then I figured Chief Shimph would say something because the guys were like, "So, what'd you think. You did a good job. You stuck in there." He didn't say anything. Then the next day, we came back from a car fire. I guess at like three in the morning and Chief Shimph used to like to read a lot and watch hockey. That was his thing. So, he's sitting in the kitchen. It's like three in the morning. Watching a hockey game rerun or something. And I'm in the kitchen by myself. He says, "What'd you think of that fire kid?" I had to look around. I didn't know who he was talking to.

So, you're excited and then you're trying to do the right thing. You want to fit in. Everybody wants to fit in. I don't care what anybody says. No one walks into the door with this attitude. So, it was a little nerve racking at times because you don't want to make mistakes. Especially when you get on the rig. You want to check the equipment correctly. You want the guys to have faith in you. Because honestly, I have faith in them. My life's in their hands. I don't know anything. They've got to know that at some point you're going to step up, learn the job, and you're going to have their back. That's important to me.

So, it was good. It was a good experience because I felt like they broke me in the right way. There was some razzing going on, but then there was some serious stuff and it all worked out.

Tarantino: Before I came on the fire department, I knew John Centanni. I knew Billy George. Knew a couple of guys, but I really wasn't friendly, friendly with them. So, I grew up with John Guida. I grew up with Vinnie Martone, went to grammar school with him. And they were much more friendly with all these guys. So, towards the end of the Academy, it's "We're going to get you to go here and we're going to get you to go here and we're going to get you to go here." I don't know anybody. I know nobody. So, sometimes they let you request where you would like to go. I didn't even request anything. I had no idea where I wanted to go, at all. I grew up in North Newark and I didn't know the city at all. A lot of people always ask "Oh, where'd you grow up?" "I grew up in Newark." "Oh, don't you know this street and that street?" I didn't know any of them. I stayed in North Newark. The first day I went to NJIT, first day, from where I grew up it's a mile and a half away, I got lost. I never came on the other side of 280, just never. So, I had no idea which firehouse.

I knew Sammy Pappalardo, I grew up with Steven Pappalardo also. He came on after me, but Sammy lived down the street from me. So, I knew the Park Avenue firehouse. I knew there was a firehouse on Mount Prospect Avenue. I didn't even know there was a firehouse over at Sixth Street, at Twenty-eight Engine. I didn't know that existed, so when they gave us the order to where we're going, I got Eleven Truck on the second tour. It was great. It was awesome. I mean I never left there for seventeen years. I didn't put a transfer paper in until I got promoted. Best thing that ever happened.

The first day is a Sunday. I walk in with two boxes of donuts. My captain is Captain Haran. My crew is Richie Heinze, John Maraguglio, and it was me. I was the third. On the engine was Al Alfano, Eddie Griff, Sal Bidot, and Jeff Lukawski.

All these nightmare stories that you hear. They treated me just fine. The one thing that I remember, Captain Haran didn't give me some big long speech about you got to do this, that, and the other thing. I thought he was the coolest guy ever. He goes, "Just come to work. Show up. I want you to show up for work. Don't call in sick. And when you're here, if I ask you to do something, just do it." I thought that was the easiest, best ever. I thought it was great.

I had my first fire about a month and a half later, good fire. There was other little bullshit stuff, but we had a job on South Orange and Speedway. It's kind of an abandoned place and we go upstairs. Twelve Truck had gotten the roof. Haran and Maraguglio are someplace else. I'm with Richie Heinze. We go to the second floor and it's kind of open. One of those big, open rooms and I can remember seeing the fire and it starts to come at me. Richie Heinze grabbing me and I was mesmerized. He pulled me back. "What the fuck are you doing?" Like that, I was like, "I don't know. I got a little mesmerized." But they were good. I loved being there.

West: I was first assigned to Engine Twenty-one on the first tour. I thought towards the last day of the Academy that I was going to go to Central Avenue, Engine Eleven on the second tour. I had people telling me that that's where I was going to go. And then when Captain Carl Duerr read the assignments, he said, "West, Engine Twenty-one, retired." The look on my face probably told the whole story. I had no clue where Engine Twenty-one was and when he said retired, I could only imagine it was a little bit of a slower firehouse. Engine Twenty-one, tour one.

I was welcomed. The Vailsburg firehouse was older gentlemen who had done their time in busy companies and gravitated towards a slower house. And it was a lot of fun, actually. It turned out to be a lot of fun. I was only there for a few short months, but it was a great way to start. You know, learning from some of the older guys and they made you really feel at home.

Approximately three months later a transfer list came out. It was very hard to get into Engine Six at the time. There was a gentleman who put in for the third tour Engine Six and at the very last minute he pulled his papers, didn't want to go. They called me and asked me if I'd be interested. I knew a guy there I was friendly with, but it was a sheer stroke of luck that this guy backed out at the last minute and it became available. I jumped on it. Engine Six tour three is where I went and that's really where I started my career. The first part was fun, but Engine Six was for me the best engine company out there. They took the job very seriously and that's really where I learned to be a fireman, at Engine Six tour three.

When I first got there, my crew was Captain Tommy Grehl, Mark Hopkins, Jimmy McCormack, John Centanni, and myself. Shortly after that Captain Tommy Grehl moved on to Special Service. Captain Richie Zieser became my captain and that was wonderful. He was a solid individual and took the job very seriously. Tommy Grehl was an excellent captain. Richie Zieser was an excellent captain. I like to think I got lucky working with those two guys as my superiors.

The first year I was on the job, while I was up in Vailsburg right before Thanksgiving in 1989, on Johnson Avenue they had three city blocks burning with thirty mile an hour winds. I was a new kid up in Vailsburg, Engine Twenty-one and here are these three city blocks burning. A conflagration I remember they called it in Firehouse magazine. We were the last engine company in the City of Newark to be called to go to that fire. I was listening and listening and listening and I couldn't believe we were not going to this fire. I eventually made it. And it was really unbelievable. The wind blowing the embers. Literally we're wetting houses down with outside lines to protect them and they were just catching fire right in front of us. It was something that was really unbelievable. So, that was early on, that was like the first couple of months on the job. It was pretty unbelievable.

1990s: Passing the Torch

Pierson: Out of the Academy I was assigned to Five Truck, but it was only temporary. I did the summer at Five Truck. It was two to three months. Then we had to go back to the Academy for one week. After that they put us back out to a full-time assignment. So, I came to Seven Engine.

Five Truck was busy because we had the projects down the street. We had some busy days. It seemed like you had a better shot at getting a fire when I was there than nowadays. Maybe first tour you might be able to catch something, maybe a kitchen fire or something. All the boxes were still in, so we were getting a lot of pulled boxes. But it was busy, kept you busy.

It was neat. I tell you the first thing I experienced was a little push and shoving match between a Battalion Chief's driver and a guy on my crew. And I thought, "These people are a little bit testy. Is this the way it's going to be?" That was the first day in. It was over Mets baseball, so you can understand that. I did feel welcomed. It was nice. They kind of took me under their wing and showed me the ropes. And it was good. I enjoyed it from the gate. The captain I had, Captain McDonnell, he would make you write down all the runs in the book. I guess it's what they used to do. I kind of took him literally. I wrote down every run in the city, a couple of pages.

Seven Engine was on Mulberry Street then. We were down there and then we moved up to West Market. I guess we were down there for five or six months. Then they did the rotational closings. So, the guys at Eleven Engine all had seniority. They all came down and we scattered. I went back to Five Truck. I was lucky. There was a spot open there and that's where I stayed for fourteen, fifteen years, until I got promoted. I have no complaints.

I think all told I was at Seven Engine about a year. I was going over the rigs with the senior man. It was only me and another guy in my class, Bobby Lynch. But he was put on the class before. But he sold it pretty good. And finally, I got it and so I asked him, "How long have you been on." He knew exactly where I was going. He started laughing. He sold it pretty good

I remember a night early on, there were two four-alarms going on at the same time, Stone Street and Tony's Palace. And we were assigned over at the Palace. That alarm came in first. The Third Battalion chief pulled up and assigned us to ember patrol. I thought my captain was going to shoot him or have an aneurism. So, we took up from that and went to Seven Truck's quarters on a move up. As soon as we pulled in, we were sent down to Stone Street. They had about three houses and a four-story brick all going. And that was chaos for a while. Jersey City ended being there and I had never seen that before. So, it was a lot of work.

Petrone: I came out of the Training Academy and went to Eighteen Engine. We were a great deal busier than we are now. We did alright. I was fortunate. I always worked for a good captain and with good guys. We went to a lot of fires and I feel like I learned a lot. Tried not to tarnish the family name. My father had a good reputation on the fire department. I walked in; I was Pete's son. That's all everybody said, "Oh you're Pete's son." I was told get there around seven thirty. We start at eight. So, I got there about quarter after seven.

I had known just a couple of the guys through my father or just through where I worked at Economy Fire. I worked for Wags (Captain John Nanartowicz). A lot of guys came through there, working there. So, I know a couple of guys that work on Avon Avenue. I went in and I sat down, minding my own business. I said hello to the guys when they came in. But I let those guys kind of dictate. I was only twenty-one years old, so I'm not going to come in and act like, "Oh, I just got out of the Training Academy. I just read this book. I know a lot." At that time, I went to Eighteen Engine, I was on the first tour. So, I went to work for Kevin Killeen, whom I had known through Economy Fire. Also had a tremendous reputation as a great fireman. And he taught me a great deal. He taught me how to draft water, not that day, but later on. But he had us out the very first day I was in the firehouse.

He took us to an abandoned building, full turn out gear. At the time it was just the rubber coats and the hip boots. Charged line into the building, advanced the charged line. The other guys who had been on for quite a while, they weren't thrilled about doing all that, but it was Killeen's idea which I thought was the right way, It's the only way to get a feel for advancing a line. You could tell somebody how it's going to feel, but you're never going to understand it until you do it.

So, we did that the first two days. We raised ladders. I don't think we had any fires those first two days, but we had one our first night in. So, it was a good experience. Like I said, I worked for good guys. Killeen was a great captain and John Perdisatt was working there at the time and Greg Sereico and Georgie Miranda. And Nine Truck was still in service. So, Mike Cawley was there and Bob Langevin, John Fedash, Al Taylor, and Courtney Ruffner. So, really it was a good bunch of guys. I felt like I was really learning a lot in a short period of time. Which I was told would be what's going to happen when I got out, by Captain Wargo and Captain Camasta.

I always felt very fortunate to work with great captains. I worked for Kevin Killeen. Then I worked for Kevin Burkhardt for seventeen years. The first fire I went to was with the first tour. I think it was the first night I worked. We were on a move up. We had a fire Down Neck. We got a move up and enroute they banged out another alarm, so we ended up going to the fire. It was in some kind of warehouse. I remember I worked with John Perdisatt. He was on the tip. He said, "Stay with me." I stayed with him and we got a good portion of the fire. He gave me the tip. Told me what to do. "If you get tired just let me know." It was a good experience. At the time I had just met John. Three days in the firehouse and I had heard good, great things about him and he didn't disappoint me.

Castelluccio: My first assignment was Twenty-seven Engine. And the reason I went there, I had a friend on the job who told me, "Come to Twenty-seven Engine." I had no clue about the job or any of the companies. I ended up going there and about a month and a half later, he ended up going to Five Truck. So, the reason he wanted me to go there was so that he could get out. I wasn't very happy with that. And I wasn't happy listening to all the guys going to fires. From there I transferred over to Fourteen Engine luckily, four months onto the job and I spent four years at Fourteen.

I was a little nervous walking into Twenty-seven the first day. I wasn't really sure. We only did two weeks in the Training Academy. And I was kind of nervous because I realized right away, the people I was working with weren't really gung-ho or full of fire, but it was exciting. I think I felt welcomed. I think a lot of the guys were on the tail end of their careers. The younger guys, I don't think they even wanted to be there. It was good. I had Captain Mike Ruane as my first captain. And he was really good. He made me feel very welcome and Lenny Gino was the battalion chief at the time. He ran out of that house. They were very open. It was a nice atmosphere.

Twenty-seven was very busy with car fires. We had a lot of car fires, not many structure fires. Everybody around us was getting two, three fires a night and I knew I had to get out as fast as possible.

Fourteen was a lot busier than Twenty-seven. We were catching a lot of four-one and four-seven boxes which was good. So, all the stuff that was burning on Pennsylvania Avenue, Wright, and all those streets. We caught a lot of that first due. On second alarms we were able to get more, but it still wasn't busy enough for me. I always wanted to go to more fires. So, after four years I left there and went to Nine Truck on Avon Avenue. It was a difficult thing because I truly loved the guys I was working with. We were tight knit. It was a family type. I actually wrote them a three-page letter when I was leaving. It was a tough decision, but it was the best decision for my career.

Snyder: My brother and father are on the fire department. I went to Eleven Engine to see my brother. I didn't go to Seventeen to see my dad, but I went to

Fourteen a lot when he was a captain. I was like a young kid. I remember Fourteen, sliding down the pole by myself. I was seven, eight. I was like, should I do it? Should I do it? And they were all downstairs doing their thing. I did it, but it was a scary thing for an eight-year-old.

I spent my first summer on Mulberry Street. That was a great house. It was a whole different thing. I went in thinking engine or truck and then all of the sudden they stick me in Rescue. I made them one and five. They were all good guys. They treated me great. They put me on the down the first night.

I remember the first few days at Rescue because there was some kind of a call for a lady committing suicide with gas smell. We got there. We forced entry for the cops. It was in a high-rise, so we forced entry with the Rabbit tool. I had the Halligan and there was nobody in the room. So, investigating further I came to a kitchen that had two doors. They were both locked. I opened the door and there was this person covered in sheets. So, I was like, we're not going to let you commit suicide. She had a sheet over her. I turned to tell the cops, "We've got somebody in here." And then next thing, I turn around, she had a hammer in her hand coming at me saying, "Get out of here." She's like, "Don't interrupt me." That was one of my first experiences.

Bartelloni: Our first day was covering the captain's test. It might have been after our first week, that Saturday. They had the captain's test in 1993. So, I went to Truck One on Mulberry Street and it was funny because obviously I didn't know many people on the fire department, but I knocked on the door. They had a dog that attacked me. I'll never forget that dog was growling. Bill Burkhardt was my first experience and he was a nice guy. Introduced me to everybody and I had a good day with them. Then we went back to the Academy and then I went to Five Engine for my first year.

Did I feel welcome when you walked into the firehouse? Absolutely, absolutely. I was just turning twenty-nine years old. I wasn't a kid. But I realized

I don't know anything about this job. So, I came in humble and pretty much maintained that. Trying to learn this job my whole career because you never stop learning.

My first year at Five Engine, I remember that my first experience wasn't a good one. We ran out of water in a building and the fire was going over our heads. Trying to get out of the building, again I'm not on long, I kind of got lost. And I'm thinking this isn't going to turn out well. I grabbed one of the firemen's jackets and said, "Where are we?" Thank God they were close. But sometimes you're new so you just can't remember the lay out of the building. Some of these guys, you could blindfold them. They could tell you what room it is. They're so good at it and they've been doing it. But when you're new, you've got to learn that.

Gail: After the first two weeks in the Academy, they put us into the field because there was a captain's test and they needed bodies in the field because a lot of people were taking the test. They didn't have enough bodies to put on fire trucks, so they put all forty or forty-one of us out in the field. We were only in the Academy a week or two. It was like nothing. I went to Engine Twenty-eight in North Newark. Man, I was green as green can be. Boy, it was funny. Didn't know anything. Went through the day shift and barely anything at all happened. It was a slow day. I don't think there was a fire in the city.

I think they treated me pretty fine. They weren't all buddy, buddy with me, but they didn't know me. It was a lowkey crew. I think it was probably an overtime person and the captain. It was like a skeleton crew because they had a lot of people taking the test. So, the captain didn't have his regular crew anyway. It wasn't like they were all buddy, buddy and I was on the outside. Because the captain probably didn't know the other firefighter that well. So, it wasn't that bad. I don't remember it as being odd.

It was as welcoming as it could be. It was good enough. I was only there for ten hours. They weren't asking me about my life and asking me about my marriage and all the other stuff. Wanting to get to know me, that's for sure. But they were like, yeah, let's get some good lunch. I guess the captain showed me around the truck a little bit. Told me where things were, gave me a couple of instructions. You stay with me and we'll do what we have to do.

Then I was at Engine Six for the summer filling in vacations. A lot of the people in Engine Six I knew from the training. They were at the training, maybe two guys there that were at the training. So, I knew them. And when I came to the tour, they said, "Hey why don't you come over here on a temporary basis." They didn't really have the spot, but they took me on a temporary basis and they made a recommendation to their deputy chief. The deputy chief said, "Sure, we can take him here." So, I kind of got lucky there. I went to a good crew with a good group of people. That's how I got to Engine Six.

After that, I went to Ladder Seven for about two years. Very different. I didn't know any of them, very unfamiliar. Different part of the city, different job. It wasn't a hard transition; it was very different. A whole different outlook. I didn't have the camaraderie there. I was definitely the new person. They were indifferent to me. It wasn't really like the, "Hey, buddy come on over. You'll have a great time." welcoming of Engine Six. Because I knew them prior.

There were a couple of fires there. We did some reckless stuff that I probably wouldn't do if I was not at the age I was. Jumping from roof to roof with the saws and throwing the saws across and cutting holes on multiple buildings. Yeah, the roofs were close, but still, you have all your gear on and all the equipment. And you know if you had to get off the roof, you had to jump back to the other building to get down the ladder. So, it definitely wasn't the safest practice. But the people inside were happy that you cut so many holes because they really felt it. They tell you as soon as you opened up that hole, I really felt it. It felt great. What a relief. So, you definitely had a purpose. It was definitely good team work. Whatever you were doing was usually helping somebody out.

Ostertag: I was at Eighteen for the first six months with Captain Durkin. Then I got bounced by Ronnie Coco. I wasn't assigned there yet. I was just brought there as a new guy. So, the transfer list wasn't out yet. So, he bounced me in January. I got there in September right out of the Academy. January, the transfer list came out or somewhere around that time. So, I went down to Engine Sixteen for six months. And then Chief Lalor called me up and told me there's a spot at Truck Five. And if I would be interested. I said, I would love to. Chief Lalor says, "Okay, well you got it." It was a little different then. "You got it. I'll put your papers in for you." I said, "Alright." So that was 1995, latter part of '95.

The first day I walked into Eighteen Engine, my crew was George Perdon, Cliff Humphrey, and Billy Brownlee. They were very warm and welcoming. And Captain Durkin, he was a little sarcastic, but he was really a great captain. We got along great.

Sixteen Engine wasn't a place that I wanted to be. It's slow. Times were a little different. I mean I was there with one of my classmates, Jeff Dixon. He was bumped down there too. And it was just a little slower pace, older guys there. Guys that just didn't want to do the job. But we made the best of it. Me and Jeff were the new guys. We started cooking. They never cooked down there. We cooked. We actually had a captain, who would always go up to his room. Never come down when we got there. We started cooking. He'd come down and eat with us. Then he'd go back to his room. But there wasn't a lot of enthusiasm down at Sixteen.

I was greeted at Five Truck with a beer. They were still on Irvine Turner Boulevard. I replaced Richie Bennett because he got promoted. So, it was Gary Miller, Jimmy Weiss, Myles McDonald, and Harry Kapinowski. I was greeted with a beer. That's how I was greeted. Very warm, welcoming again, but totally different. These guys went to jobs. They loved the job. They were workers and these guys were tough, but funny, funny guys. And you know what? They always sat around the kitchen table. Always a conversation. They all knew each other's families. The phone would ring. No cell phones then. The payphone or the house line, that was it. Ring, it would be someone's wife. Someone would answer the phone and "Hey how you doing?" Totally different. Everyone knew each other and their families. That's what it was like up there. But I think the whole department was like that back then. That's what I remember about Truck Five. And it was always in the kitchen.

Ramos: I was assigned to Truck Seven right out of the Academy as a probationary firefighter and never left. I never roamed like other firemen. I went there to stay and never left.

We were running all night. At that time, we had a lot of car fires. Besides that, respond to fires, other incidents. We were busy. I think our run count has gone down about maybe 200, 300 runs from that time, if not more.

Walking in the first night, first you're nervous. If you're not nervous, you're lying to yourself. Nervous, could not sleep. I didn't sleep in the firehouse for the first year or so. You don't know what's going on. You're listening; you don't want to miss anything. You don't want to miss a run. But I was happy, proud, all of those things. I was happy to be there, number one. I was nervous, but more happy than anything else.

I was welcomed. I walked in. Captain Payntor was my captain. Love that guy. I walked in. He goes "How are you? My name is Captain Bruce Payntor." Shook my hand. I had my bell cap on. He takes that off. I had my tie on. He took the tie off. He threw it to the ladder. He said, "Relax. Take it easy. You're going to be here a while." He took it from there, so I felt very, very welcome by Captain Payntor.

My most memorable fire is, of course, when I got injured and Mike DeLane God rest his soul, passed away. I had only been on the job three months. It was a job on Chester Street, North Newark. We pulled up to the house. The box came in, I would say, midnight. I never go upstairs to sleep, but I was going upstairs to try and lay down for a little while. As I'm upstairs by the door, the bell comes in. I come right downstairs.

I'm driving. I'm going down Broadway and I see the glow from the building before I make a right-hand turn. So, you could tell the thing was going. I make a right-hand turn onto Chester Street and there was a report of a woman trapped on the second floor. As we pull up, Captain Payton orders, since it's a rescue, to try to get the aerial to the second floor where the lady is supposed to be at. Ron Ballew was with me at the time. As I'm putting the aerial up towards the second floor there were some wires around. They were too low and I say to Ron Ballew, "We can't get the second floor." So, I say, maybe we can go to the roof. So, we go to the roof. We were up there. We were doing our job. We were cutting holes. There was fire from everywhere. It was the kind of fire where's you're in the chimney. There was no break. It was like straight up, all sides. Well, we cut one hole and are in the process of cutting a second hole, when our saw for some reason stopped working. It malfunctioned.

Captain Payntor came up to the roof. He got on the radio and asked for a second K-12. Mike DeLane was the one who brought the K-12 to us on the roof. We cut at least two more holes. And we were ordered to get down. Captain Payntor told me to get down first. So, I'm coming down the aerial. Now to climb up there the aerial was positioned close to a wire. So, we had to get down low so we could pass the wire. I come down and I go down to the wire, as I reach the turntable, I turn around. I hear Mike DeLane call my name to get the K-12. So, I go back up the aerial for the K-12 and that's the last thing I remember. I didn't remember what happened until like two or three days later when it started coming back to me. When I woke up in the ambulance, because I was knocked unconscious by the current, I thought the roof had collapsed. Because it was spongey. That's why I was in an ambulance.

Colin Archer was the EMT that night. I recall when I opened my eyes, his eyes are fixated on mine, looking like, "Are you okay, are you okay?" And then he said who he was. I asked him, "Did the roof collapse?" He goes, "No, you were electrocuted." Next thing I don't remember. I was in and out of consciousness. But that night the lady also passed away at that fire. Mike apparently hit the wire twice from what I was told after the fact. He hit it when we both came in contact with it and then I heard also at one point I guess he lost consciousness or something and hit it again. So, he actually came in contact with the wire twice. That was something that, of course, I will never forget.

Richardson: I was actually first assigned to Rescue One. I was kind of like a rover. They really didn't call it roving back then. Let's put it that way. I was sent to Rescue One on the first tour. Captain Norman Esparolini was my first captain. I had Tommy Melillo, Mike Wells, Steve LaPenta, and Norman Bellina. That was my crew. And I was being moved between Ladder One, Rescue One, and Engine Nine for a couple of months. Then they were going to move me to Engine Twenty-six because they were only one and one. Richie Bauman was the captain up there and Barry Barbera was the only other guy on Twenty-six on the first tour. They were going to bounce me up there because I was the fifth guy on Rescue. They kind of fought to keep me on Rescue. Definitely, they wanted to keep me, but they were like, "No that's not going to happen. You have to go to Twenty-six."

I was up in Twenty-six for a little while. And I would sit there and Captain Bauman would see it in me. I would be sitting there on the couch with the radio in my hand, listening to the calls. Rescue going and all these other companies going. Engine Nine's going out and they got another fire. I think he kind of knew that I wasn't going to stick around. But it was what it was.

Then I got a call one day from John Prachar. He was the captain at Ladder Five on the first tour. He car pooled with Mike Wells. Pete Petrone had just left Five Truck to go down to Special Service before he retired. And Prachar said to me, "Oh, listen, I need a guy. I hear from Mike Wells you're a pretty good guy. Do you want to come down to Five Truck?" And the balls of me, I sat there and said, "Well, you know, I am trying to get to Nine Engine or Five Engine, one of those." He goes, "You kidding me? You'd rather go to Nine Engine or Five Engine than Five Truck?" I go, "Yeah, I guess you're right." He says, "Alright, put your papers in. I'll see what I can do." We were still on the tens and fourteens and that was my days. That was the second day we were going to come in. Then we were going to come in on our nights. So, I came in that following shift. I was going to do my transfer papers and Richie Bauman turns around and takes a memo and throws it across the kitchen table at me. He's like, "I don't know who you know kid, but thanks a lot." What are you talking about? I look at the memo and I was transferred on a memo from Engine Twenty-six to Ladder Five affective the next tour. So, I was like, "Wow, you didn't even make out your transfer papers." The following day shift, I was at Five Truck. Stayed there until I got promoted in 2007. So, I was there for a lot of years.

I walked into the firehouse on Irvine Turner Boulevard. Prachar was your typical Irishman. He had Greg Sereico, John Wilson, and Tony Vanarelli.

It was a dilapidated firehouse at that point. It had been slated for demolition several times. They were going to build us a new firehouse. Prachar would say that, "Yeah, don't get too comfortable. I came on the job in '78 and they told me, 'Don't get too comfortable here because they're going to build us a new firehouse.'" And he left there, came back as a captain and he was still in the same firehouse. It was not the most well-kept.

We were coming in relieving the fourth tour. And it was his uncle that was the captain, Uncle Dan. He was the captain on the fourth tour. He had some big, heavy hitters. He didn't want to know about it. But I guess firehouse life was pretty much what you would expect. It was a bunch of guys. It was a club house, a lot of good fun. The third tour was probably the most rambunctious of the tours. They were the youngest. It was different for me because in Nine Engine there wasn't a lot of the activities. Rescue was very straightlaced. Twenty-six was pretty straightlaced. And when I came there, I saw a different side of the fire department.

But they were knowledgeable. They took me in. Whenever we did get a job, stayed with me and we're never going to get you hurt. Then Twelve Engine was there. Frank Bellina, Billy Boan was the captain. Stevie Giannos, John Paulson, and Frank Odom. That was the crew on the engine. It was a family. It was a good family.

I remember one fire; the fire had gone through the roof already, but we put the stick up anyway and Agoston goes up to the tip of the aerial. There was no roof left. I'm still a new guy, so I'm kind of like following whatever he's saying and he's waving me up, right. I run around. I grab the saw. I put the saw on the turntable. I'm looking at the fire and I go "Wow that's a pretty good fire up there." And John's sitting there waving me up and I'm looking at him, "What?" The fire's coming through the roof. What are we doing? So, I pick up the saw; I'm walking up; and he's laughing at me. He came back down. He goes, "We're not going to even be in this building." So, we set up for ladder pipe operations, but you could mess around and fool around like that because you knew the guy you were working with wasn't going to harm you. I think that was on MLK Boulevard. It was a large three-story, four-story brick. That was pretty funny.

Had another fire my first year at the very end of Irvine Turner Boulevard, they have these little two-story-townhouse, apartment type buildings. It came in and this guy's standing in his doorway, drunk out of his mind and he's trying to stop us from coming in, because it's his apartment. He's going, "You're not coming in here." John Prachar and Billy Boan come up to the door and smoke is just pouring out over this guy's head. It's black, thick, rich smoke. His apartment's on fire. Somewhere in there is on fire. That was a pretty good one.

I don't remember the exact location of the hardest fire that first year, but I remember the fire. The first death, it was a kid. We tried. We just couldn't get in. We were the truck, but the engine couldn't get in. So, I ran, got a line, and bought it up. We were opposing lines. We couldn't get down the hallway to the apartment and they couldn't push far enough up. We took a pretty good beating. Jimmy Weiss was working that night; he was the captain. By the time we pushed far enough down the hall so we could get in, Eleven Truck was coming in the window and handed the kid out. But he was gone. So, that was a tough one. They give you that ribbon. "Hey, you did a good job. Here's a ribbon you can put on your uniform." I took that and I think I might have even thrown that one away. I didn't do my job that day. I didn't get the kid.

Jackson: I went to the fourth tour and I was assigned in Vailsburg which was a selection for me because as a young kid from the city of Newark, my mother was my only parent for most of my life. There really were no male figures in my household that I could really relate to that are doing something positive. Everybody there they had kids my age and I didn't know how they were going to accept me. I'm a black kid from Newark and it was mostly Caucasian men from Newark, most of them. Who had been on the longer than I've been alive, but they embraced me. There was one guy; he was a black guy, Artie Garrett. He laid down the rules for me. What I need to do to gel with everybody and to make it in the department, to have a great career. They said, "Why'd they send this kid here? What are they thinking about? He's not going to learn anything up here. He needs to be down there on the hill learning."

But for me to come on the job new and go to Vailsburg with a bunch of guys who had been around in the '70s, who had twenty-five, thirty years on and who had kids my age. It was a blessing for me to go up there because I didn't get that many lessons on fire, but I got a lot of lessons on life. Every day when I sat at the kitchen table, it was, "Kid, this is what you should do. Kid, don't do what you see us doing. Kid, save your money. Kid, read your books." It was every day was a lesson on life with them.

Then when we did get the fire, I got my first fire on Alexander Street, they said, "Kid, get the tip." They had done it already and that fire station up there was considered the retirement home. There was everything there from horseshoes to gardening to tanning and they had all done it. They were just riding the rest of their career out.

So, I listened to those male figures and they gave me a positive look at this career. They let me know that what I was doing was right by studying. Because most of what I did up there was just read books about the job, the general orders. I would listen to them. "Kid, don't buy a car, buy a house." Guys like Richie Heinze. Guys like Captain Tokanos. Guys like Captain Al Mauriello. These guys did a lot. When I did buy my first house, my boiler was cracked. And who came there? Al Alfano, who's a plumber, brought his crew. They came over and fixed my boiler for me. It was a real, real enlightening experience for me. Then when I had an opportunity, I would take all the details. They were happy because I would go down to busier firehouses. I would get lessons on life up here and I would go down to Ninth Street, Seven Engine and get experience on the job. And I eventually transferred down there to Seven Engine.

I went to Seven Engine for a long stent and when I came back, my captain said let someone else take the details because he didn't want to be short. I asked the chief if I could get detailed down there permanently because the person was out long term. I guess the chief brought it to my captain's attention and he didn't want me to leave. They were short one day and I think my captain was out and I did take the detail down there. The chief for some reason said I'm going to leave you down there. And I wound up staying down there, put my papers in for it, and I got the position. My captain wasn't happy. He called me, "Hey, you didn't like it up here?" I liked it, but I told him, I want to learn the job.

He didn't understand at first, but we still talk now. He has called me every single birthday since I've been on this job. Every birthday we talk. We're supposed to meet for breakfast or lunch one day at Topp's Diner. He always goes there.

One of the most memorable experiences that I had as a young firefighter was a fire we had on Norfolk Street. It was an abandoned building we rode by many times. It was a three-story wood frame, but it was next to a three-or-four-story ordinary construction building. There probably was not even a foot clearance between the two of them. It was in the evening. We were on tens and fourteens, and I think we were coming to the end of our shift. It was like five o'clock and this box came in. We get there and it was ripping. This is when working together, knowing each other, and all coordinating paid off.

One guy was up on the deck pipe on the main fire building, trying to keep it from getting into the exposure on the delta side which is the occupied structure. And me and the captain went to that structure to make sure everybody was out of the upper floors. The first-floor apartment was rolling from the front door to the back door. This is one of my first fires like this. I'm on the tip, me and the captain, and we went from the front door all the way to the back. In the kitchen the fire was pushing through the window. This is how it got in this structure from the exposure building. So, it was a matter of coordination, making sure that the exterior team out there grabbed a hand line. They were trying to keep it from extending, putting out a lot of fire in the main building as companies came. Keeping it from constantly going from the main fire building to the exposure. So, we trusted in one another and me and the captain went in. We went from front to back until we didn't see anything else. We had only one thing and we put it out.

You come out; you feel good. The adrenalin was flowing. You get through it. You don't know, you might not come back out. That all goes through your mind, but you look back, you're like, "Man, I really went in there and did this?" Then you come out and see the exposure about to collapse and you see how much building you saved. And you have the chiefs telling you, "You guys did a good job."

Y. Pierre: I did not feel welcome at all walking into the firehouse. I felt very uncomfortable. It's not like in the service, fifty guys walk in to the squad bay and everybody instantly becomes friends. It wasn't like that. It was more like, we're going see what this guy's is all about, trying to get a feel of you. You're trying to get a feel of them. Meanwhile the first time someone says something that you feel is out of line, you say to yourself, "You know what? I'm not going to like this guy. We're not going to get along." But the ice starts to melt a little bit. And then you start to work with the guy. Then it gets better, it gets better. It got better.

My first assignment was at Ladder Eight. My first day in the firehouse, I walked in. I had my bag. I was in uniform and the guys were cracking a joke. They asked me if I was lost. I said, "No I don't think so." You're new on the job. You really don't know what's going on. So, you figure now maybe I'm in the wrong place. What am I doing here? And then they said, "No you must be lost because we don't have any new guys coming in this house." And then as I'm sitting there talking, the captain walked into the room. So, I looked at the captain and I let him know I'm firefighter Pierre reporting for duty. He says, "Oh, Pierre, I've been expecting you." I'm like, "Oh, my God. I'm at the right place." I thought I had to go find another place, but the captain said, "You're in the right place." They showed me my bunk, showed me upstairs, walked me around the rig, taught me different things about the rig. "Okay, this is going to be different. It's not like training anymore. This is the real thing." And I remember he said, "Now the training begins."

I didn't know what he meant and then we finally went to a car fire. I was so afraid. The car fire was in the garage. The garage was a brick garage. It was nice and hot, but when the heat was coming back at me, I'm thinking to myself, this is way too hot. I don't need to be going in there. And my captain said, "Now Yves get closer to the car, put the fire out." I'm like, "Aren't we close enough?" I must have been like, maybe thirty feet from the car. Not aware of what I got myself into still. He says, "No you got to go to the car." Now I'm trying to get very close to the car. And I heard the first tire blow. Oh my God, I almost dropped the line and just took off for home. My captain said, "Yves, it was just a tire. It's okay, relax. The fire's going to go out. Just keep water on it." As he's talking to me, I'm saying to myself, maybe it's not that bad. The fire starts to go out a little bit and I'm like, it worked. The water really worked when you put it on fire. That was my first day, my first fire. It was a car fire and I was devastated.

Farrell: My first assignment was Engine Twenty-six, tour two. I loved it. Two of my closest friends were up there. They had just gotten on the job the class before me. They had a spot opening, so I was able to get that spot. Back then you really pretty much got plugged in and assigned because they were so low on numbers that the classes they were hiring didn't rove. You got plugged into a spot because there were a lot of spots out there. Brian Donnelly is my captain and we had a good crew. We had a really good crew actually up there. Think about it. We had Eddy Haran on the truck. Brian Donnelly on Twenty-six. Billy Melodic and Mike Lubertazzi were up there with us. And you just had some really good firemen up there.

Unfortunately, back then the Burg was a little slow so you didn't go to as many fires. But you still learned the job and I think I learned how to be a fireman first rather than how to fight a fire. There are two aspects to this job. How to fight a fire and how to be a fireman. They're not totally different things. They're intertwined, but you really need to learn to be a fireman and act like a fireman, your mentality. You being a fireman mentality. And then you have to put that into your hands-on in a fire building. You learn how to be a fireman by looking at guys like Eddy Haran and Carl Pinal and even guys like Brian Donnelly, Tommy Mastroeni. Those are the guys that taught me the job. Not so much by sitting down and saying this, this, and this. But taught by example.

I can remember my first fire. It was actually a move up. Brian was aggressive. Brian wanted to go to fires. The minute they banged a signal eleven, he got on the hotline and he'd say, "We'll take a move up." My first fire was on Central Avenue. It was a move up. We moved up to Eleven Engine. On the way there, they banged the second alarm. Brian had already called available as Eleven Engine. Boom, we were the first ones in the door. Second floor, it was me, Brian, and Mike

Lubertazzi. And it was going good. It was a nice little job. It was a nice way to get your feet wet.

Roberson: First day in the firehouse I was nervous and excited at the same time. I call it nervous issues. Just bring your gear to the firehouse and just experience it. At the company I went to I met this fellow; his name is Joe McMillian. Joe Mac was my buddy. He was a gentleman at all times and a true professional. He taught me pretty much everything I know about this job. Always keep a steady polish, stay on top of your game, you know what I mean. That's why we never took anything for granted. So, every day we read, we talked fires, we worked with the rigs, the trucks and everything. I knew the truck like the back of my hand, all the appliances and things that go on the truck. And just being a gentleman, being a professional. Knowing that this is not a club house. It's not a playground. You're a professional and the public looks at you that way, as a professional. So, it's part of being a public servant.

I actually caught a fire my first day on the job. We caught a fire at one o'clock in the morning. It was an occupied structure, so you're going in there to actually use what you learned in the Academy. Put your skills to work. That was a big thing. I always tell people, it may sound bad, but in order to practice our profession, we need fires because that's our profession. That's how we practice our skills, at a fire. You just can't fire fight in the books. You have to put the work in.

At that fire, first you had to stay with the captain. He made sure I was right behind him. "Stay behind me." I'm like, "I'm right behind you, cap. Let's go to work." As we were taught, as you approach the fire you do your size up. Listen to the radio. We heard it's a three-story frame building. The fire is on the second floor and it's occupied. As soon as we're on the scene, sure enough, fire is on the second floor, blowing out the window. So, as a truck man, part of our job is to team up with the engine guys so we can open up the walls and the windows of this apartment and they can put water on the fire. The philosophy as you fight the fire is you've got to get relief for that truck and engine. It doesn't look good to put water on a fire without the room being vented. If not, you're going to get burnt from all the steam. So, it was a great experience going in and nobody got hurt, thank God. We actually pulled a couple of people out of there. It was a great experience.

Meier: I was first assigned to the Rescue Squad. I was never in that firehouse, so you feel butterflies. It's the big guys. Walking into the firehouse, I can only compare it to being a freshman in high school and being a senior in high school. When you're a freshman in high school, you walk in the door and you've got big goo-goo eyes and you've got guys that you know were through the '70s and '80s and are at their retirement age. They've seen the wars years and they've got all that experience.

I knew a couple of the faces in the firehouse. I walked in and they started showing us around the rig and kind of getting us oriented within the firehouse and then the alarm came in and we went to work. So, it was good. The first night we worked, my first hour I had a motor vehicle accident with entrapment and a two-alarm fire, so by eight o'clock I had gotten that done. Got my first fire in.

Rodrigues: My first assignment was Nineteen Engine on the fourth tour and my captain back them was Captain Jimmy Wendt. Excellent guy, excellent captain. I learned a lot from him and I went to a lot of fires back then. My first fire with Nineteen Engine was in Chancellor Avenue. I still remember. And the same night we caught another job. We were second due engine. It was in Chancellor Avenue further out. Right out of Academy, a little scared back then.

Captain Wendt used to call me Mighty Mouse because back then I was a little bigger. "I'm going to be behind you. Just make sure you do what you have to do. Don't be scared. Everything is going to be okay." Guess what, I was a little scare, but I did what I had to do. If I remember it was a two and a half story wood frame.

The fire was on the second floor, going pretty good, exposure coming out of the windows. I stretched with Salvatore Lombardo. He was another new guy. He came on like a month before me, the class of June 1996. We went up the stairs, at the top we masked up. I looked at Captain Wendt. He said "Go ahead." I just said a prayer and I went up there and we put it out. It was an exciting night. Very exciting, I was a young kid. I was only twenty-seven back then. I said this is what I want to do for the rest of my life. And I keep saying the same thing. If I'm born again, I want to be a fireman again.

Montalvo: My first assignment was Engine Twenty-seven tour four. I was there for about six months. And then I transferred over to Truck Ten. I spent a total of eight years there. And then I got stuck in the racial bias transfers where they moved guys to break up the makeup of companies so they weren't all one ethnicity. So, I got stuck in that transfer. Wound up doing that for about a year. Wound up going to Truck One. After that year, I found out there was an opening here at Engine Ten and I've been here ever since.

Walking into the firehouse was definitely an experience. Being a new guy. Being a red ass. Besides, they could tell we were kind of excited about coming into the job. We wanted to do a lot. But I actually had a bunch of old salts that pretty much were getting ready to retire. My captain had less than six months to go and the other guys that were there had maybe a year or two left on the job. So, it was interesting because you really didn't go out and do too much training. They didn't want to do any training or anything like that. It was like, "Hey listen we'll teach you the job as it comes along." But as you know, Down Neck was kind of close, so we really didn't get much.

My captain sort of led the way as I started going through the process of testing and meeting more guys. We were told, "Hey listen, you come on the job, don't tell anybody who you know. Don't tell anybody who you're related to because some people might not like him. So, just learn the job, do your job and that's it." The first couple of years that's all you're supposed to do.

At my first fire, I had the tip and a lot of guys were looking at me like. "What are you doing with the tip?" They didn't want to grab it, so I grabbed it. All I remember is I pulled out of the rig and the chief said, "Get a line there." Our guys weren't really moving too fast, so I said, "Okay." And I grabbed the tip and went in. And they caught up with me later on. I caught two jobs with them. The first one was a three bagger on Malvern Street. And that was pretty much a surround and drown for us with a two and a half. The second we used an inch and three quarter, I got the tip on that, too.

Then I went to Truck Ten. I got moved over. I got set up with Richie Dixon, Kevin Mitchko, Glen Cassidy and Robert Bowie. And these guys they used to like to go out and show me. They used to love to take me out. Okay let's go. Let's put the ladder up. This is what you do up on a roof. This is how you do it. This is how you search. So, they enjoyed the fact that they had a new guy and they enjoyed teaching. From what I can feel working with them, they enjoyed teaching me stuff. This is what we do. This is how we do it. I stayed there for eight years.

Willis: My first assignment was Engine Twenty-one in Vailsburg, the Burg. I went there right off the bat. Walking in was an adventure. First day walking in I had Captain Al Brand, Al Mauriello, and God bless his soul, Harry Tokanos. The man cared about this job and cared about the men. Al Brand was a great guy too. Harry was the disciplinary. Harry was the teacher. Harry was a good guy. He died young. But my experience was walking in the firehouse. They walked me around. Captain Brand brought me to the rig. Showed me my place. Then I went in the kitchen and washed my hands. I was told to join in and help. So, I turned around and put my hands into the bowl of barbeque sauce and ribs without it cooking.

I got an earful. And it wasn't pleasant. And I'm like, "Why are you talking to me like that? I'm not no little kid. I'm a father with children." He pulled me to the side and he asked me, "Did you wash your hands?" And I went, "Yes. I washed my hands and I wanted to help you." He apologized to me. He goes, "Whenever you're doing anything, make sure you wash your hands." This is the kind of guy Harry was, but he was a strict guy and I think he was showing he was the boss. I was a little upset about it at the moment and as time went by you realize, you're going to a fire. There's no room. No joking and this guy made sure that you knew what you were doing. He wanted you to learn the right way. He taught us the right way. I wasn't on the truck. He was the truck captain. But I would go over and learn the truck as I was learning the engine. That's the kind of guy Harry was. Miss him. I miss the guy. I mean they had a big crew, fifteen of us. We had a freak show up there.

All the guys were good. Turn around and some of my guys left firehouses to come up and work with me because we had such a good crew. Time went by and of course I moved on to a busier company. Went to Seventeen Engine. Had a good time there too. Got to meet new people. Diverse, I was the only white, Al Fleming, Al Brooks, John Brown, and me. I had a good crew. We got our fires. We got our share working in Irvington and Newark, working up on the border there. Eighteen and Seventeen worked together, hand in hand. We had fun. That's my experience in the firehouse. The guys were great to me. Treated me well. They poked at each other in fun. We had a good time and they taught me a lot. Taught me that everybody can get along. It was nice.

Twenty-one at the time was the Squirt. So, I got to learn the Squirt which was interesting, more than just an engine, with raising the ladder pipe and everything. I was pretty good. Within three months I was driving back then. Now I don't think they'll allow anybody behind the wheel for six months. You got to be on one year before you get certified. I got certified, I believe, in three months. And I was pretty good at it. Pretty good at pumping. I did my job. I can't say I was a super firefighter. But I did my job.

My first fire is the one I'll always remember. I was thirty-two turning thirty-three, one month on the job. And I remember the alarm going off. It was about twelve o'clock at night and it was Madison Avenue, end of Madison down by Clinton. I just don't remember the cross street. I remember leaving the Burg. Now you know how far Madison is from the Burg. All I saw was the sky lit up orange. And I went, "Ut-oh. This is not good." So, on the rig we rode outside at the time. The lights glaring, the siren going, panicking a little with confusion because you don't know what you're getting into the first time. Pulling up on that scene and we have a giant H shaped building fully involved. It was going and I'll never forget, I saw Ten Engine with Pauly Bartelloni walking on the edge of the roof and this thing was going. He was setting up a two-and-a-half.

I'll never forget Captain Brand fighting with the Chief Higginson. Yelling at him because he yelled at us to pull up to the building and dump water on with the two-and-a-half. I set it up and I'm holding the two-and-a-half. Our rig got stuck in the mud. We were in the mud. We got it out, but we had a fence stuck under the rig. My captain flipping out on Higginson saying we're too close to the fire. The wall is buckling. They're fighting with each other. We just moved out of the way and the whole side of the building came down. Right where I was and the thought went in my mind, "What did I get myself into? Why didn't I stay in Port Newark?" At the time, it's your first fire. To see something like that, that's rare for your first one.

I remember Paul Bartelloni, Tommy Mastroeni. and Captain Cook. Tommy Cook was my friend and neighbor Down Neck. Later on, I went up to Captain Cook and he introduced me. I said, "Man, you were walking on the edge of that roof." Paul said, "Don't worry, you'll get your turn." We played ball together, me and Paul Bartelloni, so we knew each other off the job.

Freese: My first assignment was on the third tour at Sixteen Engine. I liked the guys. It was very old school. The captain had his time to go if he wanted to. He was really old school. And my first night. It was a night actually, a fourteen-hour night. I was sitting at the kitchen table after dinner and a buddy of the captain passes by. He brings a couple of beers and my heart started racing. He put a couple of beers on the table and the captain says, "Here kid, have a beer." And I was like, "Oh no cap, I'm good. Thank you so much." Meanwhile my heart is beating so fast. I got a big lump in my throat. I didn't know what to do. He says, "No, kid, have a beer." "No, really cap, I'm good, really. Really." "It's an order. Have the beer." So, I did it. He gave me an order. I had the beer and then I walked away and I waited until they were pretty much done. And that was my first night. We didn't have any runs that night. It was pretty crazy.

I absolutely felt welcomed. I remember there was Jim Kupko, the captain, myself, and Paul Reilly. Paul Reilly was a really nice guy. As soon as I came, he made me feel welcome. He showed me around the firehouse. He showed me around the rig. He showed me how to pump. He showed me the tools. He was always working with me. He said, "Kid, if we get a job, I need somebody that knows what they're doing. You and I are going to be working together." And he made me feel really welcomed. He was an old North Newark guy, like myself. But I didn't like the assignment simply because it was a little slow. I was brand new and I wanted to be a little busier and be more aggressive and see fire, but it was a great experience. I was there for just over a year until I was able to put papers in for a transfer. I apologized to my captain. I said, "Nothing personal, cap, but I want to get a little busier and I put my papers in." From there I ended up going to Truck One on the first tour.

One Truck was Haz-mat, but I didn't mind. It's something new. It was a new certification. It was something different other than firefighting. It was emergency service as well. And actually, I was kind of interested in it. I figured it would make me that much busier. It was a different world. The culture was totally different. A lot busier, more focused, guys more into the job. Wanting to run, wanting to go to fires. There's more of a brotherhood. The cooking and eating together. Families, meeting each other's families and having yearly Christmas parties and stuff like that. Yeah, it was a whole different world and it was great.

Actually, I caught a few jobs with Sixteen, but the one job that I'll never forget was over there on Brill Street. We were first due; I took the first line in. There were three story row houses and we took the first line up to the third floor on the main fire building. There was a lot of fire, but the fire had already spread to the apartment next door, it went into the cockloft, and then it went into the exposure, A and B already. So, by the time our battalion chief and deputy got there they had an emergency evacuation. So, we evacuated and regrouped and made another attempt with the interior attack. And we found two little girls that died in the apartment right next door to where I took the first line in. So, that's one reason I'll never forget. I didn't know they were there. But the main body of fire was in the apartment I took the line into. And not only that, at the time I had two little girls almost the same exact ages as the two little girls that perished in that fire. I kind of dealt with it pretty good that night. It was my first fatality and my first big job. But the next morning, when the newspapers came out, it had the picture of the two little girls. That's when it started messing with me a little bit. I went home and hugged my daughters. I'll never forget that. I did catch a couple of jobs with Sixteen Engine. It wasn't much, but when we did it was usually a significant job.

2000s: A New Millennium, A New Department

Capt. Highsmith: My first real assignment was Engine Twelve, tour three. When I walked into the firehouse, they treated me pretty well. It was a tough day. Because the original captain was sick, so they sent another captain from Vailsburg. And it was his first permanent day there. He welcomed me and told me he's going to teach me everything he knows. It's a great job. And then Chief Carter showed up and the first thing he told me was, "I don't know who you know, but this is my God damned battalion." There was a beef going on between him and Planning that I did not know anything about. So, Planning sent me there. After the first five minutes, we got along well.

I was working under firefighter Don Alexander. He was acting captain for me for about a year. We were in Twelve Engine. There really wasn't much housework because the house was in such bad shape. But they did drill me and train me properly because I was the weak link. I had the greatest guys, Don Alexander, Mike Gibbons, Ray Rivera, me, and then the captain. I was the weak link. But they brought me up to speed.

As a fireman, in my early years, the projects were still standing and we had a fire on the twelfth floor. And I'm running up with everybody else and I got my donut roll and the project bag. I was slow getting up and when I got to the top all I could do was throw the gear down and lean up against the wall. And the guys put the fire out. It takes some time to build up to that. You don't run kid, you walk.

John Agoston one night was detailed to us. He told me we're gonna die together. I said, "Okay, we're gonna die together." And sure as anything, we had a bad job. Chief Carter ordered me out. I said, "I'm not leaving without my partner. You get him out, I'll leave." And he argued with Chief Carter. Finally Chief Carter got him to leave. We had to go through a window, slide across an icy roof, and pray that we catch the ladder. We caught it. We went down and after that Chief Carter told me John would never work on our tour again.

Carr: When I came on the old timers were like, "Hey, kid, how you doing? You sit over there. You shut up and when we need you, we'll call you." But it was basically, get yourself together. Put your gear around. Check all my equipment. Make sure I can identify all the appliances and tools on the rig. It was learning all the nuances, making sure you knew what the running assignments were, pay attention to that. Know exactly where you're going. If you know the area, don't be afraid to give anybody input about where they're going. "You stay right the F where I'm at. Stay right under me, don't you go no F-ing where. I tell you, if I got to look for you, there's going to be a problem." That terminology basically is what it was. I'm just giving it to you as raw as I can. But that environment is very endearing for the most part because it's tough love. They want to make sure that I get home to my family the next day.

At first, I roved on the third tour for a year. And my deputy chief at the time was Chief Rydzewski. I roved all over. I went to every firehouse in the city at the time except for Nine Engine and Nineteen Engine. Then when I got assigned to the second tour, I was supposed to be at Twelve Engine, but at the last minute somebody had a bigger hook than me, ended up going to Twelve Engine.

I roved when I got assigned to the second tour. And I had to go to Twenty-six Engine. So, I was at Twenty-six Engine with Al Carlucci, Anthony Campbell, Carl Pinal senior, and Tommy Condito. That's when Bernie Snyder came up, "Yeah, I'm going to send you somewhere busier. Lucky for you, Colin Archer broke his leg at a fire. So, we're going to send you down to Rescue." So, I was at Rescue for a little while with Joe D'Alise, Steve Ciasullo, Phil Martinez, and Frank Fonseca.

When my time was up at Rescue, they sent me back to the Burg and that's when Phil Manno had come up to the Burg. I was there for a while and then I left there and went to Six Engine.

When you walk into a new firehouse, you talk to the other guys. And they bring you into this room. This is Captain such and such. And then he looks at you. So, you're such and such. Okay, well kid, listen to this guy. They had a hierarchy.

The senior man was like your supervisor for the most part. He would take you around, show you everything. And then the captain was like, "Did he show you this?" "Yes, he did." "Good job. Alright so now what I need you to do, stay with me. If we get a job, you don't do anything but what I tell you to do." That's it. It was an understanding where you had the senior man. The senior man told you what it is and then you had the captain to make sure that he told you what it was and you just did what you were supposed to do. Where the captain had a well-trained unit, that was already instilled. I think most of those guys basically were getting ready to be first line supervisors themselves.

My first fire was when I came back from my honeymoon. I went down to Ladder Five and we had a fire on the corner of Court Street and MLK which was coincidentally across the street from the church that held Lawrence Webb's funeral. That was my first fire and it was with Captain Weiss. When we went inside the building, we took our Halligans and hit the ceiling and we both said, "Oh, sugar-honey-ice-tea." Tin ceilings. It was tin ceilings. That was my first job. My first job on an engine company, I was with Seventeen Engine and Marcus Johnson was the one that was always grabbing the tip. He got stuck a little bit trying to do something and I grabbed the line. I ran up to the second floor and had a limp line and was up there all by myself. They didn't realize I was moving so fast. Chief Carter came up. Now he got the line so we worked the line. I didn't really start getting more cautious until I got more time on the job. The one thing that was told to me was, the job's most dangerous at the beginning when you know nothing and at the end, when you think you know it all.

Rosario: First assignment, well for the first year they had us roving. So, roving, they had me do Ladder Eleven out of Ninth Street. I was there for two months and then I got sent to Engine Nine. Then I got pulled out of Nine and put into Administrative Services because myself and another fireman and two cops got put in for a competition on the Today Show.

So, for three months all we did was come into work and train. You know physically and with equipment, police and fire. We did that for three months and then we did this competition. We made it to the finals on the Today Show. It was the Bravest and Finest competition. We went up against Detroit, Worchester, Mass, and Phoenix, Arizona. That was a real nice feather in my cap when you first come to the service. Got a lot of guys breaking my balls because of it, but it was a great thing. I got out of there, went back to Engine Nine for a while and then got sent to Sixteen Engine. Was at Sixteen Engine for about a month and then they asked for my request, where I wanted to go. I wanted to go to Ladder One. I got sent to Ladder One, so my first real captain was Captain DeCuester, who is now Battalion Chief Five for the third tour.

My first day in the firehouse I was lucky. We caught a fire on Broad Street. Actually, it was the barber shop on Broad Street and Market Street. Signal eleven. It was just a smoky fire and it was the first time I met the guys from Truck One. Dean Gotti wasn't there at the time, but Mike Popik, and John Dugan were there and DeCuester. The crew from Sixteen took me over there and introduced me to them. "Hey, this is the probie you guys are picking up." They're all saying, "Get ready. We're waiting for you, got all your stuff set up. Soon as you come in, just get ready, we're going to run."

Of course, I brought donuts and bagels because you never come in empty handed to a new firehouse. So, from the minute I get in there, they just showed me around the firehouse, started teaching me. The big thing was Haz-mat because Ladder One and Rescue One were the Haz-mat team. So, you were dual hatted. You did fire suppression for most times and then whenever they needed you, you would go as the Haz-mat team. So, our focus was to get me ready to go to Haz-mat school, finish that, and become part of the Haz-mat team. And driving all the different vehicles because with the Haz-mat team you have the two different vehicles you have to drive.

Kupko: I had that "in" with my father being on the job. We overlapped for two and a half years together. So, certain days, lunch breaks in the Academy, some of the guys would gravitate towards me because my father would invite me over for lunch. And guys wanted to get into the firehouse and see what it was like before they actually got into the firehouse for real. So, that was nice to have when I first came in the door.

The people who knew my father were going to bust my balls a little bit harder. I think he had a fair level of respect amongst his peers on the job, so there's a certain expectation that I felt as if I had to live up to. There's pressure coming on the job feeling I don't want to embarrass my father. He was always stern when I was growing up with things like that. So, I didn't want to disappoint him, basically, is what it came down to. He was my role model growing up. I was his shadow, walking in his shoes. He could really do no wrong in my eyes, so I just wanted to live up to his expectations. Make him as proud as I could.

When we came out of the Academy, it was an election year. Sharpe James had the citywide initiative where he wanted everyone to ride around on the rigs. So, they bounced us around quite a bit. When we first came out, we were roving initially. My first stop was with Donny Volkert at Twenty-six Engine. I was there for about a month. Then I went to Four Truck with George Jorda. I was there for two or three months. And then there was an injury in the field at Ten Engine. They moved me over to Ten Engine and I was there for the remainder of that year. I believe about eight or nine months. Before I finally landed in my first official assignment which was back at Four Truck on the fourth tour.

We weren't very busy down there, maybe we did 1200 runs a year. So, your average quota for a day was maybe three or four runs. You could have days where you didn't turn a wheel at all and there were days where you went out six or seven times. Being in the Ironbound section, the fire load was down for the most part. But I did catch a few jobs down there. I did learn from George at the time. He wasn't going to go out of his way. He was ready to retire, so he couldn't go out and show you everything, but if I asked him to take me out and work on X, Y, Z, whatever the case may have been, he never told me to go screw. He was always accommodating in one way, shape, form, or another. Earlier in the day was better than later in the day.

Memorable fires, one was in, I want to say Lorsack Furniture. Which was right off of Ferry Street. Just the proximity of it, the hustle and bustle of that area of the city which is constant action at all times. Probably one of the first major incidents that I got. I had only been on the job for a year. It was a large facility, a lot of fire load in there. Mattresses up in the cockloft area, all kinds of furniture, cloth, leather couches, wood dining room tables. So, that was a pretty extensive job. I had the opportunity to work on the roof and inside. And when you came out of that building, it was almost like you were putting on a rock concert. There were three or four hundred people on the sidewalk watching what you were doing. It was in the middle of a work day. Everything just kind of grinds to a halt. And people tend to focus their attention on you.

Another one I can remember, I believe it was Elm Street, noon fire. Again, when I was still in the Ironbound section. It was in illegal apartments built above a garage in the rear of the house. And the extent of the fire wasn't evident when we pulled up. It wasn't like you could see flames lapping out of windows and down the block. But when we got in front of the structure, it became evident there was an issue in there. Right away it was brought to our attention that there was an elderly gentleman that rented out the apartment and lived in the apartment. So, immediately that life safety hazard came to mind. We made our way to the building, did a primary search, couldn't locate him. Fourteen Engine for some reason got there first that day. I remember them having the initial line into the building. And after they had knocked the fire down, the firefighter on the tip was actually laying on top of the gentleman that was renting the apartment. He didn't even realize it. He just thought it was an ottoman or something that he was on in the middle of the room. The victim had basically melted into the floor. That was my first encounter with death in the fire service. So, that left a firm impression that it's not just fun and games that you're going in to.

Mickels: My first day at the firehouse was on Mount Prospect, Ladder Six. I was very nervous. Most of the guys there were hospitable. "How you doing?" The captain showed me where to go, where to put my gear, how to check my mask, things like that. He showed me the way he wanted me to do things. It was very new to me. Especially the night, the fourteen-hour night came with sleeping in the firehouse. Back then we didn't sleep in the firehouse until we got out of the Academy. Now, I think what they're doing with the guys in the Academy is they're giving them some experience sleeping overnight in the firehouses. I think the last class did that. So, I was a little nervous sleeping with other people in the same room in expectation of something to happen, the bell to hit. So, it was nerve racking. I believe we did have a call after midnight, so that was new. I was so nervous I couldn't sleep anyway. But just to get on the truck, watching everybody moving fast and it was just so chaotic. It was all very nerve racking to me, but I think that's normal. And I wanted to do well. Did I feel welcome? Yes, I did.

Most of the old timers were very supportive. Some of them didn't want to be involved or talk to the new recruits. It was the old school mentality. Don't talk to me. You're new on the job. You don't know anything. So, some of them shied away from us and some of them actually took us under their wing to train us. Treated us like we were regular people. Some again chose to wait some years before they even wanted to talk to us or deal with us. But that was that mentality back then, very old school mentality. We had quite a few different types of personalities, characters. But most of them were very experienced men.

Gaddy: I did rove for six months and I had to go to Summer Avenue to Nine Engine. And it was raining, I mean storming raining outside. And they were saying that they had to do housework. I really didn't know any better at the time. I'm coming over there. It's my first-time roving. I was never hazed or anything like that before. And these guys are telling me that I had to go and clean the windows inside and outside. So, I'm outside in storming rain and I'm cleaning windows and I'm saying to myself, "This doesn't make any sense. This can't be right." And no one comes out there. They had me out there the whole time. And then I was like, "Am I done?" "No, you're not." So, I then took the matter up to the chief. I'm still a rookie. I can't go off on them right now. So, I know this is not right and I have no change of clothes. They have the air on. I'm freezing. So, I sat up there for a while until I couldn't take it anymore. And I went and I told Chief Kirkland. He went down and let them know, no more hazing, there will be no more hazing. So, the four tours that I did over there, I did about a month over there. I was disturbed by them. And that always stuck out with me. So, any new guys I don't do hazing. I don't call you red ass, I don't do any of that. I like to teach. I like to show.

My first permanent assignment, was Ladder Ten. Ten actually was Ladder Nine. Really. They browned out Ladder Ten. They then opened Ladder Nine with the same guys that were on Ladder Ten.

I got my first fire in two weeks. So, it was quite busy. I met a kid, Ray Martinez. He was the reason I came over to Ladder Ten. He was in a motorcycle accident shortly after I got on with him. And that kind of messed me up right there. So that made me not want to be at Ladder Ten. He was the reason why I was there. You get that connection with someone when you get on and he was the younger guy, the fun guy, and then you had the two older guys who were Carl Carpenter and Fuquan Straum and they were pretty much like the older brothers, the no nonsense. Then I had Chief Adams as my captain, he wasn't even in at that time. Ray Martinez and Fuquan Straum and Carl Carpenter on my second day, they hit the bell like ding ding ding like we got a run. And I get up running. Leave my sneakers and everything, running and they're all there laughing.

When I got assigned to Eighteen, I remember seeing Dane Rispoli, "Cousie" and when I saw him, I was like, Cous. That was kind of the ice breaker. I actually brought in donuts like they suggested. It was kind of a waste because nobody eats it. They already have their own stuff and Cous was, "Oh, you didn't have to bring that." He kind of put me under his wing and from that day on I was under his wing and being taught. So, that was my first day coming in. He sent me up to Chief Jackson, who was a captain at the time. He told me what he expected of me and what was expected of this job and he asked me something in regards to what I want in the next six years. I guess he was putting that battery in my back, being a captain, a minority captain on this job. You didn't see that at one time and now you're starting to see an influx of them along with Puerto Ricans. Of course, him being a black officer at that time and having me come from the Weequahic section where he came from, he already instilled that into me. I wasn't thinking about that at the time. I was just thinking about my first job and was I going to catch anything. I just kind of took that advice and put it on ice for a while, maybe three years and learnt the ropes of being a fireman. I then put the battery in my back and started going forward with wanting to be a captain and thinking like a captain. Yeah, my first day was pretty much easy.

I got one memorable fire that always will stick out. It was the fire that was on Norwood Street. And it was when we lost four or five kids, three adults. I think we had maybe eight, nine bodies. We pulled on the scene and went down a one way. You could see the fire pretty much going as you're coming out of the firehouse. You see the cloud of smoke. So, we were pretty aware of where we had to go and the area it was at. When we got there, the whole entire second floor, third floor was going. We run down to Engine Eleven who was in front of the house at the time and we were taking off inch and three quarters, four lengths.

The father of the kids came up to me and was stating that he left his kids in the house. We couldn't understand how he and his girlfriend/wife got out of the house, but left the kids there. When he said that to me, I just felt empty because I just knew they were gone. So, we tried and tried and tried, but the fire burnt all the way, completely down. We had exposure problems that were very heavily engulfed, the side of the house that was the exposure side on the B side started to fall on the D side of the main fire building which impaired us from making any type of extension toward the second floor. We tried to go through the first floor to go up the back, but that pretty much fell down and started collapsing. So, we had to pull out and go on defensive mode. And then we noticed that the exposure on the B side of the main fire building started to catch. We had to go into the exposure which was also occupied and evacuate people out of there. But the thing that sticks out most is the kids. When doing overhaul, you step on them and they pretty much were like unrecognizable. That's one fire that sticks with me.

Jenkins: My first assignment out of the Academy was roving. Didn't have a permanent assignment, but the first place I was sent to out of the Academy was Engine Twenty-eight on the first tour. When I walked in, I did feel welcomed. At the time I walked in, the captain was very friendly. They all made me feel very comfortable. I was at Twenty-eight for about two months. Then I went to Ladder Six. And I was there for about two months then I went from Ladder Six to Engine Nine. I was at Engine Nine for another two months and then I got sent to the Fourth Battalion with Ladder Nine. From Ladder Nine, I went to Engine Twelve and from Engine Twelve I went to Seventeen. My first permanent assignment out of the Academy was Engine Sixteen on the first tour.

For me it was very busy. For some reason these companies that I arrived in started catching fires. My first day at Twenty-eight, as soon as I walked in the door and sat down, talking to the guys, full assignment, second due at a fire. When I went to Ladder Six, we had a fire. The same when I left Ladder Six and went to Engine Nine, the second shift at Engine Nine, caught a fire. When I left there, as soon as I walked into Ladder Nine, introduced myself to the captain, had a working fire, first due. The first time I went to the roof. And at that time, at that fire, we didn't put the aerial up. So, we had to carry a ground ladder around the back, help push the ground ladder. Go up and cut the roof, me and Firefighter Al Taylor had that job. And then after that, Twelve Engine, I didn't catch any jobs. But when I went to Ten Engine, I caught quite a few jobs. Then when I got to Sixteen Engine, everybody says it's a slow house, but for some reason we were never not working that often. There were more factory fires than anything else down there.

I remember a fire when I was at Ten Engine. We were one and two. I was new on the job, caught a fire on Earl Street. We went in the building, it was an abandoned building, fire on the second floor. We went to the second floor. Nobody was there to ventilate yet, so we're trying to fight the fire. Trying to locate it. Trying to put it out. We found the fire. Once we put the fire out, we found with no venting, from the water and the type of heat, we got steam burns that came through the hood.

Figuereq: I was assigned to Twenty-eight Engine on the second tour. Walking in that morning was a little bit nerve wracking because it's new and you hear all different things. "Oh, they're going to pick on you, talk it up because you're the red ass, the new guy." But actually, the guys there in that house welcomed me with open arms. I never got that feeling. They took me in like one of their brothers, right away which was great. It was a great experience for the first day on the job.

It's kind of funny. I didn't want to go to Twenty-eight because it was a slow house, actually my first three days on the job I caught working fires. We had a three bagger my first day in the field, about three o'clock, a job right on North Sixth, right before Park Ave. That's when they had the rotational closings, so Fifteen Engine wasn't there. So, Twenty-eight was actually first due right next to the firehouse. Right out of the Academy, first day actually in the field. My heart's pumping. Don't really know what to expect besides that, "Oh crap we're going to go into a burning house." So, first thing we arrive. Jay Walker was our driver that day. He's a captain today. Angelo Guida was my senior guy and Bobby Clark; he was my captain. As soon as we arrived there, jumped out, flames were already coming right out the first floor, right out the window. Felt the heat and I was like,

"Oh, crap." But we went in and did our stuff and turned it off. My kids that evening, they came by. It was my first day. I didn't even have extra clothes. So, they came by to give me clothes. They just said that I looked like a kid in a candy store with a smile on my face. It was unfortunate for the people in the house, but for me it was something that I wanted to do, so I was excited.

Medina: I was assigned to Engine Thirteen, first tour. I live right across the street. You could hear the bells right from my house. I was really nervous. I started off kind of wrong. So, I went outside with my gear, I didn't see my car. I walk around the corner; they stole my car on my first day. So, now this is going on and I'm going to the firehouse across the street. I had to call the cops and make a report. It was screwed up, but the guys were good. I knew most of them. After that, it was exciting. I was a little nervous. I finally got to be in the firehouse.

It wasn't busy at all, to tell you the truth. But I had a good captain, Mickey Martino was my captain. Twenty Engine guy, Tact Squad, Eleven Engine, then Nine Engine in his career. Then he was a captain at Engine Eighteen. He had different shifts. When I came on the captains had one set of hours and the firefighters had another set of hours. You work with the first and second tour. Captain Martino was the guy who actually trained. It was pretty slow. We caught a few fires, but he trained me every day.

March 10, 2008, I had a lot of good fires. I'm on for a year now and I'm at Eleven Engine. We caught two fires that day. One across the street from Eleven Engine. Jose Robels was the captain. He just got promoted captain and we caught a fire in the morning right across Nineth Street, right by Eleven Engine's firehouse. And then later on about four o'clock we got another fire, three alarms. That was on Chapel, the cross street was Ferry. Chief Weiss was there. We had three houses going. First time I caught a fire like that where I was going in, heavy smoke, heavy heat and we were the only ones in there for a while. First line in the building, second alarm, we got in front of the building, incredible. This is what firefighting is all about. We might have been in there two, three hours pretty much. We went from floor to floor to floor. We put out the first floor. Went to the second floor. Then had to go back down because the exposure was going. Then we went up, messing with the two-and-a-half. Eleven Engine was on the B exposure, Eighteen was on the C exposure. It looked like there weren't too many people in there. So, we took a beating. That's why I remember.

Dugan: I was assigned to Ladder Eleven, tour one. First day in the firehouse, how was I greeted? Anybody I ran across loved my father and appreciated what he did for them in the union, so everybody treated me well. Of course, I was still a red ass, so I still got my balls busted. I didn't go in there expecting to get any special treatment, of course, and we wouldn't want any. So, do whatever you're supposed to do, do your dishes and keep your mouth shut and go along with the flow. I had some good senior firemen that took me under their wing and showed me how to do the rig and when anything would come up, they would help me out.

At the time, Chief Lalor had asked my father, "Anything I can do to help your son?" He said, "Well, can you have him in the same firehouse with me?" My father was on Engine Eleven on the fourth tour. So, I would see him when he'd be getting off and I'd be coming on. I actually caught a couple of jobs with him when he was working on a mutual swap. My first roof job, I looked off the roof and here's my dad looking at me. So, that was pretty cool. At that fire he told me, truck work is a marathon, not a sprint. Because he saw we cut the roof then I went downstairs, grabbed a hook, ran by and he says, "You can't do stuff like that." That was a memory that I'll have forever for sure.

I got that first roof with Lonzie Ellison, Junior. I brought my tank up there and had my mask on. Then when I get down, all the senior guys are like, "Hey kid what are you doing with your mask on?" I was like, "I'm not supposed to wear my mask?" And they said, "No, you don't need that." So, the next fire I had I caught the roof with Gene Hurle and it banked up. I was like, "I wish I had my mask."

After that I would bring my mask and take it off. It is kind of awkward to start opening the roof and stuff with it. But again, that's a lesson I learned.

At my first fire, my heart was racing. It was almost like being a paratrooper. When you stand up and hook up to that airplane and you're about to jump out, you can't panic. You can't be thinking about, "Oh, my God." You try to remember what they told you, your training, and do it to your best abilities.

I remember the first summer I was working, we had a huge heat wave. And we got a call for a gas leak. The cops were outside this building because they know there's a gas leak in there. We don't smell any gas. My captain was Jerry DeLane, and he says, "I don't smell any gas." But you can see two people sitting on their couches in the apartment. He had me climb through the window. And there they were, a brother and sister. They were schizophrenic and they were paranoid to open up their windows. They just baked inside their apartment. Just sitting there, one sitting on the couch, the other on a recliner. And I just looked at them like, "Wow, these are the first dead bodies I've ever seen." Other than like funerals and stuff like that. Opened the door. Jerry came in and I'm still looking at them. And he goes to open the back door. He's like yelling. I'm like, "What, what, what?" I'm all scared. "What is it?" "Oh, it's just cockroaches." When he opened the door, the cockroaches came out from the doorframe. My mind was so focused on these two people just sitting there. So, I'll always remember that.

K. Alfano: Come out of the Academy and they schedule you for your first day at the firehouse. Everyone got their assignments. Mine was Engine Twelve. We got lucky, because before the 2006 class, there hadn't been a class for a while. The fire department was at an all-time low. So, our class, when we first got on, we were lucky. About ninety-five percent of us got a spot and only a few had to rove. So, when I came on, I was ordered to go to Engine Twelve on the fourth tour. That's where I was for about eight months.

I was surprised at how much stuff the fire department handles, all the different calls. But it wasn't too busy. I would say in a twenty-four-hour shift, we were going out at least eight to ten times a day. Not all of them were fires. They still had the projects down on Prince Street. Those were some of the first fires that I caught, up in there. Fire wise it wasn't so busy, but I would say it was busier when I came on ten years ago than it seems to be now.

When I walked into the firehouse, I think Bobby Testa threw a pot at us. They just told us to introduce ourselves. Called us red asses and then showed us where to put our stuff and then told us this is where you're going to be sitting. This is what you're going to be doing and then the rest of the day, pretty much I kept my mouth shut and did whatever I was told. I chipped in. I helped around. I did cooking, whatever.

They knew I was Phil Alfano's son. Everyone knew. But my father told me, you just keep your mouth shut and just help. Do whatever is needed. If there's a mop that needs to be picked up, don't ask to do it. Just do it. Cooking comes around, just chip in. Clean, just clean. Don't ask to do anything. Just take it upon yourself and just go do it. I felt welcomed. Even before I came on the job, I knew most of the guys up here that I work with. I knew Andre, because he was in the Union down with my uncle. I knew the guys.

We had fires in those concrete building over on Spruce Street before they tore them down. Putting a ladder up to the third floor, going up in there, just putting garbage fires out. It probably took a couple of shifts before I caught my first real job. A couple of fires that I remember going in and being like, whoa. I was only down there for maybe eight months until I got moved up to Eighteen Engine. We had a job with Captain Kevin Burkhardt. It was going pretty good. We got in there and put it out, but it was like you had to crawl in there on your belly. It was in the back and I couldn't see anything. You got the hood on and everything and it's still alright, but it's getting hot. But as long as you're with your guys and you were in there, you felt safe. We got it done. We were able to put it out. But you know, there's been a few fires where it been like, "What am I doing here?" Literally, "What's going on here?"

M. Bellina: I think my going into the firehouse is different. In the Academy they're like, you should go where you're knocking your elbows. And my dad's like, no you don't do that. Just show up on time. Sit at the table. Keep your mouth shut. And listen to what goes on. If anyone talks with you, you can talk with them. If they joke, you joke with them and that's pretty much it. But I'm Frank's son, I get the benefit of the doubt. Of course, that's because of the reputation he built for himself. This job showed me that part. I just know him as a great father and a great guy. I didn't know him as a firefighter. He never brought any of that home. He never talked anything about that, so I had no idea what was going on. I've learned that not through just random people, but when I would go to the firehouse. My dad would go, "Oh, you know who you're working with?" "Oh, Captain Kormash is there." "You want to catch a job with that guy." But then Chief Kormash telling stories about my father. And he never really told stories, but saying the type of guy he was and knowing how my father held him. It showed me a lot because I didn't know.

I roved third battalion on the second tour. So, I spent a lot of time at Engine Nine. Chief Straile tried to keep me there, but I roved a lot in the third battalion. And then after like a handful of months, I went to Ladder Five on the second tour. After two or three months, I was there pretty much the entire time. Then I got transferred to the first tour. So, I came to Ladder Five.

When we came out of the Academy, people were allowed to rove in the third or the fifth. No one was allowed to come to the fourth or the first. Only one person went to the first. He's on the truck with me and he come on with me too. He was the only one in the first battalion and he stayed at Nineth Street most of the time. My father told me to try to learn the main streets and pretty much to get familiar with the cross streets and everything like that. You weren't allowed to drive for a whole year, so I think that makes it a bit more difficult to learn. And when I came on my dad was like, just listen to the radio which is the key to everything. He said, pay attention because it also helps you know the streets. If I don't know the street and I know Eighteen is the first due engine company on the box. I'll listen. I'll know it's in that area. Also pay attention to what companies are out of service. You get enough of a feeling for everything.

My perspective of busy is a little different than everybody else's because if I ever said I was busy, my father would just laugh. So, like busy in terms of going on runs and not fires, when I first got to Ladder Five on the second tour, Ten Truck was running as Nine Truck because they were redoing their house. We would go on a lot of runs covering for Ten Truck, like go to the airport. It took a while before I got my first fire. I caught nothing really significant. One day, I was on Rescue and there was an entrapment on the Turnpike. And a helicopter landed. That was like my third or fourth shift, something different.

2010s: The Modern Newark Fire Department

B. Maresca: My first assignment was Engine Nine and I've been there the whole time. It gets busy on some days, but not always busy. Walking into the firehouse my first day was different. It was a different experience than I had ever experienced before. Everyone was cool and pretty nice about it, so I felt welcomed. I was my father's son, but that was alright. My first day I think I worked with one or two guys I had already met from when I was young, so that was pretty cool.

G. Centanni: I roved the third tour. I started off in the third battalion, then I hit every battalion. I went to Engine Nine for like a year and a half before I came to Six. I was Chief John Centanni's son, so a lot of the guys he worked with were still on when I got on and they all respected him. They busted my chops a little bit, but they kind of gave me the benefit of the doubt. I guess they liked me. I felt more or less welcomed.

Nine was great. Vinnie Martone was my captain. He taught me a lot. Then a spot at Six opened up. He told me he might retire. My father was at Six, so it's always where I wanted to go, then the spot opened up and before it got taken, I was going to jump on it.

My first fire was at Engine Nine. It was in the middle of the night. It was on Linden Street. It was a three-story brick, fire on the top floor. We got the fire. I had the tip. That was my first time I was on the tip. It was all open. Seven Engine was on the second; we went to the third. More of the fire was on the third.

G. Pierre: We roved for a while. Then I ended up in the same house that my father and my uncle were in, Engine Twenty-six. I wanted to go to Eighteen. I learned later on that my father's first stop was Eighteen. I learned that later on. I had been requested to go to Bergen and Lehigh. A request to go to Ladder Ten. I declined. I got requests from Fifteen and Truck Seven. I got requests from Down

Neck, Twenty-seven/Boat One. Ladder Four requested me. Initially I was going to Engine Sixteen where I didn't want to go. I didn't want to go to Four. One transfer list said I was going to Fifteen. One said I was going to Ten. The last list I was assigned to Twenty-six. And I'm so happy I'm here. I actually live in the neighborhood and I could walk home.

I didn't want to come to Twenty-six because this is one of the firehouses where I did not feel like, "This is where I wanted to be." I came into the firehouse, everybody's kind of like quiet. "Firefighter Gregory Pierre, sir." "Alright, first of all put the horn down. Have a seat." I didn't have a captain. The whole house didn't have captain at the time. It was myself and there was a fellow firefighter that was a friend of my uncle's. We trained one time together. And it's Carl Houston and Bull and me. We were the young guys of the house. So, we're kind of like the young titans running around here, steaming and barking around the house. It's good, kind of like lifts it up. Then we got a captain, Captain Mackey. I'm happy with Mackey. Mack trained me a lot. Mack had been at Eighteen where I wanted to go. He got made captain and came over. When I saw Mack, I said, "Hey I'm good now." So, it went from the old regime to kind of like a new regime. Now it's kind of like a new Burg. Now we're pumped up. We beat Eleven Engine/Eleven Truck to a lot of boxes.

I didn't feel welcomed my first day and I didn't want to announce that I'm Yves son. I'm not one of those guys. When I came in, I really don't think they cared who I was. I was a red ass. They thought I was a red ass, honestly. It was "Alright, listen. One, don't snoot me all out. Don't come in here screaming. In the morning we do breakfast. Two, just go do something." You know what I mean. But I was already checking the rig. I'm pulling out my Scott pack. I'm pulling out my project bag. I'm going through. We're drilling. I said, "What's this? What's this? What's this? What do you do with this?" So, it was a good vibe. I had another young guy, came out of the Academy with me. He came to the truck. So, it was good we had that camaraderie. We both were kind of like hungry to learn the job. Hungry to show what we know. So, that was a good.

As far as the older guys, they didn't care, but our age is contagious, so we were told. I came into a house with a bunch of roving captains. I'm talking to the captains, "Cap, what's going on? Where you from?" "I'm from such and such." "How long you been on the job?" Been on the job this many years. "Are you going to drill me?" "No, we're not drilling." And I felt so deflated. But now they know. Now they know about us. Now they know if you come to the Burg, you're most likely going to have to drill. You come to the Burg; you know the guys are going to ask you to drill. Now the word is out. Then once I got my captain I was definitely embraced by the guys.

I remember when my first fire was. My first real fire I caught at Ladder Ten. That was my first job roving. And my thing is not being able to see and confined space that's what bothered me back then. I can climb heights. I climb twenty stories on a ladder, as long as the ladder is stable, I'll climb it. I don't mind, running up to the fire, I'm cool with that. But when I can't see, oh my God. It was the first time I was in a situation like that. It was an apartment fire. Apartments can get smoky, So, the captain asked me, "You ready for this?" "Yeah, I'm ready for this. I'm ready for this cap." So. I'm a young titan. I climb the stairs, got to the top. Ready to go and the apartment door is open. So, sitting there in the hallway, it's blacked out. When I walked into that smoke. I had a light. and I still couldn't see anything.

My heart dropped. So, Captain Hickey said, "P go back here and get so and so." I could do that. I had to go back to the rig and get a water can. The whole time I'm going, "Good, let's go get ready. You got to do this. You got to do this. You got to do this." I come back up. I still can't see anything! I was lucky enough to be in that situation. The captain really walked me through it. It was a mattress fire. We as a truck put it out with a water can. Kudos.

So, my captain was like. "He's my probie. He's an all-star. He put the fire out with a water can." We put the fire out with a water can. That was my first fire. Just the fact that I'm not comfortable with not being able to see in that smoke, that was like my first little, huh. And then the next fire and the next fire and after like each fire it went up an evolution.

Rawa: I walked in expecting, from the stories that I'd heard and the things I'd seen, I thought it was going to be tough. I'm an easy target for anything. I'm easy to pick on, but I take it well. I never really got that from anybody, honestly. It was complete respect and nothing but guys looking to help you out and make you feel comfortable. I was actually shocked. Everybody was great. I met nothing but good guys. I felt welcomed.

My roving experience was a little different from what I had expected it to be. What I got was that during that half year roving, you're going to be switching between battalions on a tour. So, you can get a chance to see the city and get a chance to meet different guys and learn different parts of the city. Then I was assigned to the second tour, Fifth Battalion. I stayed in the Fifth Battalion the entire time. So, I never changed the battalions. Ninety-five percent of my roving career was at Clinton Avenue, Ten Engine. It was great, which I loved.

When I came on, Clinton Avenue was considered the Fifth Battalion. Right now, they moved it back to the Fourth. Luckily, I had those good guys in the Fifth Battalion at the time because I enjoyed working over there. As soon as they allowed you to put in for spots, I was lucky enough to get into Rescue with Captain Joseph Gethard who was our instructor in the Academy. So, I got to continue working with him after the twelve weeks were through. Which was nice, a couple of months in Rescue, nothing to complain about, but I realized it's kind of time to set my sails on something more realistic for a new guy with zero experience.

My most memorable fire was while I was roving. It was a high-rise fire in the Colonnades. The fire was on the twelfth floor and especially being a new guy, you want to show that you can handle any situation that's thrown at you. So, you hear the twelfth floor, I'm like, I can handle it. I can run up those flights. When we got the high-rise pack on you. You got the hose on you. By the seventh floor I was completely drained, but I still never gave up. We got up there. There was not much work for us to do once we got up there. It was pretty much all taken care of. But once I got to the top flight, all the guys were fine, they seemed fine, so I tried to keep my cool. I could barely hang on, but then the captain said, "All right nothing for us to do." So, we went to head back downstairs. I picked everything up because I didn't want the captain to take anything. I wanted to show him that I'll head right back down with him. I picked it up and as soon as I took my first step down the stairs, both my feet went right up in the air over my head and I slid down the stairs probably about ten, fifteen stairs. and oh, I ate it bad. I probably should have gone to the hospital, but I think my pride took more focus than the actual pain of the fall. I slid on my tank. My back was probably bruised, but I didn't let anybody know it. They let me know it to this day every time I see them.

J. Centanni: I roved for like six months on the first tour. My first assignment was Eleven Engine, third tour. I knew a lot of the guys I worked with, so I would get my chops busted about being the chief's son. But for the most part, it was very welcoming. My dad used to bring me around. So, a lot of people knew me before. But it was a good experience. A lot of people helped me out learning stuff. It was good. It was familiar, especially this house at Nineth Street. He took me around here a lot. He was captain here and he was a fireman here. I knew how it went and everything like that. So, it was not easy but it was somewhat easy because I knew how you're supposed to act and be hard working around the firehouse.

It was really exciting because I always wanted to do it. So, the first time walking in it didn't feel like I was working. It just felt like I was visiting again, but then you get used to it. Worked with a lot of good guys here and I worked at Six Engine for a while, at Nine Engine. You had a lot of good guys and they showed you what was expected day to day.

I don't have much experience yet, but the guys I work with are very aggressive, with a lot of experience. Both the captains are great. And the firemen have a lot of fires, so you notice it's a lot faster in this area with the companies, Six, Eighteen, Eleven, Seven, Eleven Truck, Five Truck, all them. Everyone's quick to get inside, so they want the fire. And you know everyone's with you the whole time. A small department doesn't have the benefit of having that many guys in there working. You know right away you have four engines, two trucks, the Rescue. Everyone's going on a full assignment. Definitely faster. All good guys here.

My first day working, I was at Nine Engine. We had mutual aid. We went to Orange. It was us, Fifteen Engine, and Ladder Seven. It was in the daytime too. When we got there originally, they thought most of it was knocked down. There was an electrical problem in the street. They said there were problems going to the different houses. So, they just asked us to go into one of their houses. It was just the Newark guys in that building. They didn't have as many people. So, they were occupied in the other one. It was a third-floor fire. Just the front of the house, wasn't a lot, two rooms maybe. My brother actually had the tip. I was working with him. I had a hook. I was pulling the walls.

Garay: I went to Twenty-seven Engine for the first three tours and then I went to Ladder Five for another three tours. Then I went to Engine Fourteen. The chief in the Fifth Battalion tried to keep me for three days consecutively because at that time I was still nursing. So, I would bring my pump. He wanted to accommodate me more. After Fourteen I went to Five Engine. I went to Nineteen Engine also. I never got to go to Sixteen Engine in the Fifth Battalion. That's when we were placed back in the Third Battalion. There I was able to go everywhere. Park Avenue, Nine Engine, Thirteen Engine, Twenty-eight Engine, Seven Engine, and Six Engine. Then we went to the Fourth Battalion and when I got to the Fourth Battalion the chief just left me at Rescue. So, I didn't get to go to the other Fourth

Battalion companies. Because the captain at Rescue at that time was Captain Daniels and after being there for a couple of days he said, "Are you okay being here at Rescue?" I said, "Yes. It's a busy company. I like it." And he says, "Well, I'm going to ask the chief, if you don't mind, to leave you here for the rest of the time that you're at Fourth Battalion." And I said, "Okay." So, I didn't have to go back to the chief. I was at Rescue until it was time for me to go to my home company for the next transfer list.

Then I requested to go to Twenty-seven Engine for the first six months. I went to Twenty-seven Engine because they had the boat. But then the boat broke down, so we weren't having any runs. I was thinking about putting my papers in for Rescue. At the same time Captain Daniels kept asking me, "Veronica did you put your papers in? Did you put your papers in?" I said, "No Cap." But when the next list came, I put in my papers for Rescue. I've been there for the last six months. I'm not a Haz-mat tech yet. I just went to the high angle training. I received the class portion of the ice water rescue, but when we were actually going to do the drill for the ice water rescue in Branch Brook Park, the weather conditions didn't allow for it so now we have to wait until next winter.

We had a fire on Pennsylvania Avenue, fourth alarm. That was a memorable fire. I never felt that kind of heat before. As a matter of fact, I was discussing it with the guys downstairs. Being at Rescue, we have to go behind the engine companies. At that particular fire, we actually saw the fire grow in the building in front of us because the engine company was having a hard time getting water. I actually felt that agonizing heat for two, three seconds where, whoa, you start losing your mind. I was like, wow, I remember thinking to myself, "Oh my gosh, this is unbearable." I never felt that unbearable heat until I was there. To the point where even my captain kept calling, "V are you there? V are you there?" Because it got pretty ugly really quick. So that was the most memorable, I think the most uncomfortable feeling is you're just standing in there waiting for that water to get in and those seconds become minutes because you're doing nothing. When you're overhauling, when you're busy doing something it's like, okay, time is flying by. But when you're just standing there waiting for the line to be opened. Ah, my gosh, it seems like forever.

Fortunato: I was roving on the third tour. My first day I was at Seven Truck on Park Avenue. Walking into the firehouse was a cool experience, definitely a cool experience. The guys were really cool. I felt welcomed. I had a great first day.

We had a fire that day. My first day, I'm working at Seven Truck and we got a mutual aid fire to Orange. They had three houses on fire. We got there. They had knocked down the fire in one house, so we pulled the ceilings and overhauled. And then the second house started taking off on the top floor so we went up an aerial, me, Chris Wolfe, and Danny Roebuck went up and they let me cut the roof, my first day. So that was a good experience. It was definitely an eye opener doing it, but it was fun.

Earp: The first time in the firehouse? I was very nervous because I didn't know what to expect. You know being the new guy it always, "Okay, how is the day going to go? What to expect? How am I going to get along with the guys? How are the guys going to accept me?" But when I first set foot in the firehouse, I felt accepted. I felt that the guys treated me as an equal. As not just being a new guy, they'll tell me, "Oh you're a firefighter just like us." So that made me feel a little better. It eased the transition coming from the Academy into a firehouse. It made things much easier for me. As the day went along, they showed me different things and I picked up on it. And by me learning, they made me more confident, got better and each shift that I came to the firehouse I just got more and more comfortable, just felt more like one of the guys. Just felt more welcome. It didn't take long. The guys are great on this department.

I had a fire first due on the truck, on Ladder Ten. We went up to the second level of the structure. We went to the back room. The fire was in the house next to it. We were in the exposure house, so we got up there. The chief was saying we have to hit the walls. There's fire in the walls. We see smoke so from there we started breaking the walls down, pulling the ceiling and there was fire in the walls. We had Engine Five. They had to put the fire out as we were knocking the walls down.

Corales: I came in with my turnout gear, my little duffle bag, and a box of donuts for the guys. When I walked in nobody said a word to me, so I just went right to the rig to put my turnout gear there, set myself up, and introduce myself to the captain who was standing next to the rig. I put my turnout gear down. I go to shake the captain's hand and we got a full assignment. A full assignment comes in. So, before I even got to let him know who I was and my name, he just jumped in his boots. I jumped in my boots, dropped the donuts right on the floor. Left it right on the bay with my duffle bag and I'm on the rig with a driver and a captain who I don't even know. And my heart is pumping down Mount Prospect Avenue. I just remember, I don't know what I'm getting myself into. This is the way I'm taking off. That's how I got my career started.

It was just a light smoke condition. It was fine, but me not knowing and not being in the field, I thought it was the most nerve-racking situation. When I got back and got the donuts, with a little bit of oil from the bay floor, it kind of worked out. They all had a laugh about that. They told me, "You see, this is what this is about. You got to always be ready." But I definitely felt welcomed.

Alexander II: First day, everybody from my class that was assigned to a tour, came to the deputy's quarters first so they could be assign to a battalion. We met with the deputy chief and all the battalion chiefs. They had a speech for us and they talked to us a while. Then they assigned us to a different battalion chief and battalions. I ended up on Park Ave, Engine Fifteen, right there. You're so excited, but the guys, it's just another day at work for them. So, they're cool and they're lax. "Set up over here and just follow me and I'll tell you what to do and I'll look out for you." You've got the nerves going. Every time you listen to the radio go off you think, "Okay that's mine." I'm just maxing my first day, but it doesn't always work out that way.

The rest of the guys in my class and girls, they did really well. They love it. You're nervous. You don't want to step on anybody's toes. You want to find your place. You just want to wait to see what's going on. Because you know it's a different life style coming from any other job in the world. We just do things differently. That's how it is, the nature of the beast. So, I wouldn't say they were more standoffish, it's more of just, okay I need to wait and see where I fit in amongst these guys and where's my place in the hierarchy? You know it's low man, but what does that actually mean? They all love it and it's funny now because we have a group chat from our class and every major event or something significant, we get into a group chat and talk to each other, all of us. Our first day went like this. And you can expect this and you can expect that. So, we have a good group, a tight group. We always try to help each other out and it helps, it helps.

My first fire is a four-alarm fire in the South Ward on Pennsylvania Ave. We got called on the third alarm. I was on Truck Seven that day. Wow, I didn't know the sky could get that red. I did not know that was possible. Then quickly you got to get into your training. "Okay, I got to reign it in. What am I going to do? What's my assignment? What do I need to be looking for? Okay, there's fire in this building with the exposures." After you get over the moment, your training starts to kick in. Okay, what do I need? What tools do I need? If I'm on the engine, alright am I grabbing the tip? It's on my side. Am I grabbing the tip? Am I going to be the flaker? Once the nerves start to calm down a little bit, then after that, you go to work. You go to work. You get that tunnel vision. I got my assignment. I got to get my job done because my guys are counting on me to get my job done.

We were working in the B side exposure building. I was working with a senior guy because it was two probies on that day. So, one probie went with the captain; that was another guy in my class; and I went with the senior guy. We got to pull a lot of ceilings room to room. I actually got some hose work too. I had the tip for a little while.

That fire involved, I want to say three or four buildings. So, there was a lot of work to go around. It was exhausting, but it was fun.

Cruz: I have been to Eighteen Engine. My first day I got a house fire. We were coming back from a call and we smelt smoke, so we went around the block. We were looking, maybe we'd see something, but we didn't see anything. We kept going around. Luckily, we went back to the firehouse. I remember very clearly because I had not gone upstairs the whole day. It was my first day. I was nervous. What if we get a house fire or anything? So, the first moment I relaxed. I grabbed a coke. I went up the stairs. They were like, "Oh there's the TV room. You could watch, sit down, relax." The next thing you know they call us. One of the senior guys goes, "Come on we got to go. There's a fire." We didn't get it on the radio or anything. Turns out one of the neighbors from the person's house that was on fire, she ran to the firehouse from around the corner to let us know that her neighbor's house was on fire.

I ran down. I have never put on my gear so fast. I think it was about thirty seconds that I had everything on. It was right around the corner, the house that was on fire. I had trouble with my radio because it was like my first day, so I ended up giving it to the chief. And then we went in. One of the guys goes in with the tip. He went to find the fire. I was with the captain. We went to the second floor. I remember going in, the line in the rooms, and we went to the back of the house. There was a door. We thought maybe it was up the stairway, checking the back to see if there was any fire there. Then they called us. They found the fire.

When we got upstairs, they handed me the tip. It was exciting, but they had already found the fire, so it was cheating. It was a very good, exciting experience. I'm glad I got it over with on my first day. I didn't have to wait and anticipate for the first house fire. It was amazing though. Because you see how every company operates. Once the fire was put out, you see the truck come in, open up the walls, open the ceiling, then we would go back in, keep hosing everything down. Then they would come back. It was amazing how organized it was. Every company has their own job. It's amazing how it just works. Loved it. It was great.

Then after that, I worked at Rescue. I did an extrication there. And then I also worked at Ten Engine. Outside fires, didn't catch a house fire with them. With Rescue I did catch fires too. We did some ventilation and shut off the electricity and utilities. I found a dog doing search and rescue. Somebody had actually put him behind a closet and they put a weight against it. We had just gone over how we had to search every closet, every bathroom. We went to a bedroom and there's a weight pushed against the closet door. Obviously, that meant nobody had checked the closet. So, as I opened the closet, there's the dog in the closet. That dog ran out of that house so fast I can't even tell you what kind of dog it was. And now I've been in the Fifth Battalion two tours. I worked on Five Engine, mostly fives for them, false alarms. And now I'm here at Twenty-seven. I worked Five Truck also, in the Fourth Battalion. Everybody has been welcoming. Everything's been good. I put in my work. I don't hesitate when they tell me to do anything. I'm short. I make sure I reach. Even though I can't reach, I'm going to reach it somehow. If something is hard to turn, I make sure I find the strength to turn it.

Interviewees

Alexander I, Captain Donald, 2 September, 2016, transcript. (appointed 1987)

Alexander II, Firefighter Donald, 23 July, 2016, transcript. (appointed 2016)

Alfano, Firefighter George, 19 December, 2005, transcript. (appointed 1953)

Alfano, Captain Kevin, 9 August, 2016, transcript. (appointed 2006)

Alvarez, Captain Orlando, 26 July, 16 August, 2016, transcript. (appointed 1989)

Arce, Battalion Chief Orlando, 9 October, 2016, transcript. (appointed 1984)

Banta, Captain Robert, 6 July, 2000, transcript. (appointed 1974)

Bartelloni, Battalion Chief Paul, 9 July, 2019, transcript. (appointed 1993)

Bellina, Deputy Director of OEM Frank, 17 August, 2016, transcript. (appointed 1981)

Bellina, Firefighter Norman, 5 September, 2020, transcript. (appointed 1986)

Bellina, Firefighter Michael, 18 August, 2016, transcript. (appointed 2008)

Belzger, Firefighter William, 4 October, 2004, transcript. (appointed 1959)

Bisogna, Captain Joseph, 25 July, 2001, transcript. (appointed 1974)

Benderoth, Captain John, 15 November, 2005, transcript. (appointed 1967)

Bitter, Deputy Chief Richard, 27 December, 2002, transcript. (appointed 1959)

Brown, Firefighter Anthony, 14 July, 1991, transcript. (appointed 1979)

Brownlee, Battalion Chief Walter, 4 September, 2019, transcript. (appointed 1973)

Burkhardt, Captain Kevin, 9 February, 2004, transcript. (appointed 1973)

Butler, Captain James, 3 September, 1993, transcript. (appointed 1963)

Cahill, Firefighter Joseph, 25 June, 1991, transcript. (appointed 1963)

Calvetti, Battalion Chief Francis, 8 July, 2005, transcript. (appointed 1966)

Camasta, Captain Joseph, 23 July, 1991, transcript. (appointed 1974)

Cardillo, Firefighter Felix, 5 October, 2008, transcript. (appointed 1959)

Carr, Captain Delwin, 30 April, 2021, transcript. (appointed 2000)

Carragher, Deputy Chief William, 1 November, 1994, transcript. (appointed 1960)

Carter, Battalion Chief Harry, 12 June, 1991, transcript. (appointed 1973)

Castelluccio, Deputy Chief Anthony, 23 August, 2016, transcript. (appointed 1993)

Centanni, Fire Chief John, 9 November, 2016, transcript. (appointed 1986)

Centanni, Firefighter Gerard, 31 October, 2016, transcript. (appointed 2013)

Centanni, Firefighter John, 31 October, 2016, transcript. (appointed 2014)

Charpentier, Firefighter Frederick, 22 August, 1993, transcript. (appointed 1959)

Coale, Captain Michael, 12 October, 2005, transcript. (appointed 1973)

Cody, Battalion Chief James, 18 October, 1999, transcript. (appointed 1964)

Connell, Battalion Chief Anthony, 26 February, 1999, transcript. (appointed 1974)

Conover, Firefighter William, 24 April, 2005, transcript. (appointed 1948)

Conville, Captain Francis, 20 November, 2009, transcript. (appointed 1940)

Corales, Firefighter Joel, 8 August, 2016, transcript. (appointed 2016)

Cordasco, Battalion Chief Matthew, 20 June, 2016, transcript. (appointed 1989)

Cosby, Firefighter Boisy, 17 June, 2003, transcript. (appointed 1963)

Cosby, Fire Prevention Specialist Joseph, 22 August, 1991, transcript. (appointed 1969)

Cruz, Firefighter Mellisa, 24 July, 2016, transcript. (appointed 2016)

Dainty, Battalion Chief Cliff, 6 September, 2016, 21 June, 2019, transcript. (appointed 1970)

Dalton, Captain Francis, 13 October, 2008, transcript. (appointed 1963)

Daly, Captain Phillip, 4 December, 2008, transcript. (appointed 1978)

Daniels, Battalion Chief Christopher, 22 July, 2016, transcript. (appointed 1989)

Daudelin, Captain George, 24 February, 2000, transcript. (appointed 1970)

DeCuester, Battalion Chief Steven, 22 May, 2019, transcript. (appointed 1984)

DeLeon, Battalion Chief Albert, 20 February, 2021, transcript. (appointed 1988)

Denvir, Captain John, 13 September, 1993, transcript. (appointed 1959)

Deutch, Firefighter Charles, 14 November, 1993, transcript. (appointed 1953)

Doherty, Captain John, 18 April, 2006, transcript. (appointed 1949)

Doherty, Captain Patrick, 18 September, 20 September, 2000, transcript. (appointed 1970)

Duerr, Chief of Apparatus Carl, 24 February, 2008, transcript. (appointed 1958)

Dugan, Captain Kevin, 23 July, 2016, transcript. (appointed 2006)

Dunn, Deputy Chief Edward, 14 August, 1991, transcript. (appointed 1959)

Earp, Firefighter Marky, 1 August, 2016, transcript. (appointed 2016)

Elward, Firefighter James, 9 July, 2005, transcript. (appointed 1962)

Farrell, Captain Daniel, 30 July, 3 August, 2016, transcript. (appointed 1996)

Figuereq, Captain Julio, 22 August, 2016, transcript. (appointed 2006)

Fortunato, Firefighter Michael, 20 August, 2016, transcript. (appointed 2014)

Freda, Deputy Chief Alfred, 12, 25, 26 July, 1991, transcript. (appointed 1959)

Fredette, Firefighter Reggie, 3 November, 1993, transcript. (appointed 1942)

Freeman, Captain Richard, 20 August, 1991, transcript. (appointed 1956)

Freese, Captain Miguel, 11 August, 2016, transcript. (appointed 1998)

Gaddy, Firefighter Saadiq, 7, 19 August, 2016, transcript. (appointed 2006)

Gail, Deputy Chief Richard, 16 July, 2019, transcript. (appointed 1993)

Garay, Firefighter Veronica, 16 August, 2016, transcript. (appointed 2014)

Garrity, Battalion Chief Joseph, 1 May, 1992, transcript. (appointed 1964)

Gaynor, Battalion Chief Robert, 22 October, 1999, transcript. (appointed 1965)

Gesualdo, Captain Albert, 21 July, 2003, transcript. (appointed 1978)

Gibson, Captain Richard, 22 April, 2005, transcript. (appointed 1953)

Giordano, Director David, 25 September, 10 October, 2020, transcript. (appointed 1984)

Goetchius, Captain Donald, 12 February, 1999, transcript. (appointed 1986)

Greene, Captain David, 29 July, 2019, transcript. (appointed 1988)

Grehl, Deputy Chief Frederick, 7 August, 1993, transcript. (appointed 1948)

Grehl, Captain Thomas, 29 May, 2002, transcript. (appointed 1971)

Griffith, Chief Operator Robert, 31 July, 1991, transcript. (appointed 1953)

Griffith, Captain Edward, 29 September, 14 October, 2016, transcript. (appointed 1983)

Griggs, Deputy Chief John, 23 April, 2005, transcript. (appointed 1956)

Griggs, Captain John, 28 September, 2016, transcript. (appointed 1988)

Haran, Captain Edward, 5 February, 2001, transcript. (appointed 1961)

Harris, Captain William, 13 December, 1999, transcript. (appointed 1961)

Highsmith, Firefighter Gerald, 2 June, 1994, transcript. (appointed 1963)

Highsmith, Captain Gregory, 8 August, 2016, transcript. (appointed 2000)

Hopkins, Captain Mark, 23 October, 2019, transcript. (appointed 1978)

Jackson, Fire Chief Rufus, 6 August, 2016, transcript. (appointed 1995)

Jenkins, Captain Thomas, 14 November, 2019, transcript. (appointed 2002)

Johnson, Captain Otis, 21 July, 14 August, 2016, transcript. (appointed 1984)

Kelly, Captain Michael, 26 April, 15 September, 2005, transcript. (appointed 1971)

Killeen, Battalion Chief Kevin, 28 September, 2009, 12 March, 2019, transcript. (appointed 1974)

Kinnear, Deputy Chief David, 28 September, 1992, transcript. (appointed 1947)

Knight, Firefighter Gerald, 19 June, 1991, transcript. (appointed 1964)

Kormash, Deputy Chief Michael, 24 October, 2016, transcript. (appointed 1979)

Kupko, Battalion Chief James, 25 August, 2 September, 2016, transcript. (appointed 2002)

Langenbach, Deputy Chief James, 24 October, 2002, transcript. (appointed 1973)

Langevin, Firefighter Robert, 23 February, 1999, transcript. (appointed 1974)

LaPenta, Battalion Chief Steven, 30 September, 2016, transcript. (appointed 1989)

Lawless, Battalion Chief Michael, 1 March, 1999, transcript. (appointed 1966)

Lee, Battalion Chief Sylvester, 5 October, 2016, transcript. (appointed 1986)

Luxton, Captain Charles, 14 January, 1999, 1 August, 2018, transcript. (appointed 1973)

Marcell, Deputy Chief Kenneth, 22 October, 2019, transcript. (appointed 1970)

Maresca, Battalion Chief Albert, 17 August, 2016, transcript. (appointed 1987)

Maresca, Firefighter Brett, 25 August, 2016, transcript. (appointed 2012)

Masters, Firefighter Anthony, 24 March, 2004, transcript. (appointed 1947)

Masters, Captain Alan, 20 August, 2016, transcript. (appointed 1986)

Masterson, Captain Andrew, 6 April, 2005, transcript. (appointed 1949)

McCormack, Deputy Chief James, 14 June, 1991, transcript. (appointed 1949)
McDonnell, Captain Thomas, 30 March, 1999, transcript. (appointed 1970)

McGee, Captain Raymond, 22 October, 2000, transcript. (appointed 1956)

McGovern, Battalion Chief Thomas, 8 June, 2001, transcript. (appointed 1968)

McGrory, Deputy Chief Alexander, 31 August, 1991, transcript. (appointed 1957)

Medina, Captain Julio, 10 August, 2016, transcript. (appointed 2006)

Meier, Captain Donald, 9 August, 2016, transcript. (appointed 1996)

Melodick, Firefighter William, 1 June, 2001, transcript. (appointed 1970)

Mickels, Captain David, 18 September, 2020, transcript. (appointed 2002)

Miller, Battalion Chief Joseph, 16 August, 1991, transcript. (appointed 1959)

Miller, Battalion Chief Kenneth, 19 October, 2005, transcript. (appointed 1969)

Mitchell, Captain Michael, 20 October, 2004, transcript. (appointed 1978)

Montalvo, Firefighter Raymond, 5 August, 2016, transcript. (appointed 1996)

Morgan, Captain Bruce, 16 May, 2001, transcript. (appointed 1973)

Nasta, Deputy Chief Michael, 17 June, 2019, transcript. (appointed 1984)

Ostertag, Captain Steve, 29 July, 2016, transcript. (appointed 1994)

Partridge, Battalion Chief Peter, 26 July, 9 November, 2019, transcript. (appointed 1974)

Perdon, Captain George, 9 June, 2003, transcript. (appointed 1974)

Perez, Captain Joseph, 23 August, 2002, transcript. (appointed 1965)

Petrone, Firefighter Michael, 23 July, 2016, transcript. (appointed 1991)

Pianka, Firefighter George, 15 June, 2001, transcript. (appointed 1970)

Pierre, Captain Yves, 15 July, 2016, transcript. (appointed 2013)

Pierre, Firefighter Gregory, 14 August, 2016, transcript. (appointed 1995)

Pierson, Captain James, 28 August, 2016, transcript. (appointed 1991)

Pignato, Captain Nicholas, 30 May, 2000, transcript. (appointed 1974)

Prachar, Firefighter Andrew, 15 December, 2005, transcript. (appointed 1959)

Prachar, Captain Daniel, 12 August, 1991, transcript. (appointed 1968)

Prachar, Captain John, 10 July, 20 September, 2005, transcript. (appointed 1978)

Ramos, Firefighter Juan, 12 August, 2016, transcript. (appointed 1994)

Rawa, Firefighter Adam, 7 August, 2016, transcript. (appointed 2013)

Redden, Fire Chief Joseph, 16 September, 2002, transcript. (appointed 1947)

Reiss, Deputy Chief Thomas, 24 July, 2020, transcript. (appointed 1979)

Ricca, Battalion Chief Ronald, 1 June, 2000, transcript. (appointed 1974)

Richardson, Battalion Chief Scott, 2 August, 2016, transcript. (appointed 1994)

Roberson, Firefighter Luther, 22 August, 2016, transcript. (appointed 1996)

Rodriguez, Battalion Chief Deblin, 21 August, 2016, transcript. (appointed 1996)

Romano, Captain Peter, 28 September, 2008, transcript. (appointed 1972)

Rosamilia, Battalion Chief Gerard, 21 August, 2020, transcript. (appointed 1973)

Rosario, Captain Angel, 5 August, 2016, transcript. (appointed 2002)

Rotunda, Firefighter Gerald, 3 May, 2000, transcript. (appointed 1970)

Ryan, Battalion Chief John, 6 July, 2005, transcript. (appointed 1948)

Ryan, Battalion Chief Joseph P., 28 September, 1999, transcript. (appointed 1973)

Saccone, Battalion Chief Thomas, 27 November, 2000, transcript. (appointed 1969)

Sandella, Captain John, 6 August, 2020, transcript. (appointed 1978)

Schoemer, Firefighter Richard, 1 July, 2005, transcript. (appointed 1959)

Schofield, Firefighter William, 27 March, 2015, transcript. (appointed 1963)

Smith, Firefighter James, 30 June, 1995, transcript. (appointed 1959)

Snyder, Captain William, 1 August, 2016, transcript. (appointed 1993)

Sorace, Captain Michael, 18 August, 2016, transcript. (appointed 1986)

Sperli, Battalion Chief Joseph, 10 September, 2010, 21 August, 2016, transcript. (appointed 1989)

Stoffers, Battalion Chief Carl, 2 September, 1998, transcript. (appointed 1956)

Stoffers, Firefighter Raymond, 8 July, 1997, transcript. (appointed 1973)

Straile, Battalion Chief Joseph, 31 July, 2018, transcript. (appointed 1974)

Tarantino, Captain Anthony, 27 June, 18 July, 2019, transcript. (appointed 1989)

Vesey, Firefighter Edward, 15 June, 1999, transcript. (appointed 1948)

Vetrini, Captain Joseph, 14 September, 1993, 25 April, 2005, transcript. (appointed 1946)

Wall, Deputy Chief Edward, 13 September, 2000, transcript. (appointed 1954)

Wapples, Battalion Chief Arnum, 5 August, 1991, transcript. (appointed 1982)

Wargo, Captain Andrew, 26 June, 1991, transcript. (appointed 1964)

Weber, Battalion Chief William, 29 October, 2008, transcript. (appointed 1969)

Weidele, Battalion Chief William, 20 July, 2016, transcript. (appointed 1984)

West, Firefighter Charles, 12 July, 2019, transcript. (appointed 1989)

Willis, Firefighter James, 9 July, 2019, transcript. (appointed 1996)

Witte, Deputy Chief Michael, 13 August, 2016, transcript. (appointed 1978)

Zieser, Deputy Chief Richard, 25 July, 2016, transcript. (appointed 1978)

www.ingramcontent.com/pod-product-compliance
Lightning Source LLC
Chambersburg PA
CBHW022119080426
42734CB00006B/185